What Readers Are Saying About *The dRuby Book*

The dRuby Book is a fantastic introduction to distributed programming in Ruby for all levels of users. The book covers all aspects of dRuby, including the principles of distributed programming and libraries and techniques to make your work easier. I recommend this book for anyone who is interested in distributed programming in Ruby and wants to learn the basics all the way to advanced process coordination strategies.

➤ **Eric Hodel**
Ruby committer, RDoc and RubyGems maintainer

dRuby is the key component that liberates Ruby objects from processes and machine platforms. Masatoshi himself explains its design, features, case studies, and even more in this book.

➤ **Yuki "Yugui" Sonoda**
Ruby 1.9 release manager

dRuby naturally extends the simplicity and power Ruby provides. Throughout this book, Rubyists should be able to enjoy a conversation with dRuby that makes you feel as if your own thoughts are traveling across processes and networks.

➤ **Kakutani Shintaro**
RubyKaigi organizer, Ruby no Kai

Any programmer wanting to understand concurrency and distributed systems using Ruby should read this book. The explanations and example code make these topics approachable and interesting.

➤ **Aaron Patterson**
Ruby and Ruby on Rails core committer

A fascinating and informative look at what is classically a total pain in the neck: distributed object management and process coordination on a single machine or across a network.

➤ **Jesse Rosalia**
Senior software engineer

The dRuby Book

Distributed and Parallel Computing with Ruby

Masatoshi Seki
translated by Makoto Inoue

The Pragmatic Bookshelf
Dallas, Texas • Raleigh, North Carolina

Pragmatic Bookshelf

Our Pragmatic courses, workshops, and other products can help you and your team create better software and have more fun. For more information, as well as the latest Pragmatic titles, please visit us at *http://pragprog.com*.

The team that produced this book includes:

Susannah Pfalzer (editor)
Potomac Indexing, LLC (indexer)
Kim Wimpsett (copyeditor)
David J Kelly (typesetter)
Janet Furlow (producer)
Juliet Benda (rights)
Ellie Callahan (support)

Printed in the United States of America.
ISBN-13: 978-1-934356-93-7
Printed on acid-free paper.
Book version: P1.0—March 2012

Contents

Part III — Process Coordination

Part IV — Running dRuby and Rinda in a Production Environment

Foreword

In 2004, Ruby on Rails became public. The world was surprised by its productivity and by the magic of Ruby that enabled Ruby on Rails. Many people knew Ruby before Rails, but few realized the power of the language, especially metaprogramming.

But Rails is not the first framework to realize the power of Ruby. dRuby came long before Rails. It uses metaprogramming features for distributed programming. Proxy objects "automagically" delegate method calls to remote objects. You don't have to write interface definitions in XML or any IDL. dRuby is a good example of a very flexible system implemented by Ruby. In this sense, Rails is a follower.

Even though dRuby has a long history, its importance hasn't been reduced a bit in recent years. In fact, distributed programming is getting more important. We have access to more and more computers over the Internet. In the "cloud" age, we should find a way to utilize those enormous numbers of computers. And we already have the answer: dRuby.

dRuby is not known outside of Japan as much as it should be. I hope this book helps people learn the lesser-known technology proven by history. And you will see the power and magic of dRuby and Ruby.

Yukihiro "Matz" Matsumoto
Japan, November 2011

Acknowledgments

For the Japanese Edition

I would like to thank the development team of Ohmsha, Ltd., for publishing the dRuby book again; Akira Yamada, Kouhei Sutou, and Shintaro Kakutani for reviews; and the fireflies from Houki River for encouraging me.

For the English Edition

I would like to thank Makoto Inoue for translating this book, Dave Thomas and Susannah Pfalzer of Pragmatic Bookshelf for giving me the opportunity to publish the English edition, Hisashi Morita and Shintaro Kakutani for advice based on knowledge of the Japanese edition, and all the reviewers—Eric Hodel, Ivo Balbaert, Sam Rose, Kim Shrier, Javier Collado, Brian Schau, Tibor Simic, Stefan Turalski, Colin Yates, Leonard Chin, Elise Huard, Jesse Rosalia, and Chad Dumler-Montplaisir.

Preface

Stateful web servers are a core concept of dRuby. dRuby lets you pass normal Ruby objects and call their methods across processes and networks seamlessly. With dRuby, you'll experience the world of distributed computing as a natural extension of Ruby.

The most widely used distributed system in the world is probably the Web. It's one of the most successful ways to distribute documents around the world—and dRuby's history is related to the Web. Back when Ruby was still in version 1.1, a web server called shttpsrv was available. shttpsrv was similar to WEBrick, but WEBrick was so innovative that Shinichiro Hara—one of the core committers of Ruby and the author of shttpsrv—decided to ditch the new version of shttpsrv in favor of WEBrick (which now comes as part of Ruby's standard libraries). But I really liked the small and cool web server called shttpsrv, so I wrote a servlet extension for it. With this extension, shttpsrv transformed from an ordinary web server to a special TCP server with state. And that is how dRuby started.

This is the third edition of *The dRuby Book* (the previous two editions were in Japanese). For this edition, I've rewritten the book to cover the latest dRuby information and new libraries. If you are looking for theoretical definitions of distributed objects or detailed comparisons of various systems, look elsewhere! This book is full of hands-on exercises and interesting code examples. I hope you put this book to use by writing code as you read and discovering new things along the way.

Ruby changes your thinking process, and so does dRuby. dRuby is not just a tool to extend a method invocation. You'll discover new techniques, programming styles, and much more as you learn how dRuby works.

dRuby will show you a side of Ruby you've never seen before. Let's explore together!

Who This Book Is For

You'll gain a lot from this book if you are...

- Interested in finding out about the benefits of writing apps using dRuby
- Excited by the concept of "distributed systems" such as NoSQL but think most of the existing systems are too complicated
- Interested in client-server network programming and web programming but are interested in a more lightweight alternative to Ruby on Rails or Sinatra
- Interested in adding concurrent programming, such as multithreading, messaging, and the Actor model, to your applications

You don't need to know much about distributed systems as a prerequisite for reading this book, but you should know the basic Ruby syntax, know the standard Ruby classes, and be able to write some simple code.

More important, you don't need big infrastructure to apply what you will learn in this book. I created most of the libraries to solve problems I was having. Because many personal computers come with multicore processors these days, everyone can benefit from multiprocessing libraries such as dRuby. dRuby and my other libraries will give you some basic constructs to build tools that will make your personal computing environment flexible and powerful. After reading this book, you'll be ready to start making your own distributed tools.

Environment

All the sample programs have been tested on OS X with Ruby 1.9.2. Some of the code runs differently depending on your operating system (especially on Windows machines). I'll mention the differences as we go along.

Throughout this book, we'll do lots of experiments using the interactive Ruby shell (irb). When invoking irb, we pass the `--prompt simple` option to switch the command prompt to a simpler version (>>). Also, we have omitted some of the output prompts (=>) for a more concise display. Finally, you may want to specify `--noreadline` if you are an OS X user and experience problems using dRuby from irb (for more details, see *OS X and readline*, on page 5).

What's in This Book

This book covers a wide range of topics related to distributed computing and more. The main focus is on dRuby, but you'll also find out about other libraries I created, such as ERB, Rinda, and Drip, and how to integrate them with dRuby. You'll learn about some advanced Ruby techniques, such as multithreading, security, and garbage collection. dRuby exposes some unique problems that you might not often encounter, so you'll find out how to deal with those situations too.

Chapter 1, *Hello, dRuby*, on page 3
: The fun part starts here. We'll launch multiple terminals and access dRuby via irb. You'll learn how to use dRuby and write some simple programs to explore the power of dRuby.

Chapter 2, *Architectures of Distributed Systems*, on page 15
: You'll learn about distributed object systems in general and how dRuby is different from others.

Chapter 3, *Integrating dRuby with eRuby*, on page 31
: eRuby is a templating system often used to render HTML. ERB is an implementation of eRuby that I wrote, and it's also part of the Ruby standard libraries. In this chapter, I'll explain how easily you can integrate ERB with dRuby.

Chapter 4, *Pass by Reference, Pass by Value*, on page 57
: Even though dRuby is a seamless extension of Ruby, there are a few differences. In this chapter, you'll learn two ways of exchanging objects over processes: by reference and by value.

Chapter 5, *Multithreading*, on page 77
: You need to know about multithreading to have a better understanding of how dRuby works. When using dRuby, multiple processes work in coordination with multithreading. In this chapter, you'll learn about threading in Ruby and how you can synchronize threads, which is important for avoiding unexpected bugs.

Chapter 6, *Coordinating Processes Using Rinda*, on page 111
: Linda is a system for multiple processes to coordinate with one another. In this chapter, you'll learn how to coordinate processes via TupleSpace using Rinda, the Ruby implementation of Linda.

Chapter 7, *Extending Rinda*, on page 137
: Rinda started as a port of Linda, but I added a few extra functionalities I thought necessary while developing applications with Rinda. You'll also learn about a service registration service called Ring, which comes with Rinda.

Chapter 8, *Parallel Computing and Persistence with Rinda*, on page 165
: After releasing Rinda, I created an extension library called *more_rinda* that adds parallel computing capability and a persistence layer to Rinda. They are not part of Ruby standard libraries but have interesting extensions—with some drawbacks. I'll explain why. If you're interested in parallel computing or NoSQL, this is a chapter you shouldn't miss.

Chapter 9, *Drip: A Stream-Based Storage System*, on page 181
: If more_rinda is the trial and error of all my attempts at the art of distributed programming, Drip is my solution. Drip is a stream-based storage system, with fault tolerance and a messaging system built in. I will explain the basic usage of Drip by comparing `Queue` and `Hash` and also talk about the design policy behind Drip.

Chapter 10, *Building a Simple Search System with Drip*, on page 197
: We'll create a simple desktop search system using Drip. You will experience how you can use Drip as both a storage system and a process coordination tool. We will also talk about the `RBTree` data structure we used in the search system, which Drip uses internally.

Chapter 11, *Handling Garbage Collection*, on page 221
: You may not need to worry about garbage collection when you use Ruby daily, but there are a few things you have to know when you use dRuby. Ruby has a garbage collection system that cleans up unused objects, but this doesn't consider how dRuby passes references across processes. In this chapter, you'll see how to protect dRuby referenced objects from garbage collection and what you have to know about garbage collection when you are building applications.

Chapter 12, *Security in dRuby*, on page 229
: dRuby lets you communicate with other processes seamlessly, but this also means you have to be more careful about security to prevent unintended access. You'll learn what dRuby does and doesn't do when it comes to security and what you have to do at the application level. I'll also explain how to use dRuby over networks using SSH port forwarding.

Everyone should read Chapter 1, *Hello, dRuby*, on page 3 and Chapter 6, *Coordinating Processes Using Rinda*, on page 111 to get a basic understanding of dRuby and Rinda. If you already use dRuby and are seeking some practical tips, then you'll find the following chapters packed with detailed explanations: Chapter 4, *Pass by Reference, Pass by Value*, on page 57; Chapter 5, *Multithreading*, on page 77; Chapter 11, *Handling Garbage Collection*, on page 221; and Chapter 12, *Security in dRuby*, on page 229. If you're new to dRuby, you might find the level of detail in these chapters overwhelming. Feel free to read only the first section of these chapters and jump to the following chapters. You can always refer to these chapters as a reference when you encounter problems using dRuby.

Newly added for this English edition or greatly modified are the following chapters: Chapter 3, *Integrating dRuby with eRuby*, on page 31; Chapter 8, *Parallel Computing and Persistence with Rinda*, on page 165; and Chapter 9, *Drip: A Stream-Based Storage System*, on page 181. They're packed with unique ways to use each library and also contain many new concepts.

Conventions Used in This Book

Ruby method names follow the convention of the Ruby manual. For example, `String.new` represents a class method, and `String#chomp` represents an instance method. The arguments are just examples, and you should add your own arguments when working on the code.

The book's website[1] has a place to submit errata for the book and to participate in its discussion forum. You'll also find the source code for all the projects we build. You can click the box before the code excerpts to download that snippet directly.

Let's get started!

1. http://pragprog.com/titles/sidruby

Part I

Introducing dRuby

Welcome to the world of dRuby. In this part, you'll learn dRuby's basic concepts and architecture through a few simple applications. You'll see how Ruby and dRuby make distributed programming easy.

CHAPTER 1

Hello, dRuby

Let's get familiar with dRuby. dRuby stands for "distributed Ruby." It's one of the standard libraries that comes with the Ruby core code, and you can use it to write distributed programming apps without the hassle of installing and configuring additional components. In this chapter (because it's an unwritten rule), we'll start with "Hello, World" and then create a small reminder application that you can access from multiple terminals.

1.1 Hello, World

Let's create a server that prints out strings. Then we'll code a simple client and use it to make the server print "Hello, World." The client and server will each run in a separate process (and to make that easy, we'll run each process from a separate terminal window).

Creating the Printing Server

puts00.rb is the puts server.

puts00.rb

```
require 'drb/drb'
class Puts
  def initialize(stream=$stdout)
    @stream = stream
  end

  def puts(str)
    @stream.puts(str)
  end
end
uri = ARGV.shift
DRb.start_service(uri, Puts.new)
puts DRb.uri
DRb.thread.join()
```

Let's go through the script:

1. On line 1, we require the drb library.
2. We create a class called Puts on line 2. This class contains the puts method that we'll make available to the client.
3. On line 12, we start the dRuby service. We provide the URI (which the user passes in on the command line). The URL is the address the client uses to connect to the server. We also provide the object that will be tied to the URI. You'll find out more about the URI in *The dRuby URI, Services, and Clients*, on page 7.
4. A dRuby service runs in a separate thread. One of the most common mistakes new dRuby programmers make is to forget that their program will simply exit unless they make sure to wait until the thread stops executing. On line 14, we use DRb.thread.join to keep the script up and running.

We're going to use one terminal window to run the server. Let's call it terminal 1. In that window, run puts00.rb, passing it the URI of the service.

```
# [Terminal 1]
% ruby puts00.rb druby://localhost:12345
druby://localhost:12345
```

The server process waits for the request to arrive. Make sure that the server doesn't terminate, even after it prints out the URI of the service.

Using the Service from irb

The next step is to write the client. Rather than writing a program file, we'll just use irb. Open another terminal (terminal 2) and type the following:

```
# [Terminal 2]
% irb
irb(main):001:0> require 'drb/drb'
=> true
irb(main):002:0> there = DRbObject.new_with_uri('druby://localhost:12345')
=> #<DRb::DRbObject: ... >
```

We start by requiring the drb library—the client and the server both need it. We then create a dRuby object (of class DRbObject) by calling DRbObject.new_with_uri (refer to *OS X and readline*, on page 5 if you encounter a problem getting the prompt back), passing it the same URI we used when creating the server. We store this object in the variable there.

Now we can use this dRuby object to access methods on the server. It's as if the client has access to the Puts object we created on the server.

OS X and readline

If you use OS X and have problems getting a prompt after there = DRbObject.new_with_uri(uri), then it may be a problem with the readline library. To work around the problem, specify --noreadline.

```
irb --noreadline
```

The OS X readline library prohibits Thread from switching, and this may be causing problems when you use dRuby from irb.

```
irb(main):003:0> there.puts('Hello, World.')
=> nil
```

We called the puts method of the Puts server (see Figure 1, *Puts server and irb client*, on page 6). You should see "Hello, World." printed on terminal 1 where the server is running.

```
% ruby puts00.rb druby://localhost:12345
druby://localhost:12345
Hello, World.
```

That's pretty cool. We needed only a few lines of code to create a simple distributed server.

If you didn't notice any difference, try other characters. Make sure you observe the server terminal while you are typing in irb.

Back in irb on terminal 2, let's call the server again.

```
# [Terminal 2]
irb(main):004:0> there.puts('R is for Ruby.')
=> nil
```

You should see the second message appear on terminal 1.

The there variable in the client refers to the Puts service object. By sending the puts method to the there variable, you invoke the puts method in the server, and it prints the object you pass to standard output.

What happens if you stop the server? Try it—type Ctrl-C on terminal 1 and make sure you get back to a command prompt.

Now, back on terminal 2, call there.puts again.

```
# [Terminal 2]
irb(main):005:0> there.puts('Hello, again.')
DRb::DRbConnError: druby://localhost:12345 - #<Errno::ECONNREFUSED....
```

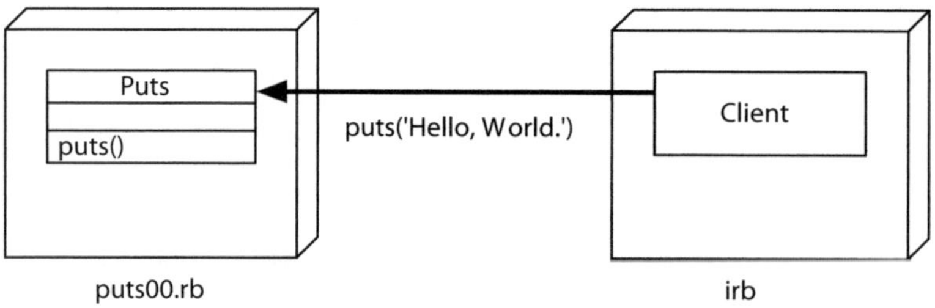

Figure 1—Puts server and irb client

dRuby raised an exception. DRbConnError means that there is a communication error between dRuby processes. The client failed to invoke the method because the server is stopped.

Let's start the server again in terminal 1.

```
# [Terminal 1]
% ruby puts00.rb druby://localhost:12345
druby://localhost:12345
```

Try there.puts again.

```
# [Terminal 2]
irb(main):006:0> there.puts('Hello, again.')
=> nil
```

This time, there is no exception, and you should see "Hello, again." printed on terminal 1.

```
# [Terminal 1]
% ruby puts00.rb
druby://localhost:12345
Hello, again.
```

Let's stop irb for now.

```
# [Terminal 2]
irb(main):007:0> exit
```

Creating the Script Version of the Client

As a final "Hello, World" experiment, let's rewrite this as a script.

hello00.rb

```
require 'drb/drb'

uri = ARGV.shift
there = DRbObject.new_with_uri(uri)
there.puts('Hello, World.')
```

As you can see, this script contains most of the same code that you typed into irb, except it gets the URI from the command line. Let's try it. Run hello00.rb in terminal 2.

```
# [Terminal 2]
% ruby hello00.rb druby://localhost:12345
```

You should see "Hello, World" appear on terminal 1.

So far, we've experimented with a simple dRuby example, and we've seen how easy it is to write a client-server model script. It's time to go a little further.

The dRuby URI, Services, and Clients

In the previous example, we used druby://localhost:12345 as a URI, but we haven't seen what this actually means. In this section, we'll learn about the relationship between the dRuby URI and the URI specified in DRb.start_service.

A dRuby URI defines the path to a dRuby server. It consists of the protocol (always druby), an optional hostname, and an optional port number.

```
druby://[hostname]:[port number]
```

When you create a service (using DRb.start_service), you give it a URI. dRuby arranges things so that clients that subsequently specify that URI will be connected to this service. Each active DRbServer has one unique URI.

```
DRb.start_service(uri, front)
```

To connect a client to a service, pass that service's URI to DRbObject.new_with_uri.

```
there = DRbObject.new_with_uri(uri)
```

An object that's associated with the URI is called the *front object* because it acts as an entrance to the service (see Figure 2, *The front object is the gateway to the application*, on page 8). All the method calls that are created by DRbObject.new_with_uri() go to this front object. When you write an actual application, you don't directly associate the model object of the application; rather, you have a proxy object that handles access control or batches multiple operations.

1.2 Building the Reminder Application

Let's create a simple task list application in which anyone can create, read, and delete entries. To keep it simple, the user interface is irb.

Let's define the Reminder class first. It has three methods: Add, delete, and to_a. Each item has a unique ID that's used when deleting an item.

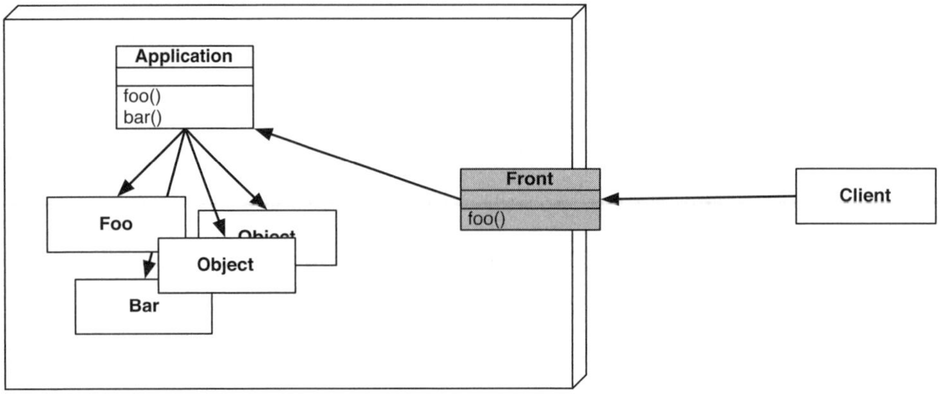

Figure 2—The front object is the gateway to the application.

reminder0.rb

```
class Reminder
  def initialize
    @item = {}
    @serial = 0
  end

  def [](key)
    @item[key]
  end

  def add(str)
    @serial += 1
    @item[@serial] = str
    @serial
  end

  def delete(key)
    @item.delete(key)
  end

  def to_a
    @item.keys.sort.collect do |k|
      [k, @item[k]]
    end
  end
end
```

Let's start the Reminder server via irb. We'll run it in terminal 1.

```
# [Terminal 1]
% irb --prompt simple -I . -r reminder0.rb -r drb/drb
```

```
>> front = Reminder.new
>> DRb.start_service('druby://localhost:12345', front)
>> DRb.uri
=> "druby://localhost:12345"
```

Next we'll use irb in terminal 2 as a client to this server.

```
# [Terminal 2]
% irb --prompt simple -r drb/drb
>> r = DRbObject.new_with_uri('druby://localhost:12345')
>> r.to_a
=> []
>> r.add('13:00 Meeting')
=> 1
>> r.add('17:00 Status report')
=> 2
>> r.add('Return DVD on Saturday')
=> 3
>> r.to_a
=> [
[1, "13:00 Meeting"],
[2, "17:00 Status report"],
[3, "Return DVD on Saturday"]
]
```

Let's start another client in a third terminal session and add and delete items.

```
# [Terminal 3]
% irb --prompt simple -r drb/drb
>> r = DRbObject.new_with_uri('druby://localhost:12345')
>> r.to_a
=> [
[1, "13:00 Meeting"],
[2, "17:00 Status report"],
[3, "Return DVD on Saturday"]
]
>> r.delete(2)
>> r.to_a
=> [[1, "13:00 Meeting"], [3, "Return DVD on Saturday"]]
>> r.add('15:00 Status report')
>> r.to_a
=> [
[1, "13:00 Meeting"],
[3, "Return DVD on Saturday"],
[4, "15:00 Status report"]
]
```

The two clients are accessing the same shared data. This is because both terminals 2 and 3 share the same Reminder object, which exists on the server (terminal 1). The clients both have a remote reference to them (see Figure 3, *Clients at terminals 2 and 3 operate the reminder at terminal 1*, on page 10).

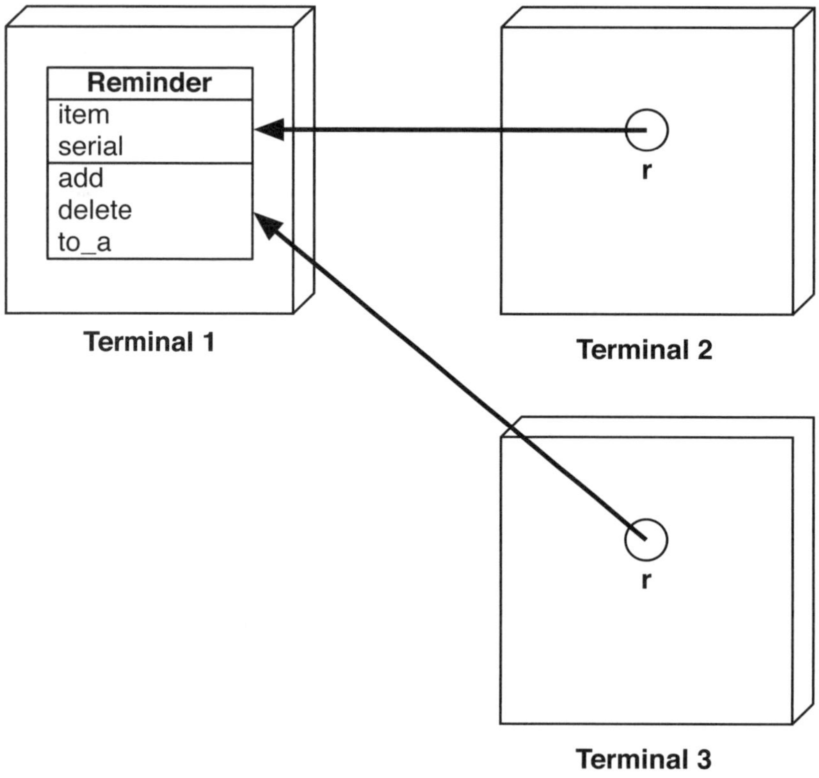

Figure 3—Clients at terminals 2 and 3 operate the reminder at terminal 1.

Next let's check the object's life span. Stop both client sessions by typing `exit` at the irb prompt. Then restart the client in terminal 2.

```
# [Terminal 2]
% irb --prompt simple -r drb/drb
>> r = DRbObject.new_with_uri('druby://localhost:12345')
>> r.to_a
=> [
[1, "13:00 Meeting"],
[3, "Return DVD on Saturday"],
[4, "15:00 Status report"]
]
```

This is as we expected. The actual `Reminder` object exists on the server, so quitting and restarting the clients doesn't have any impact on the data stored in it.

One of the benefits of using dRuby for your system is being able to share the state of a object across multiple processes. You could use dRuby as an alternative way to create persistence. For example, you could combine a short-running Common Gateway Interface (CGI) script and a long-running dRuby server when you write a web application.

To simplify the client operation, let's write a ReminderCUI script. ReminderCUI is a character-based user interface that you can use via irb. This class has a list method to show all the items and a delete method to delete an item after confirmation.

reminder_cui0.rb

```
class ReminderCUI
  def initialize(reminder)
    @model = reminder
  end

  def list
    @model.to_a.each do |k, v|
      puts format_item(k, v)
    end
    nil
  end

  def add(str)
    @model.add(str)
  end

  def show(key)
    puts format_item(key, @model[key])
  end

  def delete(key)
    puts "[delete? (Y/n)]: #{@model[key]}"
    if /\s*n\s*/ =~ gets
      puts "canceled"
      return
    end
    @model.delete(key)
    list
  end

  private
  def format_item(key, str)
    sprintf("%3d: %s\n", key, str)
  end
end
```

Let's start ReminderCUI at terminal 3 and do some experimentation (see Figure 4, *The ReminderCUI at terminal 3 operates the reminder at terminal 1*, on page 13).

```
# [Terminal 3]
% irb --prompt simple -I . -r reminder_cui0.rb -r drb/drb
>> there = DRbObject.new_with_uri('druby://localhost:12345')
>> r = ReminderCUI.new(there)
>> r.list
 1: 13:00 Meeting
 3: Return DVD on Saturday
 4: 15:00 Status report
=> nil
>> r.add('Request Ruby Hacking Guide to library')
>> r.list
 1: 13:00 Meeting
 3: Return DVD on Saturday
 4: 15:00 Status report
 5: Request Ruby Hacking Guide to library
=> nil
>> r.delete(1)
 [delete? (Y/n)]: 13:00 Meeting
n                                        #  Type "n"
canceled
=> nil
>> r.delete(1)
 [delete? (Y/n)]: 13:00 Meeting
y                                        #  Type "y"
 3: Return DVD on saturday
 4: 15:00 status report
 5: Request Ruby Hacking Guide to library
 => nil
```

Using irb, you can create a multiclient program interface easily. We'll add a web interface for this in Chapter 3, *Integrating dRuby with eRuby*, on page 31, so hold on!

In this section, we created a simple distributed application using dRuby. By now, you should have a pretty good idea of how dRuby works. But before we leave this introductory chapter, let's dig a little deeper into the URIs we've been using to access our dRuby servers.

The Hostname and Port Number

The hostname and port number components of the URI are optional on the call to DRb.start_service.

If the hostname is specified, the connection is associated with that network interface. If omitted, TCPServer will automatically assign the hostname.

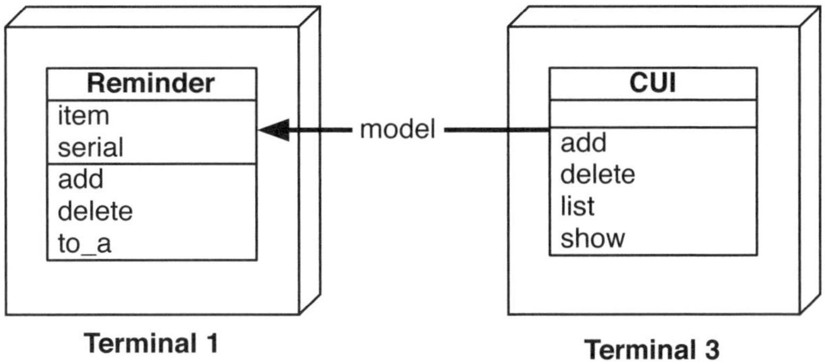

Figure 4—The ReminderCUI at terminal 3 operates the reminder at terminal 1.

If the port name is 0, the first available port will be automatically assigned.

If nil is passed instead of a URI, then it acts as if both the hostname and the port number were omitted.

Here are some examples:

- 'druby://hostname:12345': Both are specified.
- 'druby://:12345': A hostname is omitted.
- 'druby://hostname:0': A port number is omitted.
- 'druby://:0': Both a hostname and a port number are omitted.
- nil: Both a hostname and a port number are omitted.

You can always find the host and port that were used by start_service by calling the method DRb.uri. Let's try this in irb.

```
% irb -r drb/drb
irb(main):001:0> DRb.start_service('druby://localhost:12345'); DRb.uri
=> "druby://localhost:12345"
irb(main):002:0> DRb.start_service('druby://:12346'); DRb.uri
=> "druby://yourhost:12346"
irb(main):003:0> DRb.start_service('druby://localhost:0'); DRb.uri
=> "druby://localhost:52359"
irb(main):004:0> DRb.start_service('druby://:0'); DRb.uri
=> "druby://yourhost:52360"
irb(main):005:0> DRb.start_service(nil); DRb.uri
=> "druby://yourhost:52361"
irb(main):006:0> exit
```

Now let's try the "Hello, World" example without a URI. This time, use --prompt simple to simplify the irb prompt.

Start the server in terminal 1. Don't pass a URI to it.

```
# [Terminal 1]
% ruby puts00.rb
druby://yourhost:52369 #  Auto generated URI
```

Now start the client in terminal 2, using the URI displayed by the server.

```
# [Terminal 2]
% irb --prompt simple -r drb/drb
>> uri = 'druby://yourhost:52369'
>> #  Specify the same hostname and port number as in the terminal 1
>> there = DRbObject.new_with_uri(uri)
>> there.puts('Hello, World.')
```

You should see "Hello, World." pop up on terminal 1.

When we first tried the "Hello, World" app, we used localhost as the hostname, so we were able to run the clients on the same machine as the server. This time, we've used an externally accessible name, so you can try running a client on a separate machine that is networked with the server. Just specify the URI of the server, the same way you did when running the client locally.

1.3 Moving Ahead

In this chapter, we learned the following:

- We can use dRuby out of the box, because it comes with Ruby. All we need to do is require drb/drb to load the library.
- We use DRb.start_service to start a service.
- The URI identifies DRbServer.
- Each DRbServer object can associate with one object to expose it to the public.
- Clients create reference objects by specifying the URI.

Now that we understand the basics of writing a distributed app with dRuby, in the next chapter we'll step back and study the concept of distributed systems in general. We'll see how dRuby hides the complexity of these systems, thanks to the power of Ruby.

CHAPTER 2

Architectures of Distributed Systems

In this chapter, we'll walk through the concept of distributed object systems and see how dRuby fits in. First you'll learn about distributed object systems in general, and then you'll see the similarities and differences between dRuby and the other distributed object systems out there.

2.1 Understanding Distributed Object Systems

Client-server systems are among the most well-known ways to build distributed systems or applications. A *distributed object system* is an enhancement of this client-server model. It's a library in which you can build distributed applications using object-oriented programming.

When you write a distributed application, you have to pay special attention to network programming. If you don't, you may end up spending more time dealing with network programming issues than building application logic.

Many developers have tried coming up with libraries that let you easily program distributed applications by hiding these complex interprocess networking protocols. Let's take a look at the available libraries.

Remote Functions with RPC and RMI

Remote Procedure Call (RPC) is a way to call remote functions as if you were calling local functions (see Figure 5, *How RPC works*, on page 16). It generates a client stub from interface descriptions. The client stub hides network programming logic so that you don't have to worry about the location of the server or how to connect.

In Figure 5, *How RPC works*, on page 16, the *client stub* converts function calls into network communication. The "server stub" receives the communication from the client, invokes the main function, and then returns the result.

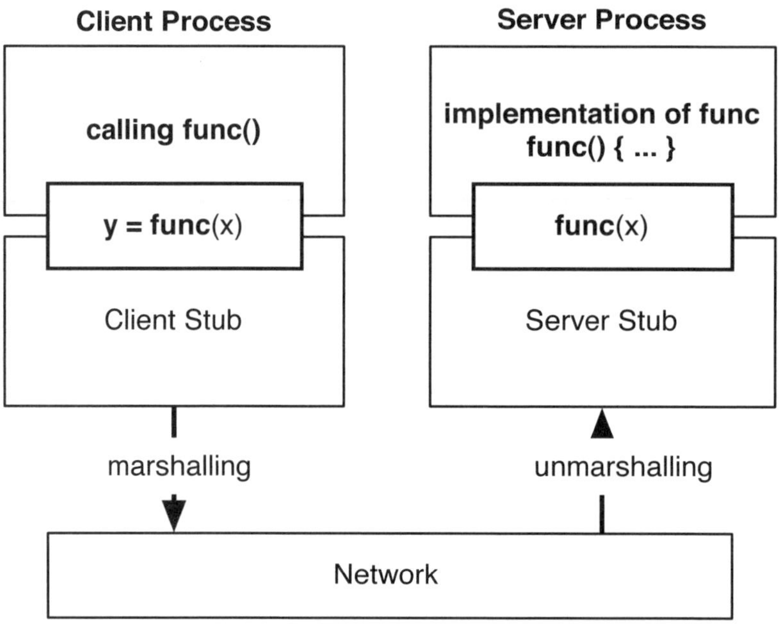

Figure 5—How RPC works: Client -> Stub -> Network -> Stub -> Server

The server stub is often called the *skeleton* or *framework*. It not only executes the incoming function request but also acts as a listener to wait for any incoming calls.

Remote Method Invocation (RMI) is a way to extend method invocation remotely, and the concept is very similar to RPC (see Figure 6, *How RMI works*, on page 17). The main difference is how you think about the concept. RPC "calls" remote functions, whereas RMI "sends" a message to remote objects. RMI also provides a client stub and a server stub to hide the interprocess communication layer. The server stub is in charge of network server programming and identifies which object should receive the call.

Clients can call methods without worrying about the location of the receiver object. You can also use the remote object reference as if it existed locally. For example, you can set a reference of a remote object into a variable or pass it as a method argument. The type of library where you can treat remote objects and local objects equally is called a *distributed object* or a *distributed object system*. A *distributed object* is also referred to as a *remotely located object* (in contrast to a local object).

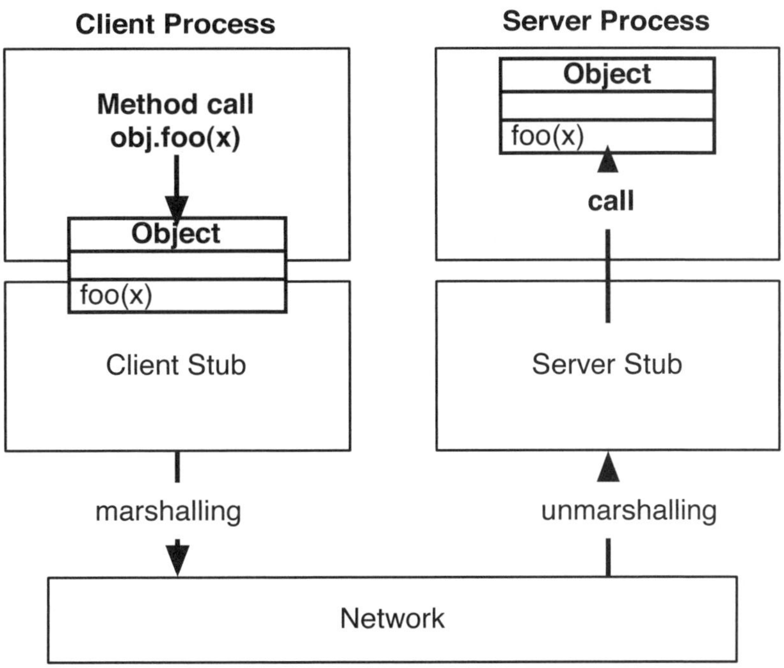

Figure 6—How RMI works: Client -> Stub -> Network -> Stub -> Server

Distributed Objects from a Programming Perspective

So far, we've learned the semantics of distributed systems. Let's now think about how these distributed systems affect our programming style.

When we write normal programs, all objects, variables, and methods are allocated inside one process space. Each process area is protected by the operating system (OS), and they can't access each other (see Figure 7, *Location of objects and processes for a normal system*, on page 18).

In a distributed object system, we treat other processes or objects in other machines as if they were in the same process space (see Figure 8, *Location of objects and processes within a distributed object systems*, on page 19).

How local processes and remote processes behave differently depends on their implementation. For example, some systems may be able to pass remote objects into arguments or return remote objects, but others may not. Some systems may require you to take extra steps when local objects communicate with remote objects.

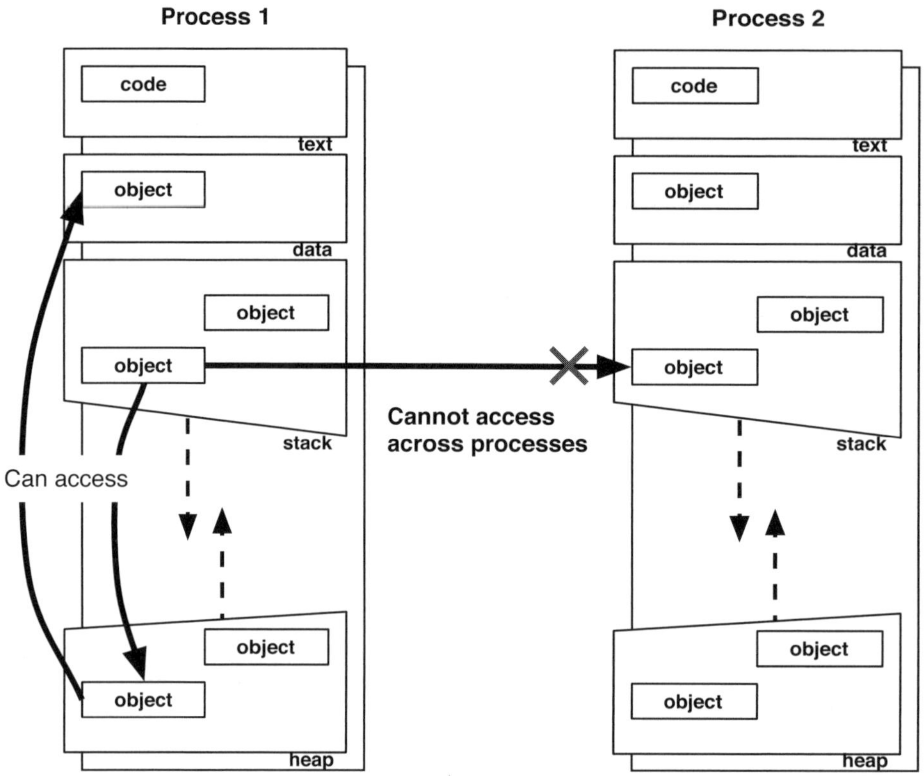

Figure 7—Location of objects and processes for a normal system. Objects can't access each other across processes.

Furthermore, there are often differences between "objects" in distributed systems and "objects" in programming languages. The smaller the difference is, the more seamless it will be to switch between programming languages.

The Popular Distributed Object Systems

Distributed Component Object Model (DCOM), Common Object Request Broker Architecture (CORBA), and Java RMI are widely known, and of course dRuby is also a distributed object system.

While Java RMI and dRuby are tightly coupled with their hosting languages, DCOM and CORBA are language-independent systems. C++, Java, and non-OOP languages such as C can use them.

DCOM, CORBA, and Java RMI require us to define the interface for stub generation because they are statically typed languages. For example, DCOM

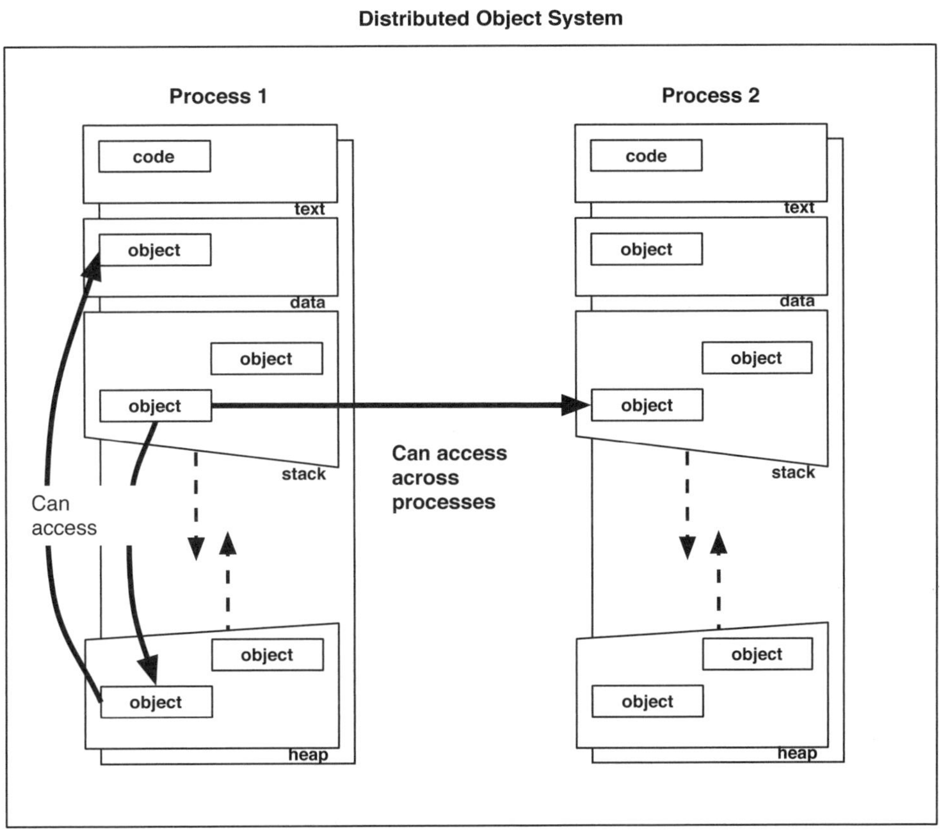

Figure 8—Location of objects and processes within a distributed object systems. Objects can access each other across processes.

and CORBA require us to write an interface using a language called Interactive Data Language (IDL); see Figure 9, *Writing interfaces using IDL*, on page 20. Once we generate stubs from IDL, we need to link them to all the clients that may use these remote objects in advance.

Dynamically typed languages, such as Cocoa/Objective-C and dRuby, don't need IDL because methods are linked at execution time. We also don't need to link to the stub of every single class. Instead, we link to only one class for the client and one for the server. This sounds so easy compared to statically typed languages, but you need to be aware of one thing. When you want to copy an object of unknown remote class (rather than just calling remote methods), then the class definition of the remote object must exist locally.

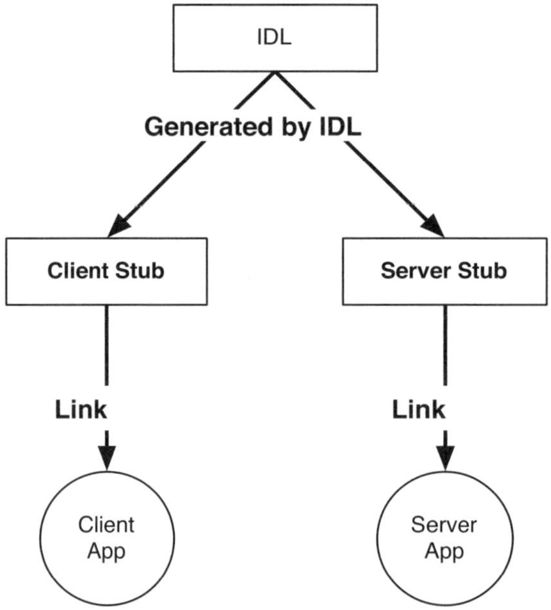

Figure 9—Writing interfaces using IDL

Your programming style becomes very different between a system that needs to know the interface in advance and a system that doesn't need to know it.

So far, we've seen the different flavors of distributed systems in other languages. Some are language dependent, and others aren't. Also, distributed systems in statically typed languages tend to require the interface of remote objects to be defined as IDL, while dynamic languages don't. Next, let's see how dRuby fits into this distributed system paradigm.

2.2 Design Principles of dRuby

I designed dRuby to extend Ruby method invocation over networks. dRuby is a library to implement distributed objects in Ruby.

dRuby has the following characteristics:

- Limited to Ruby
- 100 percent written in Ruby
- No IDL required

Let's look at these concepts a little more closely.

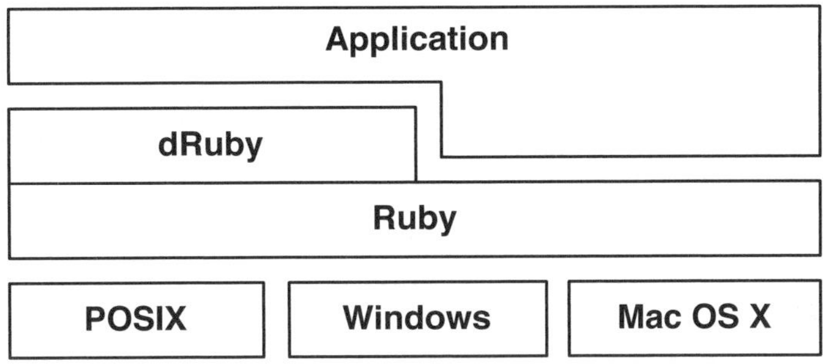

Figure 10—The software layers. Observe where dRuby sits above the operating systems.

Pure Ruby

dRuby is a distributed object system purely targeted to Ruby. It sounds limiting, but this also means you can run dRuby in any environment where Ruby can run (see Figure 10, *The software layers*, on page 21). This is very similar to Java RMI, which also can run anywhere Java can run.

Figure 11, *An example of a system across multiple OSs*, on page 22 shows the architecture of a complex system across different operating systems.

dRuby is written purely in Ruby without using any C extension libraries—another bonus. Ruby comes with network, thread, and marshaling-related libraries as part of its standard library, so I was able to write everything in Ruby. The first version of dRuby had only 160 lines (the current dRuby has more than 1,700 lines including RDoc), and the core part of the library is still the same (see *The First dRuby*, on page 23). The concise codebase of dRuby demonstrates how easily you can write a complex library by using just Ruby's standard libraries.

Feels Like Ruby

I paid special attention to the compatibility between dRuby and Ruby. Many features of Ruby remain in dRuby, too.

Ruby is very dynamic. You don't need to use inheritance most of the time because the variables of Ruby aren't typed. Ruby looks up methods at execution time (method invocation time); these characteristics also apply to dRuby. dRuby doesn't have type-in variables, and method searches are done at execution time. Because you don't need to prepare the list of methods and their inheritance information, you don't need to write IDL.

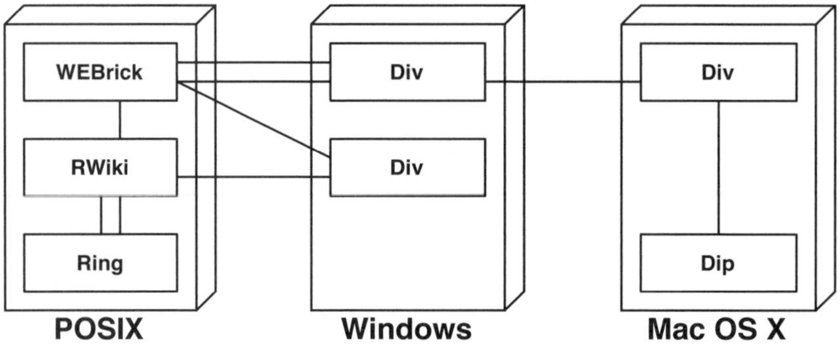

Figure 11—An example of a system across multiple OSs. Div, Ring, Dip, and RWiki are applications that use dRuby.

dRuby's core mission isn't about changing the behavior of Ruby, apart from extending Ruby method invocation across networks. With this functionality, you can have as much ease and fun programming in dRuby as you do with Ruby. For example, you can still use a block for method calls and use exceptions as well. Other multithreading synchronization methods, such as Mutex and Queue, are also available remotely, and you can use them to synchronize multiple processes.

Pass by Reference, Pass by Value

Having said all that, sometimes you need to know the difference between Ruby and dRuby.

In Ruby, objects are all exchanged by reference when you pass or receive method arguments, return values, or exceptions.

In dRuby, objects are exchanged either by reference or by the copy of the original value. When an object is passed by reference, the operation to the object will affect the original (like a normal Ruby object). However, when passed by value, the operation doesn't affect the original, and the change stays within the process where the object is modified (see Figure 12, *Passing by reference and passing by value*, on page 24).

This difference doesn't exist in Ruby, and you have to pay special attention to this when you program with dRuby.

If I really wanted to make dRuby look the same as Ruby, I could have designed dRuby to always pass by reference. However, remote object method invocation requires some network overhead, and doing small object operations all via

The First dRuby

The first version of dRuby was created in 1999 and posted to the Japanese Ruby user mailing list.[a] The email is written in Japanese, but you can see some snippets of source code that look very similar to dRuby now.

```
# Starting drb server.
DRb.start_server('druby://hostname:port', front)
# Connecting to the remote server
ro = DRbObject.new(nil, 'druby://server:port')
ro.sample(1, DRbEx.new(2), 3)
```

The original source code is about 160 lines, and about 50 lines of the core code will give you clear idea about how dRuby works internally.

```
class DRbObject
  def initialize(obj, uri=nil)
    @uri = uri || DRb.uri
    @ref = obj.id if obj
  end
  def method_missing(msg_id, *a)
    succ, result = DRbConn.new(@uri).send_message(self, msg_id, *a)
    raise result if ! succ
    result
  end

  attr :ref
end
```

DRbObject acts as a proxy object, so it doesn't have any methods. Therefore, method_missing receives all the method calls and sends them to the DRbConn class.

```
class DRbConn
  include DRbProtocol

  def initialize(remote_uri)
    @host, @port = parse_uri(remote_uri)
  end
  def send_message(ref, msg_id, *arg)
    begin
      soc = TCPSocket.open(@host, @port)
      send_request(soc, ref, msg_id, *arg)
      recv_reply(soc)
    ensure
      soc.close if soc
    end
  end
end
```

DRbConn acts as a TCPSocket server. It transfers the message to the remote server—so simple. If you're interested in the internals of dRuby, read the rest of the original code to get a better idea about the structure of the library before jumping into reading the current version of dRuby, which is more than 1,700 lines.

a. http://blade.nagaokaut.ac.jp/cgi-bin/scat.rb/ruby/ruby-list/15406

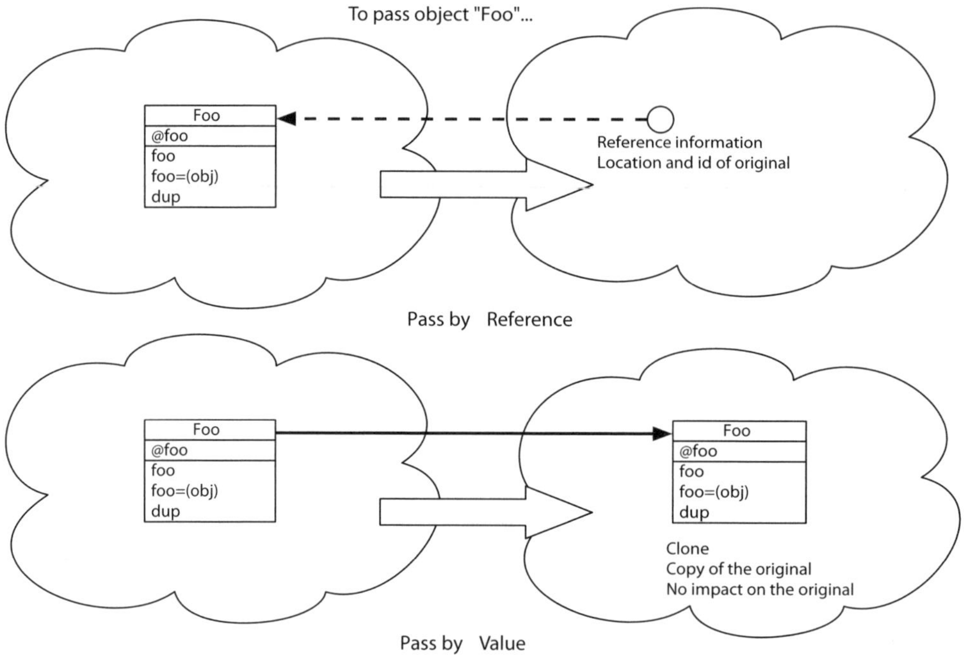

Figure 12—Passing by reference and passing by value

RMI isn't effective. It's vital to pass the copy of the object in certain situations to increase your application's performance. Also, if you keep passing by reference, you'll never get the actual value from the remote server. Instead, you'll be looping forever, trying to find out the object's state.

It might sound a bit complicated, but don't worry. You don't have to specify whether you plan to pass by value or by reference—dRuby does it for you. Because dRuby automatically selects the reference method, you don't have to write a special method for dRuby.

You'll see more detail about automatically passing by value or by reference in Chapter 4, *Pass by Reference, Pass by Value*, on page 57.

2.3 dRuby in the Real World

With dRuby, you can create distributed systems as if you were doing normal Ruby programming, which helps you turn your ideas for complex distributed systems into working applications quickly. dRuby offers a generic way to achieve RMI. Some people use dRuby to sketch their initial system and then swap with more specialized middleware as their systems grow. For inspiration, the following are some real-world examples of dRuby systems.

Hatena Screen Shot

Hatena[1] is Japan's leading Web 2.0 company and provides various services, such as a blogging system and a social bookmark system. Hatena used to provide a service called Hatena Screen Shot, which generates a screenshot of a given URL and provides it as a thumbnail. The architecture of this service was unique because it consisted of different operating systems. The web frontend was built on Linux, and the screen-capturing component was built with a Windows Internet Explorer component. This is a good example of integrating a cross-platform system using dRuby. The system was also architected to be able to run screen-capturing services in parallel so that the component could scale horizontally by simply adding more Windows machines.

Twitter

Twitter used dRuby and Rinda before it built its own queuing system called Starling in Ruby (until the system was replaced by another in-house system written in Scala). At SDForum Silicon Valley Ruby Conference 2007, Blaine Cooke presented a talk called "Scaling Twitter."[2] In the presentation, Cooke mentioned dRuby as "stupid easy and reasonably fast" (though he also described it as "kinda flaky").

Buzztter

Buzztter[3] is a web service to analyze tweets from Twitter, which extracts trending keywords. The service started in 2007, before Twitter started its own "Trending Topics." The service still provides a useful way to extract topics from Japanese tweets because Japanese sentences don't have word separation and are therefore harder to analyze. Buzztter consists of multiple subsystems, and it used Rinda (Chapter 6, *Coordinating Processes Using Rinda*, on page 111) as middleware to consume tweets from Twitter's REST API. The system used Rinda for two years, eventually replacing it with RabbitMQ[4] in 2009. In November 2007, Rinda handled 125,000 tweets (72MB) a day.

1. http://www.hatena.ne.jp
2. Slide: http://www.slideshare.net/Blaine/scaling-twitter, video: http://video.google.com/videoplay?docid=-7846959339830379167
3. http://buzztter.com
4. http://www.rabbitmq.com

RWiki

RWiki is a wiki system written with dRuby and still actively used in my workplace. It's been running for more than ten years, and the system stores more than 40,000 pages in memory (more than 1GB). RWiki doesn't use an RDBMS but logs pages in plain text. RWiki persists the data by recovering the log when the system restarts. RWiki uses Ruby Document (RD) as a document format. Once you write your wiki page, the page is stored as a Ruby object, and you can retrieve the content of the page (not just the entire source but also various components, such as chapters, sections, links, incoming links, and other customized attributes) via method invocations. RWiki acts as a wiki via HTTP but acts as an object database via dRuby. We use the object database in several ways. For example, we've been using agile methodologies for years, and we store user stories[5] and request tickets in the RWiki. Then we connect to RWiki pages via dRuby from a separate process to automatically generate TestSuite or aggregate statistical information of all the request tickets.

Libraries

Many libraries use dRuby to take advantage of its interprocess communication capability. Here are some examples:

god
: https://github.com/mojombo/god: Process monitoring system.

RSpec
: http://rspec.info/rails/runners.html: Testing framework. With the --drb option, you can speed up tests by preloading the entire Rails app.

BackgrounDRb
: http://backgroundrb.rubyforge.org: Job server and scheduler. This tool off-loads longer-running tasks from the Ruby on Rails application.

They are all open source and good examples to study for how to use dRuby in various ways.

2.4 Moving Ahead

In this chapter, we learned about distributed object systems in general and then compared dRuby with other systems. You'll find that dRuby hides most of the complexity of building distributed systems so that you can write a

5. http://www.extremeprogramming.org/rules/userstories.html

distributed program as an extension of normal Ruby programming. Having said that, there are a few differences to bear in mind, especially how to pass Ruby objects.

In the next chapter, I'll introduce another library I wrote called ERB. ERB is a template library that we'll use to add a web interface to the Reminder app we created in Chapter 1, *Hello, dRuby*, on page 3.

Part II

Understanding dRuby

In this part, you'll integrate dRuby with other components to make more complex applications. Through various exercises, you'll learn what you need to consider when communicating with multiple processes.

CHAPTER 3

Integrating dRuby with eRuby

In this chapter, you'll learn how to integrate dRuby into ERB, an implementation of the eRuby templating library. eRuby is a templating system used to embed Ruby scripts into documents; it's handy for creating templates or rendering web pages and is an excellent companion to dRuby. We'll first learn the basics of eRuby and ERB, and we'll then work through some examples to integrate them with the Reminder dRuby script we created in Chapter 1, *Hello, dRuby*, on page 3.

You may already be familiar with ERB through web frameworks such as Rails; I'll show you some cool ways of using ERB with dRuby.

3.1 Generating Templates with ERB

You probably see lots of templates from day to day, used for things such as bills, meeting agendas, HTML, and domain-specific languages (DSLs) such as program generators.

In this chapter, we'll learn various ways to generate templates using ERB.

Let's look at a sample email first.

```
-----------------------------------------
Qty Item
      Shipping Status
-----------------------------------------
1 Recollections of erb
       - Shipped June 22, 2008
1 Great BigTable and my toys
       - Shipped July 18, 2009
1 The last decade of RWiki and lazy me
       - Just shipped
-----------------------------------------
```

```
You can print the receipt and check the status of this
order (and any of your other orders) online by visiting
your account at http://www.druby.org/m_seki

http://www.druby.org
```

If we want to turn the preceding example into a reusable template, we can combine String concatenation and a String literal, as follows:

shipping_notify_pre.rb

```
class ShippingNotify

  def initialize
    @account = ''
    @customer = ''
    @items = []
  end
  attr_accessor :account, :customer, :items

  def to_s
    str = <<EOS
Dear #{customer}

This note is just to let you know that we've shipped
some items that you ordered.

-----------------------------------------
Qty Item
      Shipping Status
-----------------------------------------
EOS
    items.each do |qty, item, shipped|
      if shipped == Date.today
        status = 'Just shipped'
      elsif shipped < Date.today
        status = 'Shipped ' + shipped.strftime("%B %d, %Y")
      else
        status = 'NA'
      end
      str << "#{qty} #{item}\n"
      str << "       - #{status}\n"
    end
    str << <<EOS
-----------------------------------------

You can print the receipt and check the status of this
order (and any of your other orders) online by visiting
Your Acount at http://www.druby.org/#{account}

http://www.druby.org
EOS
```

```
    return str
  end
end

if __FILE__ == $0
  greetings = ShippingNotify.new

  greetings.account = 'm_seki'
  greetings.customer = 'Masatoshi SEKI'
  items = [[1, 'Recollections of erb', Date.new(2008, 6, 22)],
           [1, 'Great BigTable and my toys', Date.new(2009, 7, 18)],
           [1, 'The last decade of RWiki and lazy me',  Date.today]]
  greetings.items = items

  puts greetings.to_s
end
```

As you can see, lots of string literals are scattered across the script. There are two problems with embedding the partial templates into a script: it's hard to read, and it's hard to exchange scattered templates.

Many templating languages take an opposite approach. Rather than embedding documents into scripts, they embed scripts into documents, which is the approach eRuby takes.

eRuby is a templating system for embedding Ruby script into text files, and ERB is a Ruby library to write eRuby. There is also an "eruby" library implemented in C, but ERB is the one included in the Ruby standard libraries.

You can use eRuby not just to print out HTML but also to print out any text files (however, it won't detect invalid HTML files).

Here's how to embed a Ruby script:

<% ... %>
: Execute the Ruby script.

<%= ... %>
: Embed the result after evaluating the statement.

Other characters
: Embed to strings as they are.

Not only can you use the result of the statement, but you can also control flow and iterations. Let's rewrite the previous example using ERB. The following example splits the previous example into two programs. shipping_notify.erb is a template, and shipping_notify2.rb has all the data and logic.

shipping_notify.erb

```
Dear <%= customer %>

This note is just to let you know that we've shipped
some items that you ordered.

-----------------------------------------
Qty Item
      Shipping Status
-----------------------------------------<%
    items.each do |qty, item, shipped|
      if shipped == Date.today
        status = 'Just shipped'
      elsif shipped < Date.today
        status = 'Shipped ' + shipped.strftime("%B %d, %Y")
      else
        status = 'NA'
      end
%>
<%= qty %> <%= item %>
       - <%= status %><%
    end
%>
-----------------------------------------

You can print the receipt and check the status of this
order (and any of your other orders) online by visiting
your account at http://www.druby.org/<%= account %>

http://www.druby.org
```

The interesting code is around items.each. You can embed iterations and conditions into eRuby, not just string literals. Here is the refactored ShippingNotify class:

shipping_notify2.rb

```
require 'erb'
class ShippingNotify
  def initialize
    @account = ''
    @customer = ''
    @items = []
    @erb = ERB.new(File.read('shipping_notify.erb'))
  end
  attr_accessor :account, :customer, :items

  def to_s
    @erb.result(binding)
  end
end
```

```
15 if __FILE__ == $0
16   greetings = ShippingNotify.new
17 
18   greetings.account = 'm_seki'
19   greetings.customer = 'Masatoshi SEKI'
20   items = [[1, 'Recollections of erb', Date.new(2008, 6, 22)],
21            [1, 'Great BigTable and my toys', Date.new(2009, 7, 18)],
22            [1, 'The last decade of RWiki and lazy me',  Date.today]]
23   greetings.items = items
24 
25   puts greetings.to_s
26 end
```

Let's compare the differences. First, the majority of templating strings are gone, except for data initialization into the items variable on line 20. Also, the initialize constructor has a statement to instantiate the ERB object on line 7.

```
@erb = ERB.new(File.read('shipping_notify.erb'))
```

ERB.new takes the eRuby script as an argument, converts it into a Ruby script, and then generates an ERB object that evaluates the Ruby object. In this example, you just created an ERB object from the shipping_notify.erb file. You can evaluate the ERB object as many times as possible, but we want to evaluate only once in this example, so we put it into the @erb variable inside the initialize method. Next, let's look into the to_s method.

```
def to_s
  @erb.result(binding)
end
```

The method calls the result method with a strange parameter called binding. binding is a predefined variable that includes all environmental information in the current scope, such as self, variables, and methods. This lets eRuby access instance variables and instance methods of the scope that calls the eRuby script.

In the preceding example, the eRuby script is evaluated in the same scope as ShippingNotify#to_s so that the eRuby script can access the account, customer, and items methods.

When you evaluate ERB, you can pass a binding. This means the eRuby script can access the application that uses eRuby. Thanks to this feature, you don't have to worry about where to put support methods (the methods that the eRuby script uses) and how to pass them into the eRuby script.

Let's move to the part of the shipping_notify.erb code that's responsible for displaying these support methods within eRuby.

```
if shipped == Date.today
  status = 'Just shipped'
elsif shipped < Date.today
  status = 'Shipped ' + shipped.strftime("%B %d, %Y")
else
  status = 'NA'
end
```

These methods don't fit properly with the rest of the code because the code has an if statement to calculate the shipping date.

Let's extract them into a method and move them into the ShippingNotify class.

```
class ShippingNotify
  ...

  def shipping_status(shipped)
    if shipped == Date.today
      'Just shipped'
    elsif shipped < Date.today
      'Shipped ' + shipped.strftime("%B %d, %Y")
    else
      'NA'
    end
  end

  ...
end
```

Then, let's change the eRuby script to call this method.

```
-----------------------------------------
Qty Item
      Shipping Status
-----------------------------------------<%
    items.each do |qty, item, shipped|
%>
<%= qty %> <%= item %>
       - <%= shipping_status(shipped) %><%
    end
%>
-----------------------------------------
```

ShippingNotify is a View class to display text. It moves any string templating functions to an external eRuby script so that you can minimize mixing template and code. Looking at this from a different angle, the eRuby script moves any logic out of the template to make the template clean.

The following is the refactored code:

shipping_notify3.rb

```
require 'erb'

class ShippingNotify
  def initialize
    @account = ''
    @customer = ''
    @items = []
    @erb = ERB.new(File.read('shipping_notify3.erb'))
  end
  attr_accessor :account, :customer, :items

  def shipping_status(shipped)
    if shipped == Date.today
      'Just shipped'
    elsif shipped < Date.today
      'Shipped ' + shipped.strftime("%B %d, %Y")
    else
      'NA'
    end
  end

  def to_s
    @erb.result(binding)
  end
end

if __FILE__ == $0
  greetings = ShippingNotify.new

  greetings.account = 'm_seki'
  greetings.customer = 'Masatoshi SEKI'
  items = [[1, 'Recollections of erb', Date.new(2008, 6, 22)],
           [1, 'Great BigTable and my toys', Date.new(2009, 7, 18)],
           [1, 'The last decade of RWiki and lazy me',  Date.today]]
  greetings.items = items

  puts greetings.to_s
end
```

Let's review what we've done so far.

When coding a template, we tend to mix lots of string concatenation inside the document so that we can scatter several pieces of code logic inside the template. It will become slightly better if we combine String concatenation and a String literal using a "here" document.[1] In our code sample, anything surrounded by "EOS" is treated as strings, even when the code goes across

1. http://en.wikipedia.org/wiki/Here_document

multiple lines. Both styles embed strings into the script. eRuby takes an opposite approach by embedding script into strings. ERB can evaluate eRuby with binding, so it is easier to integrate with your application without adding each variable you want to pass to the template into the eRuby script.

There are different opinions about how much eRuby should be in charge and how much Ruby should. If you try to remove as much logic as possible from your eRuby script, it will just become string replacement. If you introduce new syntax for iteration and condition statements, then it is almost the same as introducing a new language.

We learned one possible way of integrating an application with eRuby using binding. You can use other methods aside from result to evaluate ERB. Here are all the ways you can integrate with ERB (also see Figure 13, *All the methods to evaluate the ERB object*, on page 39):

ERB.new(eruby_script, safe_level=nil, trim_mode=nil)
: Generates an ERB object from eruby_script. You can specify the safe level (see more details about the safe level in *Setting the Security Level with $SAFE*, on page 230) of eval and trim_mode (whether you trim the whitespace of the output or not).

run(b=TOPLEVEL_BINDING)
: Runs ERB with binding and prints to standard output.

result(b=TOPLEVEL_BINDING)
: Runs ERB with binding and returns a string.

src
: Runs ERB with binding and returns the converted Ruby script.

Let's try the src method.

```
% irb -r erb
irb(main):001:0> ERB.new('Hello, World. <%= Time.now %>').src
=> "#coding:UTF-8\n_erbout = ''; _erbout.concat \"Hello, World. \";
 _erbout.concat(( Time.now ).to_s);
 _erbout.force_encoding(__ENCODING__)"
```

The output is a bit hard to read, but it concatenates a string into the _erbout variable. When you run the result method, ERB evaluates this script. This is an expensive operation because you have to call eval, which executes every time the Ruby script is parsed. To avoid the repetitive call, you can turn the eRuby script into a method by wrapping the returning string with the method definition.

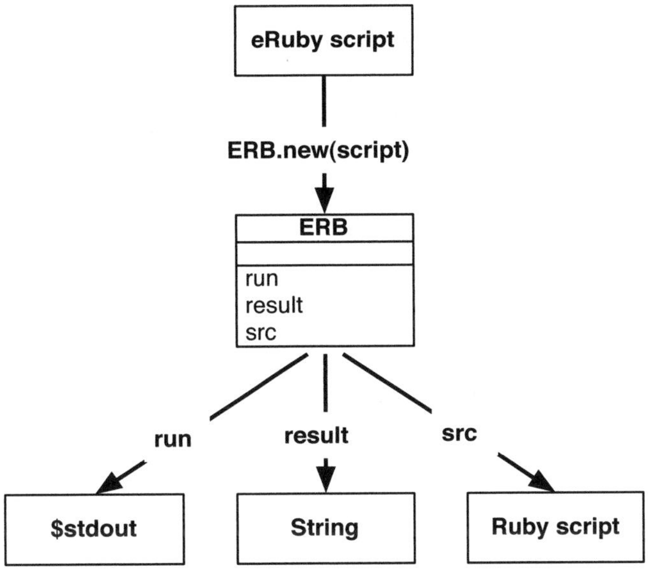

Figure 13—All the methods to evaluate the ERB object

Let's turn ShippingNotify into a method. You don't have to change the eRuby script.

shipping_notify4.rb

```
require 'erb'
class ShippingNotify
  def initialize
    @account = ''
    @customer = ''
    @items = []
  end
  attr_accessor :account, :customer, :items

  def shipping_status(shipped)
    if shipped == Date.today
      'Just shipped'
    elsif shipped < Date.today
      'Shipped ' + shipped.strftime("%B %d, %Y")
    else
      'NA'
    end
  end
  extend ERB::DefMethod
  def_erb_method('to_s', 'shipping_notify3.erb')
end
```

Once you extend ERB::DefMethod, def_erb_method becomes available. This method takes a method name, an eRuby script filename, or the ERB object as arguments, and it defines the method into the environment where this method is called (the ShippingNotify class in this case).

shipping_notify4.rb
```
extend ERB::DefMethod
def_erb_method('to_s', 'shipping_notify3.erb')
```

The caller of def_erb_method is the ShippingNotify class. It defines the content of shipping_notify3.erb as a to_s method.

So far, we learned the basic of templating and how to use ERB. Separating some logic into its own class and passing it to ERB via binding is a good way to keep the template clean. In the next section, you'll learn how to use ERB and dRuby with WEBrick::CGI so that you can publish your application via the Web.

3.2 Integrating WEBrick::CGI and ERB with dRuby

WEBrick::CGI enables you to write a CGI script with the same interfaces as a WEBrick servlet. (Rack is a similar library that's also popular.) In this example, we'll create a CGI script with WEBrick::CGI and learn how it interacts with dRuby.

Here is a simple example of how to use WEBrick::CGI:

my_cgi.rb
```
#!/usr/local/bin/ruby
require 'webrick/cgi'
require 'erb'

class MyCGI < WEBrick::CGI
  def initialize(*args)
    super(*args)
    @erb = create_erb
  end

  def do_GET(req, res)
    build_page(req, res)
  rescue
    error_page(req, res)
  end

  def build_page(req, res)
    res["content-type"] = "text/html"
    res.body = @erb.result(binding)
  end
```

```
  def error_page(req, res)
    res["content-type"] = "text/plain"
    res.body = 'oops'
  end

  def create_erb
    ERB.new(<<EOS)
<html>
 <head><title>Hello</title></head>
 <body>Hello, World.</body>
</html>
EOS
  end
end

MyCGI.new.start()
```

Let's create a class, inherit WEBrick::CGI, and then implement the do_GET() method. To use the class, instantiate it and then call the start method. The req and res arguments passed to the method are the same as the one we use for the WEBrick servlet.

So, how do you run CGI in your environment?

This is an example of running CGI in my environment (OS X):

```
$ vi my_cgi.rb
$ chmod +x my_cgi.rb
$ sudo cp my_cgi.rb /Library/WebServer/CGI-Executables/
```

You will see "Hello, World." printed to the browser if you access the page from http://localhost/cgi-bin/my_cgi.rb.

The my_cgi.rb script embedded ERB into the CGI script to make this example simple to explain. When you actually write the code, you should move the eRuby part into a different file.

Reminder CGI interface

In this section, we'll make a simple ERB-based CGI interface of the Reminder app we created in Section 1.2, *Building the Reminder Application*, on page 7.

The CGI script will have the following functionalities as the command-based version we created earlier:

- List to-do items
- The ability to add an item
- The ability to delete an item

First let's implement the "List to-do items" functionality. We'll make an ERB class to list items with <ul>:

```
<ul>
<li>1: 13:00 Meeting</li>
<li>3: Return DVD on Saturday</li>
<li>4: 15:00 Status report</li>
<li>5: Request Ruby Hacking Guide from the library</li>
</ul>
```

We can write code to insert a row at <li> iteratively. Assuming there are items in ary, here is the code:

```
<ul>
<% ary.each do |k, v| %>
<li><%= k %>: <%= v %></li>
<% end %>
</ul>
```

To test this code, we need a test server with some sample data (test_reminder.rb).

test_reminder.rb

```
require './reminder0'
require 'drb/drb'
require 'pp'

reminder = Reminder.new
reminder.add('Apply to RubyKaigi 2011')
reminder.add('Buy a pomodoro timer')
reminder.add('Display <a>')
DRb.start_service('druby://localhost:12345', reminder)

while true
  sleep 10
  pp reminder.to_a
end
```

This time, we'll create a Ruby script, rather than playing with irb. This script first creates a Reminder object, adds test data, and then starts dRuby. Run the script; it should print out the content of Reminder every ten seconds. We'll keep this script up and running. For the production environment, you should use DRb.thread.join.

```
% ruby -I. test_reminder.rb
[
 [1, "Apply to RubyKaigi 2011"],
 [2, "Buy a pomodoro timer"],
 [3, "Display <a>"]
]
....
```

Next, let's write a script to display the data (erb_reminder.rb).

erb_reminder.rb

```
require 'erb'
require 'drb/drb'

class ReminderView
  extend ERB::DefMethod
  def_erb_method('to_html(there)', 'erb_reminder.erb')
end

there = DRbObject.new_with_uri('druby://localhost:12345')
view = ReminderView.new
puts view.to_html(there)
```

The preceding code includes the erb_reminder.erb script and also talks to the dRuby service started at terminal 1.

erb_reminder.erb

```
<ul>
<% there.to_a.each do |k, v| %>
<li><%= k %>: <%= v %></li>
<% end %>
</ul>
```

Let's run the script in a different terminal.

```
% ruby erb_reminder.rb
<ul>

<li>1: Apply to RubyKaigi 2011</li>

<li>2: Buy a pomodoro timer</li>

<li>3: Display <a></li>

</ul>
```

It should display the list using <li> tags. But wait—it printed out < and > as they appear. It should escape tags like this:

```
<li>3: Display &lt;a&gt;</li>
```

Escaping

ERB::Util provides several methods to help escape HTML tags and encode URL parameters.

Command	Meaning
ERB::Util.html_escape(s)	Escapes &, “, <, >
ERB::Util.h(s)	An alias of ERB::Util.html_escape(s)
ERB::Util.url_encode(s)	Converts strings into URL-encoded strings
ERB::Util.u(s)	An alias of ERB::Util.url_encode(s)

u and h look strange, but they are used like this:

```
<ul>
<% there.to_a.each do |k, v| %>
<li><%= k %>: <%=h v %></li>
<% end %>
</ul>
```

When you write < %=h ... % > , it has the same meaning as escaping HTML. This looks like eRuby extends the Ruby syntax, but this is just a normal method invocation, as in the following code:

```
<%= h(...) %>
```

To use these methods, you need to include ERB::Util.

erb_reminder2.rb

```
require 'erb'
require 'drb/drb'

class ReminderView
  include ERB::Util
  extend ERB::DefMethod
  def_erb_method('to_html(there)', 'erb_reminder2.erb')
end

there = DRbObject.new_with_uri('druby://localhost:12345')
view = ReminderView.new
puts view.to_html(there)
```

Let’s try it again.

```
% ruby erb_reminder2.rb
<ul>

<li>1: Apply to RubyKaigi 2011</li>

<li>2: Buy a pomodoro timer</li>

<li>3: Display &lt;a&gt;</li>

</ul>
```

As you can see, the tags for the third item are properly escaped. This is because we used the h method to escape embedded strings.

Automatically Escaping Special Characters

You can customize the behavior of the concatenated objects or concatenated methods by using inheritance. Here is an example: ERB4Html is an ERB class specialized to HTML that automatically escapes HTML.

erb4html.rb

```
require 'erb'

class ERB
  class ERBString < String
    def to_s; self; end

    def erb_concat(s)
      if self.class === s
        concat(s)
      else
        concat(erb_quote(s))
      end
    end

    def erb_quote(s); s; end
  end
end

class ERB4Html < ERB
  def self.quoted(s)
    HtmlString.new(s)
  end

  class HtmlString < ERB::ERBString
    def erb_quote(s)
      ERB::Util::html_escape(s)
    end
  end

  def set_eoutvar(compiler, eoutvar = '_erbout')
    compiler.put_cmd = "#{eoutvar}.concat"
    compiler.insert_cmd = "#{eoutvar}.erb_concat"
    compiler.pre_cmd = ["#{eoutvar} = ERB4Html.quoted('')"]
    compiler.post_cmd = [eoutvar]
  end

  module Util
    def h(s)
      q(ERB::Util.h(s))
    end
```

```
      def u(s)
        q(ERB::Util.u(s))
      end

45    def q(s)
        HtmlString.new(s)
      end
    end
  end
```

This script has two main classes. ERBString on line 4 quotes strings when concatenating strings, and HtmlString on line 24 does HTML escaping. set_eoutvar on line 30 sets various configurations when ERB converts from eRuby to Ruby. ERB4Html overrides set_eoutvar to use HtmlString for string concatenation.

Automatic HTML escaping using ERB isn't perfect. You have to think about what to do when you want to pass HTML that's already escaped. And, you have to do URL encoding as well.

To help with these situations, I added the u and h methods to ERB4Html::Util, which act similarly to methods in ERB::Util. The methods in ERB4Html::Util call methods in ERB::Util and then mark them as "processed." Another method, called q, only does the marking.

Here is the example of ReminderView, which uses ERB4Html:

```
class ReminderView
  include ERB4Html::Util
  erb4html = ERB4Html.new(File.read('erb_reminder.erb'))
  erb4html.def_method(self, 'to_html(there)')
end
```

Some people say that automatic escaping avoids cross-site scripting (XSS) when you forget to manually add h, but I'm not convinced that automatic escaping using ERB4Html improves your life. What if you actually do not want to escape these tags? What happens if you handle HTML that's already escaped? Basically, you should consider your options; whether you should automatically escape or not depends on your preferences.

I'll show you one more example. The following ERB class will raise an exception if tainted strings are concatenated:

```
class ERBRestrict < ERB
  class RestrictString < ERB::ERBString
    def erb_concat(s)
      raise SecurityError if s.tainted?
      concat(s)
    end
  end
```

```
  def set_eoutvar(compiler, eoutvar = '_erbout')
    compiler.put_cmd = "#{eoutvar}.concat"
    compiler.insert_cmd = "#{eoutvar}.erb_concat"
    compiler.pre_cmd = [
      "#{eoutvar} = ERBRestrict::RestrictString.new('')"
    ]
    compiler.post_cmd = [eoutvar]
  end
end
```

This class is implemented using a subclass of ERBString, similarly to when we implemented ERB4Html. In Ruby, if an object comes from an external resource, it gets marked as "tainted" (it returns true when tainted? is called). ERBRestrict raises an exception when you try to concatenate tainted strings. This may suit you better if you want to keep unexpected things from happening. You can customize h to "untaint" the string once escaped.

The following is the full code for ERBRestrict:

erbr.rb

```
require 'erb'
class ERB
  class ERBString < String
    def to_s; self; end

    def erb_concat(s)
      if self.class === s
        concat(s)
      else
        concat(erb_quote(s))
      end
    end

    def erb_quote(s); s; end
  end
end
class ERBRestrict < ERB
  class RestrictString < ERB::ERBString
    def erb_concat(s)
      raise SecurityError if s.tainted?
      concat(s)
    end
  end
  def set_eoutvar(compiler, eoutvar = '_erbout')
    compiler.put_cmd = "#{eoutvar}.concat"
    compiler.insert_cmd = "#{eoutvar}.erb_concat"
    compiler.pre_cmd = ["#{eoutvar} = ERBRestrict::RestrictString.new('')"]
    compiler.post_cmd = [eoutvar]
  end
end
```

We've now seen two ways to customize ERB. ERB4HTML automatically escapes HTML, and ERBRestrict raises an exception when trying to concatenate tainted strings.

3.3 Putting Them Together

Let's combine the CGI script that we created first and the ReminderView that we just created.

Download the code files from http://pragprog.com/titles/sidruby, and browse to the reminder_view.rb file.

Set up this script in your web server and run it. It should show the list of items in the browser. Now you're ready to make things pretty.

Making the View Look Prettier

Displaying the list with <ul> looks too simple. Let's change the code to display with the <table> tag. Let's change ReminderView#create_erb as follows and display the CGI:

```
def self.create_erb
    ERB.new(<<EOS)
<html><head><title>Reminder</title></head>
<body>
<table border='1'>
<% @db.to_a.each do |k, v| %>
<tr><td><%= k %></td><td><%=h v %></td></tr>
<% end %>
</table>
</body>
</html>
EOS
  end
```

As you can see, you can easily change the view by replacing the eRuby script.

The table looks good, but it will look even better if it alternates the background color for each row. Let's first create a class that displays two different colors, one after another. Name the class BGColor.

```
class BGColor

  def initialize
①   @colors = ['#eeeeff', '#bbbbff']
    @count = -1
  end
  attr_accessor :colors
```

```
②   def next_bgcolor
      @count += 1
      @count = 0 if @colors.size <= @count
      "bgcolor='#{@colors[@count]}'"
    end

③   alias :to_s :next_bgcolor
  end
```

BGColor alternates the background between #eeeeff and #bbbbff.

① colors=(ary): Sets an array of background colors.

② next_bgcolor: Returns background color strings (for example, bgcolor='#eeeeff'). Returns a different color every time the method is called.

③ to_s: Alias to next_bgcolor.

Then add the bg_color method to instantiate BGColor from ReminderView.

```
class ReminderView
  ...
  def bg_color
    BGColor.new
  end
end
```

Once the bg_color method is added, we can call the method from the ERB template. Let's add bg_color in the tr tag to set the background color attribute.

```
<html><head><title>Reminder</title></head>
<body>
<table>
<% bg = bg_color
   @db.to_a.each do |k, v| %>
<tr <%= bg %>><td><%= k %></td><td><%=h v %></td></tr>
<% end %>
</table>
</body>
</html>
```

The cool thing about this approach is that you can hide the logic to swap colors and use <%= bg %> as if it were just another tag. The trick is that <%= statement %> calls to_s of the object internally, so <%= bg %> returns the result of bg.to_s, which is an alias to next_bgcolor.

Adding and Deleting Items

So far, we've implemented code to list items. In this section, we'll implement code to add items. Let's build the view first. We'll add a text field to add items at the bottom of the item lists.

```
class ReminderView
  ...
  def self.create_erb
    ERB.new(<<EOS)
<html><head><title>Reminder</title></head>
<body>
<form method='post'>
<table>
<% bg = bg_color
   @db.to_a.each do |k, v| %>
<tr <%= bg %>><td><%= k %></td><td><%=h v %></td></tr>
<% end %>
<tr <%= bg %>>
<td><input type="submit" name="cmd" value="add" /></td>
<td><input type="text" name="item" value="" size="30" /></td>
</tr>
</table>
</form>
</body>
</html>
EOS
  end
  ...
```

Let's add the ReminderView#create_erb method. Once added, let's run the CGI and make sure that the form is added.

Next, let's think about parsing the CGI request and adding it to the Reminder server. We'll follow these steps:

1. Check the command type of the query. We'll handle only adding for now.
2. Retrieve text from the text field.
3. If there is a string, then normalize the encoding and add the item to the Reminder server.

Let's add the code to implement the preceding logic.

```
class ReminderCGI < WEBrick::CGI
  def do_request(req, res)
①   cmd ,= req.query['cmd']
    case cmd
    when 'add'
      do_add(req, res)
    end
  end

  def do_add(req, res)
②   item ,= req.query['item']
    return if item.nil? || item.empty?
```

```
③     item.encode('utf-8')
      return unless item.valid_encoding?
      @db.add(item)
    end
```

Did you notice the ,= expression at ① and ②? This ,= req.query[key] is an idiom often used for Ruby CGI scripts (see *Multiple Assignment*, on page 52).

If item has strings assigned, then the string is normalized at ③, before being added to the Reminder server.

Note that I set the encoding of this CGI and Reminder server to utf-8. You can see it as a Content-Type of the HTML. This means you also have to convert outside strings to utf-8 format. In this example, you convert the string into UTF with encode and then make sure it is converted to the valid encoding using the valid_encoding? method.

So far, our code shows the list of items, and we can add a new item. The last step is to delete an item.

Let's add logic to do_request to delete the item when delete is specified as a command.

```
def do_request(req, res)
  cmd ,= req.query['cmd']
  case cmd
  when 'add'
    do_add(req, res)
  when 'delete'
    do_delete(req, res)
  end
end
```

Here is the definition of do_delete:

```
def do_delete(req, res)
  key ,= req.query['key']
  return if key.nil? || key.empty?
  @db.delete(key.to_i)
end
```

Next, add a view layer to generate a link to the command.

```
<% bg = bg_color
   @db.to_a.each do |k, v| %>
<tr <%= bg %>>
  <td><%= k %></td>
  <td><%=h v %></td>
  <td><%=a_delete(k)%>X</a><td>
</tr>
<% end %>
```

Multiple Assignment

Ruby lets you assign values to multiple variables. The value may or may not be an array, and this trick allows the first value to be retrieved from that array; it retrieves a single value if it's not an array. The following is an example:

```
irb --prompt simple
>> name, age = ['seki',20]
=> ["seki", 20]
>> name
=> "seki"
>> age
=> 20
>> name, age = 'sora',12
=> ["sora", 12]
>> name
=> "sora"
>> age
=> 12
>> name, age = nil
=> nil
>> name
=> nil
>> age
=> nil
```

It is worth noting that multiple assignment doesn't raise any exceptions even when the value is nil.

a_delete is a utility method to generate a link to delete an item. It takes a key of the item to delete. (In a real system, you should not delete an item via a link, because a web bot can automatically follow the link and delete the item.)

```
class ReminderView
  ...
  def make_param(hash)
    hash.collect do |k, v|
      u(k) + '=' + u(v)
    end.join(';')
  end

  def anchor(query)
    %Q+<a href="?#{make_param(query)}">+
  end

  def a_delete(key)
    anchor('cmd' => 'delete', 'key'=>key)
  end
```

Download the complete script and browse to reminder_final.rb to see the finished product!

We've come a long way. If you just want to write a website, it's easier to use an existing framework. But what I wanted to show you here is how you can add a web view on top of dRuby so that you can access dRuby in various ways. Using frameworks will constrain you to do things in a certain way, but using dRuby and ERB directly will give you more flexibility.

3.4 Adding an Error Page

We've now created all the features we need. In this section, we'll create an error page for debugging purposes. So far, we have an error_page method that returns an "oops" string when an error happens.

Take a look at the do_GET method. This method receives req, builds a page, and calls the error_page error when exceptions are raised.

```
def do_GET(req, res)
  do_request(req, res)
  build_page(req, res)
rescue
  error_page(req, res)
end
```

The current error_page method simply returns "oops," as shown in the following code. To actually see the error page, stop your ReminderCGI server, and browse the page.

```
def error_page(req, res)
   res["content-type"] = "text/plain"
   res.body = 'oops'
end
```

When actually running a site, the site should redirect to a static error page or say something better than "oops."

Let's modify error_page and display debugging error messages. Some web servers may write the error into error logs. We'll make an error display class to help you debug. It will display error pages like those you see when you run Ruby on the Web.

```
class ErrorView
  include ERB::Util

  def self.create_erb
    ERB.new(<<EOS)
<html><head><title>error</title></head>
<body>
<p><%=h error %> - <%=h error.class %></p>
<ul>
```

```
<% info.each do |line| %>
<li><%=h line %></li>
<% end %>
</ul>
</body>
</html>
EOS
  end

  extend ERB::DefMethod
  def_erb_method('to_html(req, res, error=$!, info=$@)', create_erb)
end
```

ErrorView converts exception information ($!, $@), which you receive when rescue is raised, and turns it into HTML.

Change error_page to return the result of ErrorView#to_html, instead of "oops."

```
def error_page(req, res)
 res["content-type"] = "text/html; charset=utf-8"
 res.body = ErrorView.new.to_html(req, res)
end
```

It should now display where the DRb::DRbConnError exception was raised.

3.5 Changing Process Allocation

Before we finish this chapter, let's look at some different ways of using CGI and dRuby. We'll change the layout of objects between processes and see a slightly different world.

So far, you have two processes, the Reminder server and the CGI client. The Reminder process lives for a longer time, while the CGI process lives for a short time. It bothers me that CGI has a relatively shorter life yet has so much work to do. To help with that, let's split CGI into a very small CGI process and CGI server.

First we'll modify the CGI script and turn it into a CGI server. Do you remember the last part of CGI?

```
if __FILE__ == $0
  reminder = DRbObject.new_with_uri('druby://localhost:12345')
  ReminderCGI.new(reminder).start()
end
```

Let's rewrite this to be a ReminderCGI server, rather than creating ReminderCGI, and call the start method.

cgi_reminder_d.rb
```
#!/usr/local/bin/ruby
require 'cgi_reminder'
require 'drb/drb'

reminder = DRbObject.new_with_uri('druby://localhost:12345')
cgi = ReminderCGI.new(reminder)
DRb.start_service('druby://localhost:12346', cgi)
DRb.thread.join
```

All the CGI server does is generate ReminderCGI and publish druby://localhost:12346 as a front object. Now let's move on to a very small CGI process.

cgi_reminder_s.rb
```
#!/usr/local/bin/ruby
require 'drb/drb'

DRb.start_service('druby://localhost:0')
ro = DRbObject.new_with_uri('druby://localhost:12346')
ro.start(ENV.to_hash, $stdin, $stdout)
```

The script first starts its own dRuby server, creates a remote object of the CGI server, and calls its start method. The arguments for start contain all the magic. start takes an ENV variable (converted to a hash), standard input, and standard output. When the remote ReminderCGI#start receives these parameters, then ReminderCGI behaves as if it were in the context of this CGI.

This trick relates to Chapter 4, *Pass by Reference, Pass by Value*, on page 57, but here's a brief explanation. Both $stdin and $stdout are File objects. When these variables are sent via Remote Method Invocation (RMI), they get passed by reference (the value of DRbObject) automatically. ENV is a singleton object, and it cannot be passed by value. To work around this, we converted ENV into a Hash with the to_hash method.

Let's start test_reminder_2.rb in one terminal and cgi_reminder_d.rb from another terminal and then execute the CGI from the browser.

This process layout gives us an object that lives across multiple CGI requests, and therefore it runs setup tasks only once. In this example, you can hold the ReminderCGI object across multiple CGI requests, so you need to convert ERB into a Ruby script only once.

We'll conclude this chapter by combining the Reminder server and the ReminderCGI server into one process. Let's move ReminderCGI into test_reminder_2.rb.

Here is the revised version:

test_reminder_2.rb
```
require './reminder0'
require 'drb/drb'
require 'pp'
require 'cgi_reminder'

reminder = Reminder.new
reminder.add('Apply to RubyKaigi 2011')
reminder.add('Buy a pomodoro timer')
reminder.add('Display <a>')

cgi = ReminderCGI.new(reminder)
DRb.start_service('druby://localhost:12346', cgi)

while true
  sleep 10
  pp cgi.to_a
end
```

Let's think about what this structure means. This architecture looks as if the Reminder application has ReminderCGI as a user interface. This architecture is very similar to a GUI application. CGI is equivalent to a user interface in a GUI, and an HTTP request is similar to any event (such as a button click) that happens to the GUI interface.

3.6 Moving Ahead

In this chapter, we learned about the eRuby templating system and how to use its implementation library, ERB, with dRuby and CGI. We also experimented with three different ways of allocating Reminder and ReminderCGI into processes. I hope you found it easy to make these changes, because dRuby is designed to act just like Ruby. There are many ways to architect the layout of objects into processes, and dRuby can help you when designing your system architecture.

In the next chapter, you'll learn two different ways to exchange objects across processes: passing by reference and passing by value. You may encounter unexpected behavior if you aren't aware of these differences, so let's find out more details.

CHAPTER 4

Pass by Reference, Pass by Value

In this chapter, we'll learn two different ways to exchange objects: passing by reference and passing by value. We briefly discussed this topic in *Pass by Reference, Pass by Value*, on page 22, but we'll discuss it in greater detail in this chapter. The difference is especially important when you use dRuby, so let's start with some background to make sure you understand how it all works.

4.1 Passing Objects Among Processes

In dRuby, you pass objects to another process via method arguments and receive objects via a return value. You can do this either by reference or by value. In this section, let's explore the difference.

Passing Objects in Ruby

You usually *pass by reference* in Ruby. Let's try it with irb.

```
% irb --prompt simple
>> def foo(str); str.upcase!; end
>> my_str = "Hello, World."
>> foo(my_str)
=> "HELLO, WORLD."
>> my_str
=> "HELLO, WORLD."
```

In the preceding example, we defined a method called foo, which calls upcase! internally. When we assign "Hello, World." into the my_str variable and call the foo method, then my_str now becomes "HELLO, WORLD." This is because the upcase! method inside the foo method manipulated the string.

How about *pass by value*, which passes a copy of the object? Let's try again with irb.

Call by Sharing

Strictly speaking, Ruby passes by reference. However, what Ruby passes is a reference value of an object so that you can modify the object that the reference value is pointing to with Ruby's destructive method (= methods ending with !). Another example of modifying the caller value is when you modify a Hash value as follows:

```
>>  a = {b:'c'}
=> {:b=>"c"}
>> def foo(d); d[:b] = 'C'; end
=> nil
>> foo(a)
=> "C"
>> a
=> {:b=>"C"}
```

Technically speaking, *call by sharing* or *call by object sharing*[a] is more correct name, but I will use the phrase *passing by reference* as a more generic meaning that is easier to compare with how dRuby works.

a. http://en.wikipedia.org/wiki/Evaluation_strategy#Call_by_sharing

```
>> my_str = "Hello, World."
=> "Hello, World."
>> foo(my_str.dup)
=> "HELLO, WORLD."
>> my_str
=> "Hello, World."
```

If you give a copy of the object to the method arguments, then it becomes passed by value. You pass only the copy of my_str to the foo method, so my_str stays as "Hello, World." You can see that the original value had no impact on the foo method.

When you call a method in Ruby, it always chooses to pass by reference. To pass by value, you have to call the dup method on your own (see Figure 14, *Passing by reference in a normal situation and passing by value using dup*, on page 59).

Passing Objects in dRuby

Now let's look at how this differs in dRuby.

Passing Objects with Marshal

dRuby uses the Marshal class to pass an object to other processes. Marshal consists of a dump method that serializes an object into byte strings and a load method that deserializes it (see Figure 15, *Using Marshal to create a copy of*

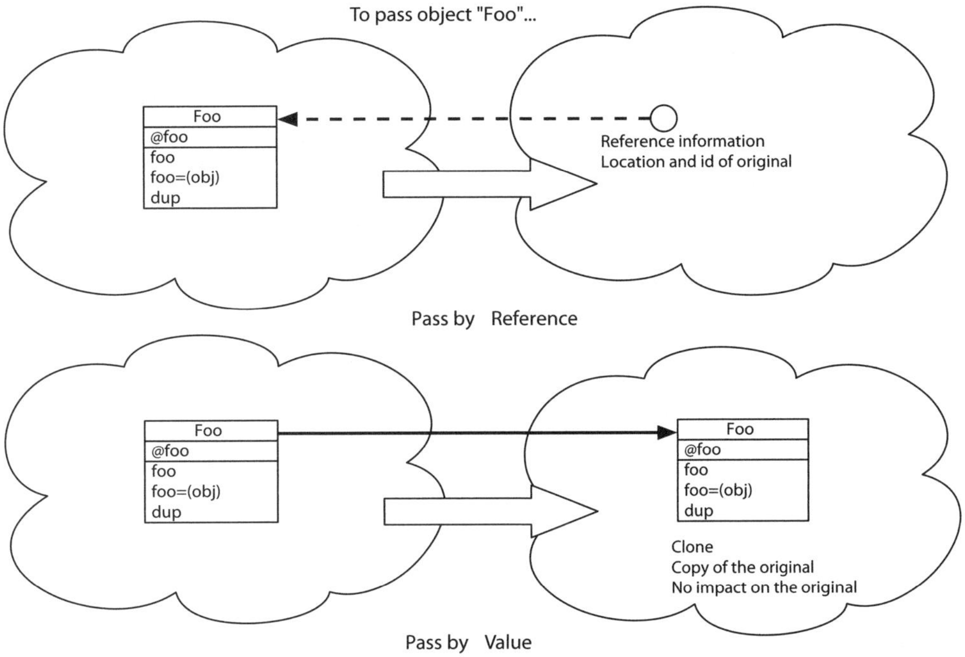

Figure 14— Passing by reference in a normal situation and passing by value using dup

an object, on page 60). You can also use Marshal to make a deep copy (which makes a different object with the same values).

Let's play with Marshal.

```
% irb --prompt simple
>> class Foo
>> attr_accessor :name
>> end
>> it = Foo.new
>> it.name = 'Foo 1'
>> it
=> #<Foo:0x40200e34 @name="Foo 1">
>> str = Marshal.dump(it)
# Copy this string of bytes to the second terminal
=> "\x04\bo:\bFoo\x06:\n@nameI\"\nFoo 1\x06:\x06ET"
>> foo = Marshal.load(str)
# "foo" and "it" has different id !!
=> #<Foo:0x401f4008 @name="Foo 1">
```

Let's try again with a different terminal, but this time let's copy the byte string we created using Marshal.dump.

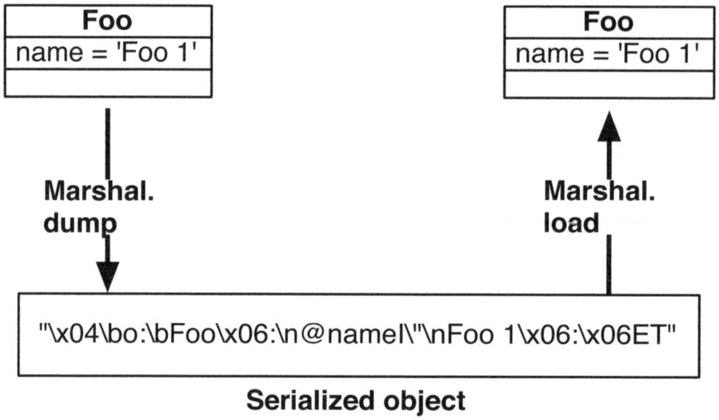

Figure 15—Using Marshal to create a copy of an object

```
% irb --prompt simple
# Define Foo class at terminal 2
>> class Foo
>> attr_accessor :name
>> end
>> # Copy and paste the dump result at terminal 1
>> str = "\x04\bo:\bFoo\x06:\n@nameI\"\nFoo 1\x06:\x06ET" # Paste here.
>> Marshal.load(str)
# You got the copy of Foo object
=> #<Foo:0x4021c0a8 @name="Foo 1">
```

Make sure that you assigned the copied string into str. It should load the Foo object that you marshaled earlier.

Pass by Reference Value

In the previous example, we exchanged the object byte string using copy and paste manually. However, you can exchange objects across processes (and even machines) via sockets. dRuby uses Marshal to call methods, pass arguments, and return values of other objects (see Figure 16, *Marshal object and transfer via socket*, on page 61).

When you use Marshal.dump and Marshal.load, Ruby always creates new objects. Does this mean dRuby always passes by value?

The answer is yes and no. When you pass by value, you simply serialize an object. When you pass by reference, instead of serializing the object, you serialize an object containing a reference to the original object. In other words, passing by reference passes the value of an object holding a reference. You

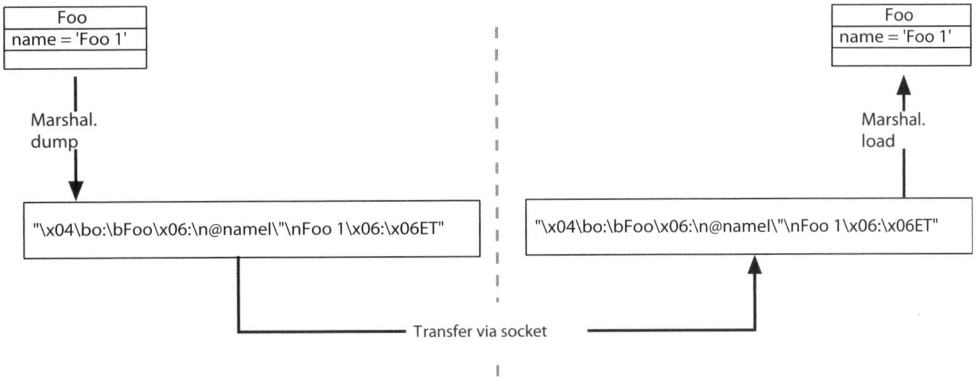

Figure 16—Marshal object and transfer via socket

can say that passing by reference passes the value of the reference object (see Figure 17, *Passing by reference implemented by passing the value of the reference*, on page 62).

Remember that we used DRbObject to connect to the DRb server in *Using the Service from irb*, on page 4? Well, DRbObject is the object that has the reference of the original object. DRbObject has two constructors for different purposes. The first one is the DRbObject.new_with_uri method, which allows you to create a reference object remotely using a URI. Another way is to use DRbObject.new(obj), which creates a reference object in its own process.

```
% irb --prompt simple -r drb/drb -r pp
>> DRb.start_service
>> ary = [1, 2, 3]
[1, 2, 3]
>> ref = DRbObject.new(ary)
[1, 2, 3]
```

DRbObject.new(obj) creates a reference object that refers to a specific object. We need to start up a server with DRb.start_service because we created a reference object for other processes to access. DRb.start_service allocates the URI for the server.

Let's observe the inside of the ref object.

```
>> pp ref

=> #<DRb::DRbObject:...
 @ref=537879846,
 @uri="druby://localhost:41708">
 => [1, 2, 3]
```

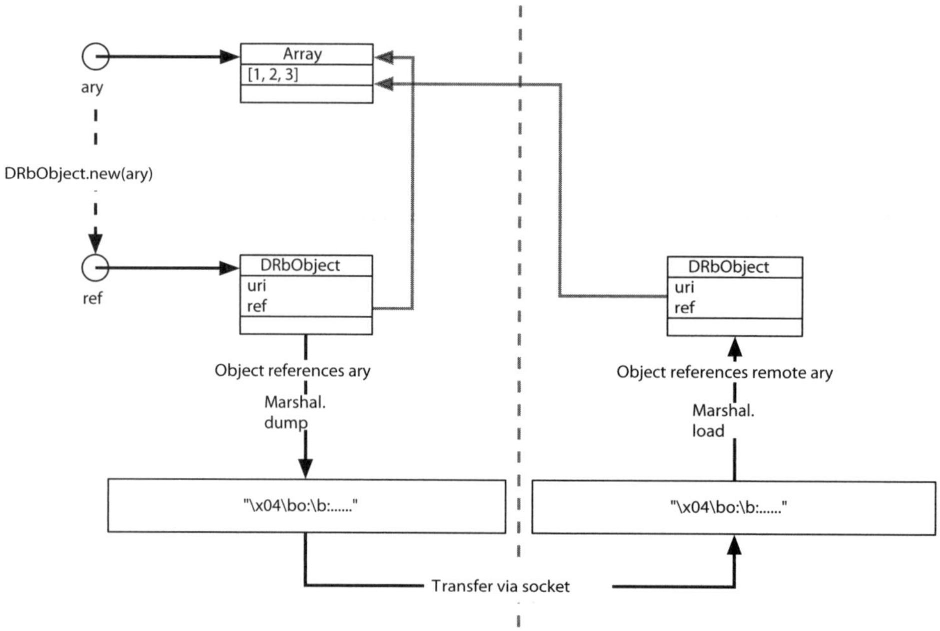

Figure 17—Passing by reference implemented by passing the value of the reference

DRbObject contains two instance variables. The first one is @uri, which holds its own URI, and the other is _id_, which holds its identification number.

```
>> ary.__id__
=> 537879846

>> exit
```

You should be able to see that _id_ contains the reference information.

Next, we'll pass objects between two terminals, so make sure you have two terminals up and running. Let's call the first terminal (the server) terminal 1 and call the second one (the client) terminal 2. At terminal 1, we'll run DRb.start_service by assigning Hash as a front object. The URI will be associated with the Hash object, which is inside the front variable. You can treat this process as you would a server that contains a certain object.

```
# [Terminal 1]
% irb --prompt simple -r drb/drb
>> front = {}
>> DRb.start_service('druby://localhost:1426', front)
=> #<DRb::DRbServer:0x ..... >
>> DRb.uri
=> "druby://localhost:1426"
```

"druby://localhost:1426" is the URI for the service at terminal 1. You can access this via terminal 2. Let's also start up a server at terminal 2.

```
# [Terminal 2]
% irb --prompt simple -r drb/drb
>> DRb.start_service
>> there = DRbObject.new_with_uri("druby://localhost:1426")
=> #<DRb::DRbObject:0x2ac5fe94 @uri="druby://localhost:1426", @ref=nil>
```

You can create a reference by assigning a URI. @uri holds druby://localhost:1426, which is used to specify DRbServer, and its reference variable is set at @ref=nil. When @ref is set to nil, it refers to a front object that is tied into a special URI.

OK, now let's assign "Hello, World." a value of key 1 in the there hash object.

```
# [Terminal 2]
>> str = "Hello, World."
>> there[1] = str
=> "Hello, World."
```

Let's examine the front object at terminal 1.

```
# [Terminal 1]
>> front
=> {1=>"Hello, World."}
```

Yes! The front object displays "Hello, World."

The String object "Hello, World." is transferred by dRuby in byte string format and restored at terminal 1. "Hello, World." should have been exchanged by value.

You might wonder how to prove that it's really passed by value. Let's do another experiment. Let's change the original string using a destructive operation. You should also check that the ID of the str is the same before and after the operation.

```
# [Terminal 2]
>> str.__id__
=> 358800978
>> str.sub!(/World/, 'dRuby')
=> "Hello, dRuby."  # Destructive substitution.
>> str.__id__
=&gt; 358800978        # <= Make sure that they are still the same object.
```

Let's see how this impacted the object at terminal 1.

```
# [Terminal 1]
>> front
=> {1=>"Hello, World."}
```

The value of the front object remains as "Hello, World." The destructive operation at terminal 2 didn't affect terminal 1.

Let's also try changing "Hello, World" at terminal 1.

```
# [Terminal 1]
>> front[1].sub!(/World/, 'Ruby')
=> "Hello, Ruby."
>> puts front[1]
Hello, Ruby.
=> nil
```

```
# [Terminal 2]
>> str
=> "Hello, dRuby."
```

Phew—it has no impact either.

Next, we'll pass by reference on purpose. Use DRbObject.new() to create a reference object (DRbObject). Specify the reference of the str object and set it to key 2 of the there hash.

```
# [Terminal 2]
>> there[2] = DRbObject.new(str)
=> "Hello, dRuby."
```

Let's see what's inside front.

```
# [Terminal 1]
>> require 'pp'
>> pp front
{1=>"Hello, Ruby.",
 2=>
  #<DRb::DRbObject:0x00000100a22550
     @ref=2157043220,
        @uri="druby://yourhost:1426">}
```

You can see that front[2] is DRbObject. (irb in 1.8 used to print out the internals of an object, but the behavior has changed in Ruby 1.9. We'll use pp for inspection instead.) So, what happens if you try to print it?

```
>> puts front[1]
Hello, Ruby.
=> nil
>> puts front[2]
Hello, dRuby.
=> nil
```

front[2] contains DRbObject, which is a reference. It prints out "Hello, dRuby."

Are you still with me? To summarize what happened: puts is called, and it calls the to_s method of the object in the argument and returns the result. So, in this case, it called front[2].to_s and then printed out the result. This method invocation against DRbObject is transferred to its original object, which is "Hello, dRuby." in terminal 2. The flow is shown in Figure 18, *Calling a method from terminal 1 to terminal 2*, on page 66.

```
# [Terminal 1]
>> front[2].to_s
=> "Hello, dRuby."
```

OK, let's check what happens if we modify "Hello, dRuby." at terminal 2 and see how it impacts terminal 1.

```
# [Terminal 2]
>> str.sub!(/dRuby/, 'Ruby and dRuby')
=> "Hello, Ruby and dRuby."
```

```
# [Terminal 1]
>> front[2].to_s
=> "Hello, Ruby and dRuby."
```

Yay, str.sub! at terminal 2 changes terminal 1. This is just like the Ruby we know.

Hmmm, so what happens if we do it the other way around? Let's try to change strings from terminal 1.

```
# [Terminal 1]
>> front[2].sub!(/Ruby and dRuby/, 'World')
=> "Hello, World."
```

```
# [Terminal 2]
>> str
=> "Hello, World."
```

front[2].sub!() at terminal 1 changed strings at terminal 2 just as we expected.

In this section, we experimented with intentionally passing by reference. We'll continue the experiments, so keep irb open on both terminals!

Which Is a Server and Which Is a Client?

Remember that front[2].sub!() was calling an object at terminal 2? You may wonder which is the server and which is the client. When you observe method invocation from the dRuby point of view, the one that receives the method is the server and the one that sends the method is the client.

```
there[1] = "Hello, World."
```

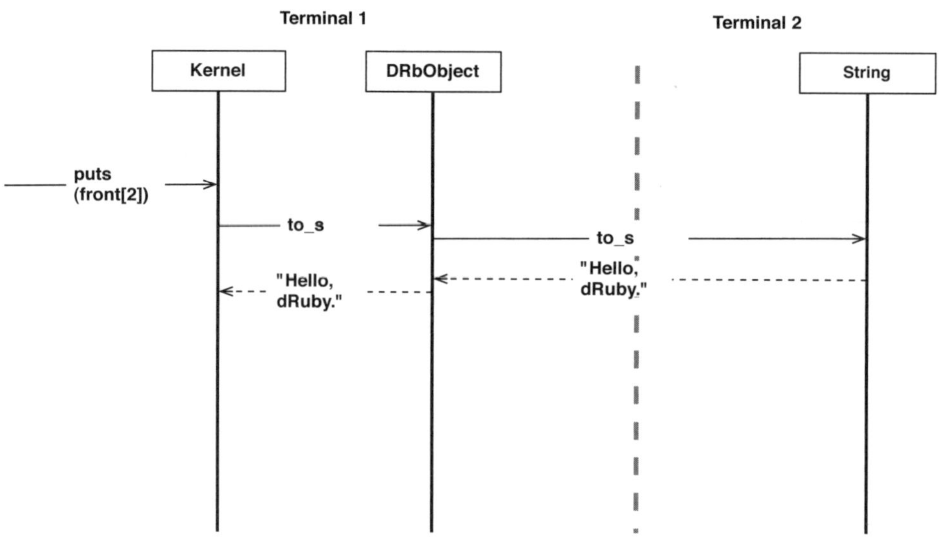

Figure 18—Calling a method from terminal 1 to terminal 2

When the setter or getter of there is called at terminal 2, terminal 1 is the server because the real object of there is at terminal 1, and terminal 2 is the client.

```
front[2].sub!
```

How about this case? The receiver will be terminal 2 because that's where the string of front[2] exists, and terminal 1 is the client.

When processes join dRuby, either process can act as a server or a client.

Now let's quit irb at terminal 2 and call front[2].sub! from terminal 1. It should raise a DRb::DRbConnError error because terminal 1 lost the connection to terminal 2.

Here's a summary of what we learned in this section:

- In dRuby, any script can easily become a server.
- Any script can become either a server or a client.
- The one that calls the method is a client, and the one that receives is a server, just like the normal method sender-receiver relationship.

Joe asks:
Why Do You Need DRb.start_service on the Client Side?

So far, we've been calling the DRb.start_service method even when a client connects to a server. You might be wondering why.

```
DRb.start_service
DRbObject.new_with_uri('druby://:1234')
```

The client code can access a remote object from the server side without calling the method, like this:

```
irb(main):015:0> h = DRbObject.new_with_uri('druby://:1234')
=> #<DRb::DRbObject:0x10031cd00 @ref=nil, @uri="druby://:1234">
irb(main):013:0> h
=> #<DRb::DRbObject:0x100348c98 @ref=nil, @uri="druby://:1234">
irb(main):014:0> h['a']
=> 1
```

So, why do we pass DRb.start_service? This will make sense once you understand how to pass by reference. Now let's try to iterate the hash.

```
irb(main):018:0> h.map{|a| a}
DRb::DRbConnError: DRb::DRbServerNotFound
  from /usr/lib/ruby/1.9/drb/drb.rb:1658:in `current_server'
  from /usr/lib/ruby/1.9/drb/drb.rb:1726:in
```

Hmmm, we got a DRb::DRbServerNotFound error message. This is because we can't perform a Marshal.dump on the Enumerator object that the map method returns, and therefore it passes by reference. This means that the server now requests that the client iterate the object. However, the server fails to connect to the client, because the client itself does not start up the service. Let's try the same operation after we run DRb.start_service.

```
irb(main):019:0> DRb.start_service
irb(main):020:0> h.map{|a| a}
=> [["a", 1]]
```

It should work as expected. I do recommend that you run DRb.start_service even on the client side to avoid this kind of situation.

4.2 Passing by Reference Automatically

It would be very inconvenient if you had to use DRbObject.new() every time you needed to pass by reference. No worries, because dRuby has an automatic mechanism to find out which way is suitable and selects the correct mechanism for you. If dRuby can serialize an object using Marshal.dump, then you should pass by value. If not, pass by reference.

Simple, right? Let's check the behavior by doing a few experiments.

Can't Dump

When you use Marshal, there are certain objects that you can't dump, such as IO, Thread, and Proc. Let's try with ($stdout).

```
% irb --prompt simple
>> Marshal.dump($stdout)
TypeError: can't dump IO
...
```

A TypeError exception is raised. This is because $stdout is an instance of IO, so you can't dump. The error happens even when it's possible to dump the object you're going to dump, but the object contains a reference to an object that can't dump. Here is the example of an Array with $stdout:

```
>> ary = []
=> []
>> Marshal.dump(ary)
=> "?004 ...."
>> ary[0] = $stdout
=> #<IO:0x ..... >
>> Marshal.dump(ary)
TypeError: can't dump IO
...
```

Let's see what happens if we pass $stdout to a different process via dRuby. Let's start two terminals.

```
#[Terminal 1]
% irb --prompt simple -r drb/drb
>> front = {}
>> DRb.start_service('druby://localhost:12345', front)
=> #<DRb::DRbServer:0x ..... >
>> DRb.uri
=> "druby://localhost:12345"
```

As we tried earlier, we pass Hash to a front object and start a server from terminal 1.

```
# [Terminal 2]
% irb --prompt simple -r drb/drb
>> DRb.start_service
=> #<DRb::DRbServer:0x ..... >
>> DRb.uri
=> "druby://localhost:1121"
>> there = DRbObject.new_with_uri('druby://localhost:12345')
=> #<DRb::DRbObject:0x ..... >
```

OK, a client is ready at terminal 2. Let's pass $stdout to terminal 1.

```
# [Terminal 2]
>> there[:stdout] = $stdout
=> #<IO:<STDOUT>>
```

You can't do `Marshal.dump`, but no error is raised. Let's check what happened to `$stdout`, which is passed to terminal 1.

```
# [Terminal 1]
>> front[:stdout]
=&gt;&gt; #<IO:0x007ffe7206fd10>
>> front[:stdout].class
=> DRb::DRbObject
```

`front[:stdout]` becomes a `DRbObject` instead of a `IO`. The `@uri` of `DRbObject` points to `DRb.uri` of terminal 2. You can see that `front[:stdout]` at `DRbObject` is a reference that refers to an object at terminal 2.

So, what just happened? When `$stdout` is passed from terminal 2 to terminal 1, dRuby captures the `Marshal.dump` failure and passes by reference instead of by value.

Let's check if the reference of `$stdout` at terminal 2 is really passed to terminal 1. Try printing out a string to `front[:stdout]`. Did it display the string in terminal 2?

```
# [Terminal 1]
>> front[:stdout].puts("Hello, DRbObject")
```

```
# [Terminal 2]
>> Hello, DRbObject
```

As expected, `"Hello, DRbObject"` appears at terminal 2. `front[:stdout]` is actually `$stdout` of terminal 2. Phew.

This is how dRuby behaves when it sends an object that cannot do `Marshal.dump`. dRuby automatically chooses to pass by reference without specifying it.

Also, if you try to access a dRuby object that contains a reference to your own process (rather than the target), then dRuby returns the real object rather than the `DRbObject` object. Let's check out the reference to `$stdout`.

```
# [Terminal 2]
>> there[:stdout]
=> #<IO:<STDOUT>>
>> there[:stdout].class
=> IO
```

This is an `IO` instance, not `DRbObject`, which has the same ID as `$stdout`.

```
# [Terminal 2]
>> there[:stdout] == $stdout
=> true
```

DRbUndumped

In the previous section, we learned how dRuby passes by reference if you can't do Marshal.dump to an object, such as IO, Thread, and Proc.

However, you may sometimes want to pass your own class by reference even though the object can be dumped. DRbUndumped is a helper module to tell dRuby to pass by value. You can either include a class or extend an object you want to pass by reference; then the object can't be dumped. Let's try it.

First we prepare the Foo class (foo.rb).

foo.rb

```
class Foo
  def initialize(name)
    @name = name
  end
  attr_accessor :name
end
```

We require foo.rb and then start the dRuby service.

```
# [Terminal 1]
% irb --prompt simple -r drb/drb -r ./foo.rb
>> front = {}
>> DRb.start_service('druby://localhost:12345', front)
```

```
# [Terminal 2]
% irb --prompt simple -r drb/drb -r ./foo.rb
>> DRb.start_service
>> there = DRbObject.new_with_uri('druby://localhost:12345')
```

Make sure that the instance of Foo can be dumped via Marshal.dump.

```
# [Terminal 1]
>> foo = Foo.new('Foo1')
>> Marshal.dump(foo)
=> "?004?006 .... "
>> front[:foo] = foo
=> #<Foo:0x .... >
```

```
# [Terminal 2]
>> there[:foo]
=> #<Foo:0x .... >
>> there[:foo].name
=> "Foo1"
```

When you look at there[:foo], it's an actual instance of Foo, rather than the reference.

```
# [Terminal 2]
>> there[:foo].name = 'Foo2'
```

```
# [Terminal 1]
>> foo.name
'Foo1'
```

Because foo is a copy of the object in terminal 1, changing the value at terminal 2 doesn't affect terminal 1.

Next let's extend DRbUndumped. foo should be passed by reference.

```
# [Terminal 1]
>> foo.extend(DRbUndumped)
>> Marshal.dump(foo)
TypeError: can't dump
  ....
```

Once we mix DRbUndumped into the foo instance and then do Marshal.dump, then foo raises a TypeError error. Pass foo from terminal 2 to terminal 1, and it should send by reference.

```
# [Terminal 2]
>> there[:foo]
=> #<DRb::DRbObject:0x .... >
>> there[:foo].name
=> "Foo1"
>> there[:foo].name = 'Foo2'
=> "Foo2"
>> there[:foo].name
=> "Foo2"
```

```
# [Terminal 1]
>> foo.name
=> "Foo2"
```

there[:foo] returned DRbObject instead of Foo. If you use there[:foo].name= to change @name, then it will impact foo. This means that it is passing by reference as we expect.

When you want to include it in a instance, you use extend. When you want to include it in a class, you use include.

Let's try the include way as well. First, make sure that an instance of Foo can do Marshal.dump.

```
# [Terminal 1]
>> bar = Foo.new('Bar1')
>> Marshal.dump(bar)
=> "?004?006 .... "
```

Mix DRbUndumped with include.

```
# [Terminal 1]
>> class Foo
>>   include DRbUndumped
>> end
>> Marshal.dump(bar)
TypeError: can't dump
   ....
>> Marshal.dump(Foo.new('Foo'))
TypeError: can't dump
   ....
```

Now any instances made out of Foo fail to Marshal.dump. Because they fail to Marshal.dump, the instances of Foo are always passed by reference.

```
# [Terminal 1]
>> front[:bar] = bar
```

```
# [Terminal 2]
>> there[:bar]
=> #<DRb::DRbObject:0x .... >
>> there[:bar].name
=> "Bar1"
>> there[:bar].name = 'Bar2'
=> "Bar2"
>> there[:bar].name
=> "Bar2"
```

```
# [Terminal 1]
>> front[:bar].name
=> "Bar2"
```

4.3 Handling Unknown Objects with DRbUnknown

In the previous section, we learned that dRuby passes by value if an object can be Marshal.dumped. However, what happens if the receiver of the object doesn't know about the class definition of the object? In this section, we'll learn about handling unknown objects. We'll use the same foo.rb sample. Let's start terminal 1 as a server and terminal 2 as a client and then pass the Foo object from the client.

```
# [Terminal 1]
% irb --prompt simple -r drb/drb
>> front = {}
>> DRb.start_service('druby://localhost:12345', front)
```

```
# [Terminal 2]
% irb --prompt simple -r drb/drb -r ./foo.rb
>> DRb.start_service
>> there = DRbObject.new_with_uri('druby://localhost:12345')
>> foo = Foo.new('Foo1')
>> there[:foo] = foo
=> #<Foo:0x ..... ">
```

irb at terminal 1 doesn't know the class definition of Foo. We just set an instance of Foo on front[:foo]. Let's see what kind of object is passed to terminal 1.

```
# [Terminal 1]
>> front[:foo]
=> #<DRb::DRbUnknown:0x.... @buf="?004?00.....", @name="Foo">
```

Hmmm, front[:foo] isn't an instance of Foo. It says it's an instance of DRbUnknown.

When an unknown object is loaded via Marshal.load and an exception is raised, dRuby captures it and loads DRbUnknown instead. DRbUnknown knows two things. One is the string buffer that failed to be loaded, and the other is the name of the class or module.

You can use the following methods to find out information about each:

DRbUnknown#buf
: Buffer of the serialized string that Marshal.load failed to load

DRbUnknown#name
: Name of the unknown class or module names

DRBUnknown#reload
: Retries Marshal.load

When dRuby receives an unknown class, it creates the DRbUnknown object automatically. You can't call the method against DRbUnknown, but you can transfer DRbUnknown.

Let's pass the DRbUnknown object from terminal 1 to terminal 2.

```
# [Terminal 2]
>> bar = there[:foo]
=> #<Foo:0x .... @name="Foo1">
>> foo.__id__ == bar.__id__
=> false
```

Terminal 2 received a new Foo instance, instead of DRbUnkown. (We compare by looking at the value of _id_.)

When dRuby does Marshal.load to the DRbUnknown object, it tries to Marshal.load against the buffer, and it returns the real object instead of DRbUnknown when successful.

Let's transfer the object using the third terminal.

```
# [Terminal 3]
% irb --prompt simple -r drb/drb
>> DRb.start_service
>> there = DRbObject.new_with_uri('druby://localhost:12345')
>> unknown = there[:foo]
=> #<DRb::DRbUnknown:0x.... @buf="?004?00.....", @name="Foo">
>> unknown.name
=> "Foo"
```

Terminal 3 does receive DRbUnknown because it doesn't know about the Foo class definition. The result of unknown.name is Foo. Now require foo.rb, and try it again.

```
# [Terminal 3]
>> unknown.reload
=> #<DRb::DRbUnknown:0x.... @buf="?004?00.....", @name="Foo">
>> require 'foo'
>> unknown.reload
=> #<Foo:0x .... @name="Foo1">
```

When you first did unknown.reload, you received DRbUnknown. When you tried it again after requiring the class, then it returned Foo. dRuby tried reloading the object.

Let's send the object again from terminal 1. This time, it should receive Foo, instead of DRbUnknown.

```
# [Terminal 3]
>> foo = there[:foo]
=> #<Foo:0x .... @name="Foo1">
```

Good! Since it now knows the definition of Foo, it did receive Foo.

By using DRbUnknown, you can keep unknown objects, even though you can't call their methods.

Why do we need such functionalities? Consider a Queue service. The Queue is responsible for transferring objects from one process to another. If DRbUnknown did not exist, then the proxying Queue service would require the class definitions of every class that may go through the `Queue`. `DRbUnknown` becomes very handy in such cases.

4.4 Moving Ahead

In this chapter, we learned the following:

- There are two different ways to exchange objects across processes, passing by reference and passing by value.
- dRuby chooses which way to pass by checking whether an object can be serialized by `Marshal.dump`.
- You can change the default exchange method by using `DRbUndumped`.
- If a process receives unknown objects, `DRbUnknown` will let you save and transfer these unknown objects.

In the next chapter, you'll find out about multithreading in Ruby and see how dRuby makes use of it.

CHAPTER 5

Multithreading

In many systems, each thread shares the same memory address space. Systems can switch the flow of control, but they can't switch memory space. So, threads tend to have less overhead and are often called *lightweight* processes.

With multithreading, you can easily write applications that handle multiple events, such as a network or GUI application. However, multithreading causes problems that don't happen in single-threaded mode.

dRuby-based systems are often composed of multiple processes. When serving as a server, dRuby has no idea when clients will call the server methods. This situation is similar to what happens when programming in a multithreaded environment. In this chapter, we'll learn about multithreading in Ruby, communication between threads, and how to apply these techniques when programming in dRuby.

Before you start this chapter, keep in mind that multithreading is a difficult topic in general; don't be surprised if you feel overwhelmed by the number of topics covered in this chapter. Feel free to skip whenever you like. However, do read Section 5.4, *Passing Objects via Queue*, on page 104 to understand how to use Queue to communicate in a multithreaded environment, because we'll compare Queue with other concepts in Chapter 6, *Coordinating Processes Using Rinda*, on page 111 and Chapter 9, *Drip: A Stream-Based Storage System*, on page 181.

5.1 dRuby and Multithreading

Multithreading is vital in dRuby. In this section, we'll take a look at the relationship between dRuby and multithreading.

Always in Multithreading Mode

dRuby generates threads by first having DRb.start_service generate a server thread that waits for method calls from other processes. Then, every time the server thread receives a method call from the client, the server generates a new thread that takes care of executing the method call.

While the server is handling other remote method calls, it creates a new thread and executes it when there's a call from a client.

Let's see how process A calls process B (see Figure 19, *How remote method calls work*, on page 79).

```
there = DRbObject.new_with_uri('...')
there.foo()
```

When there is a request to process B, then a server thread at DRbServer receives the request. DRbServer then creates a new method invocation and delegates the task to it in a separate thread. As soon as it gets delegated, the server thread comes back and prepares for the next method call (see Figure 20, *Implementing a remote method call*, on page 79).

Thanks to this mechanism, dRuby can receive different calls and execute them while it's in the middle of processing other calls. Let's think about the following code:

```
ary = DRbObject.new_with_uri(..)
ary.each do |x|
  x.foo()
end
```

Because dRuby has no constraints—such as blocking other method calls while performing a method call—it doesn't cause a deadlock when two processes call each other (see Figure 21, *Two processes calling each other*, on page 80). This architecture enables you to call remote methods with block arguments.

The main goal of dRuby is to extend Ruby's method invocation to a distributed environment. I implemented dRuby so that objects can call each other just as they do in normal Ruby scripts. For this reason, you have to pay particular attention to multithreading when using dRuby. Always bear in mind that the server script may receive method calls at any time.

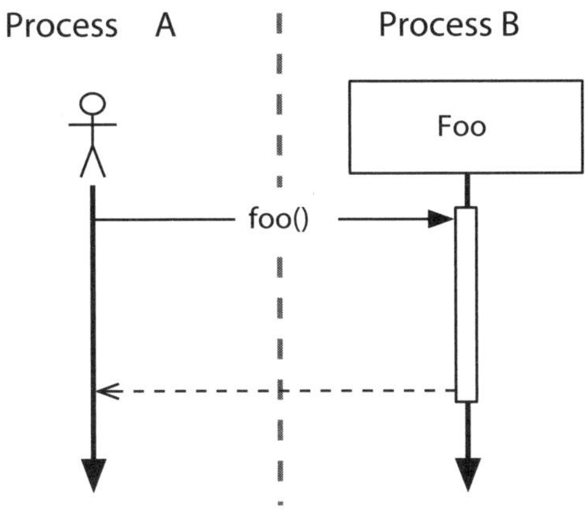

Figure 19—How remote method calls work

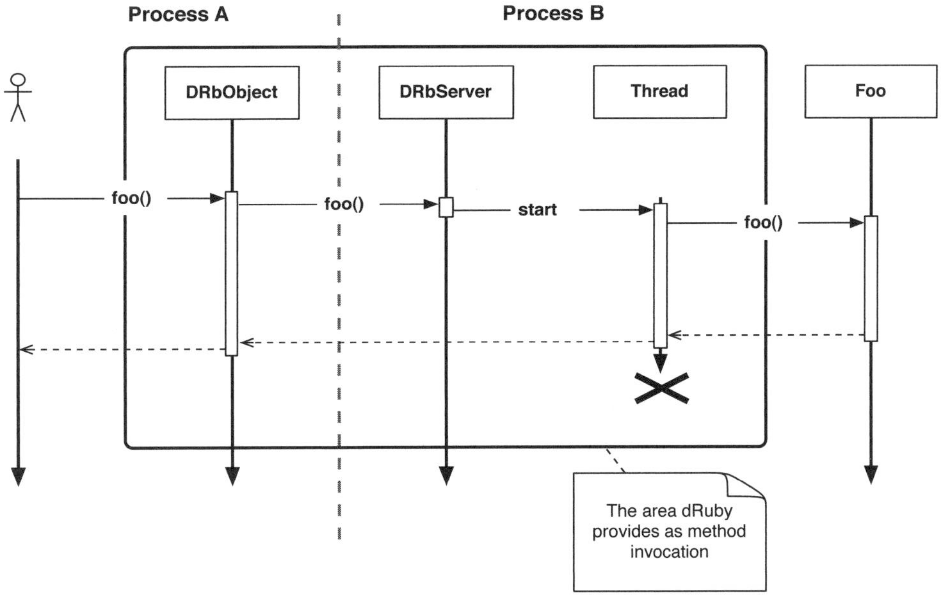

Figure 20—Implementing a remote method call

5.2 Understanding the Thread Class

When a Ruby interpreter executes a script, a main thread starts (see Figure 22, *Main thread at start-up*, on page 81). The main thread is in charge of processing the main script. The main thread is invoked in the very beginning,

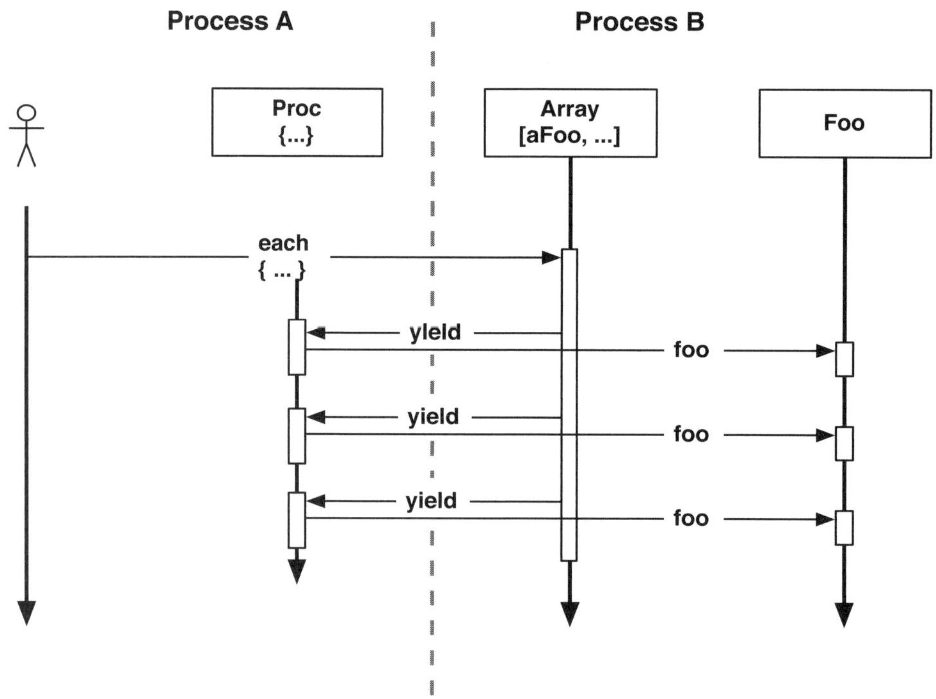

Figure 21—Two processes calling each other

and when the main thread ends, then the script also ends. The main thread is the longest-living thread within a script's life cycle.

Ruby threading works by passing a block to the `Thread` class. You can pass parameters to the block by passing arguments in `Thread.new`.

```
thread = Thread.new(1,2,3) do |x, y, z|
  # Operations to be threaded.
end
```

This creates a "program flow" (see Figure 23, *Launching the second thread*, on page 81).

A thread has various states, such as `running` or `sleep`. When the thread is waiting for `IO` or other threads, then it goes into sleep mode. A thread often goes back and forth between `run` and `sleep` mode and eventually finishes (see Figure 24, *States of a thread*, on page 82).

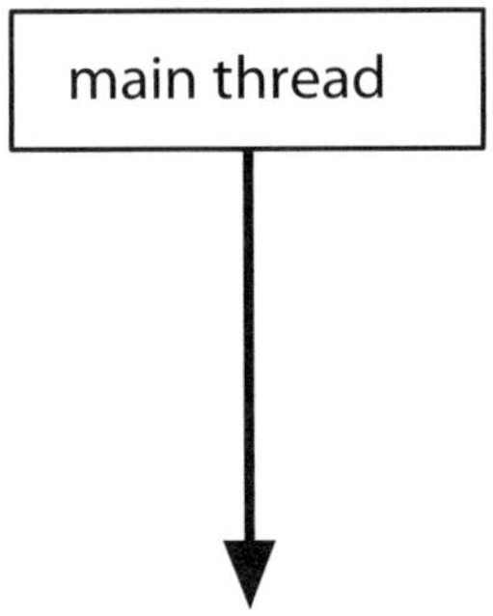

Figure 22—Main thread at start-up

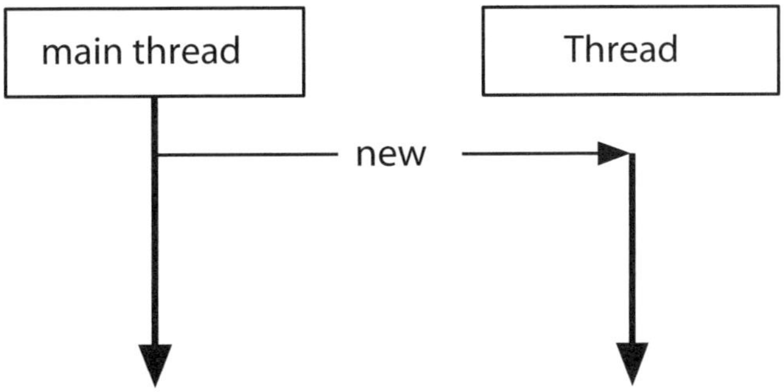

Figure 23—Launching the second thread

When a thread ends, it contains the end state. If the thread was terminated by an exception, then it will raise an exception when you try to access the value.

You can check the state of a thread using the `alive?`, `status`, and `value` methods.

alive?
: Returns `true` or `false`

status
: Returns the following state code:

- `"run"` running.
- `sleep` sleeping.
- `aborting` aborting.
- `false` finished normally.
- `nil` terminated by exception.

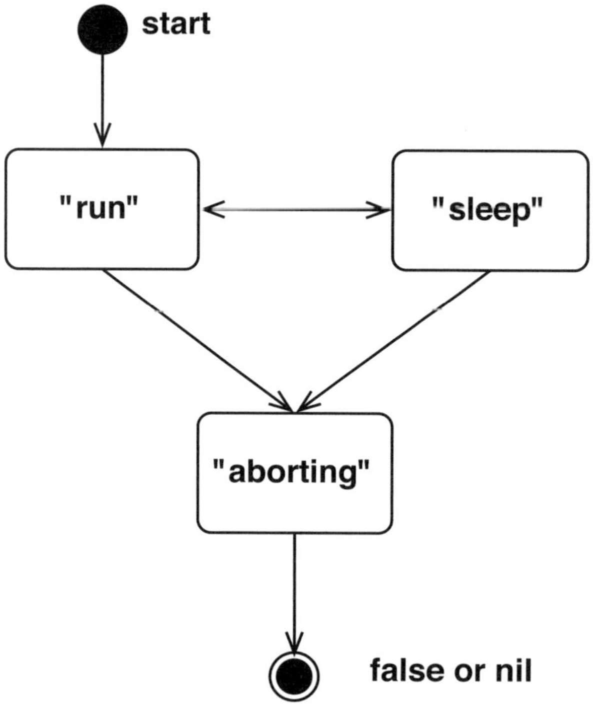

Figure 24—States of a thread

stop?
: Returns true when the thread ended or is asleep.

value
: Waits until the thread ends and returns the value. If the thread is already finished, then it returns the value immediately. If it was terminated by an exception, then it raises an exception. You can access value at any time, and an exception will be raised every time you access the value.

value waits and returns the value. If all you want is to wait until the end of the thread, then you can use the join method. When the join method is called, it blocks the calling thread until the receiver thread ends (see Figure 25, *Threads waiting to join*, on page 83).

To control the state of the thread, you can use the following methods:

exit
: Terminate the thread.

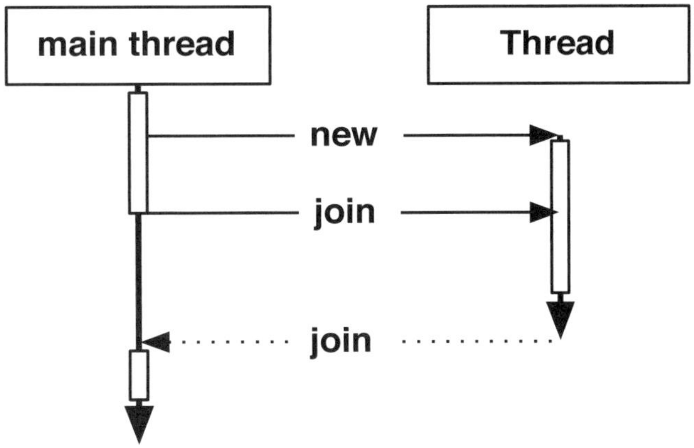

Figure 25—Threads waiting to join

wakeup
: Change the thread in running mode.

run
: Get the thread into running mode. Switch thread.

raise
: Raise exception to the thread.

There are no methods to get other threads into sleep mode. If you want to get your own thread into sleep mode, then you can use the sleep or stop (a class method of the Thread class) method. If you use the sleep method, then you can stop the execution up to the specified time (or forever).

You can also investigate all threads within a process with the following class methods:

Thread.list
: Lists all live threads

Thread.main
: Returns the main thread

Thread.current
: Returns the currently running thread

Let's try this with irb.

When irb first starts, it should have only one thread as the main thread.

```
% irb --prompt simple
>> Thread.list
=> [#<Thread:0x40.... run>]
>> Thread.list[0] == Thread.main
=> true
>> Thread.current == Thread.main
=> true
```

Here is the code to generate numbers from 0 to 9. However, this uses sleep for each iteration.

```
>> th = Thread.new { 10.times {|x| sleep; p [Thread.current, x]} }
=> #<Thread:0x... sleep>
```

The thread of th is in sleep mode. The Thread.list, status, alive?, and stop? show you the statuses of each thread.

```
>> Thread.list
=> [#<Thread:0x..... sleep>, #<Thread:0x.... run>]
>> th.status
=> "sleep"
>> th.alive?
=> true
>> th.stop?
=> true
```

Let's wake up th via the wakeup method.

```
>> th.wakeup
=> #<Thread:0x2.... run>
[#<Thread:0x2.... run>, 0]>>
```

th is now in running mode and prints out 0. Because both the main thread and the th thread print out strings, the screen output may not be indented properly. th should now be in sleep mode as it moves to the next iteration.

```
>> th.status
=> "sleep"
```

Let's change the status of th into run mode. run changes the thread immediately, so the output styling may differ from when using wakeup.

```
>> th.run
[#<Thread:0x2..... run>, 1]=> #<Thread:0x2..... run>

>> th.run
[#<Thread:0x2..... run>, 2]=> #<Thread:0x2..... run>

>> th.wakeup
=> #<Thread:0x2..... run>
[#<Thread:0x2..... run>, 3]
```

Next, let's terminate by raising an exception to th.

```
>> th.raise('stop!')
=> nil
>> Thread.list
=> [#<Thread:0x..... run>]
>> th.status
=> nil
>> th.alive?
=> false
>> th.stop?
=> true
```

Since it was terminated by an exception, th.status should return nil. Thread.list returns only a live thread, so it should return only the main thread. th is already terminated, alive? should return false, and stop? should return true.

How about th.value? It should raise the same exception as the one raised by th.raise(RuntimeError: stop!).

```
>> th.value
RuntimeError: stop!
        from (irb):7
        from (irb):11:in `value'
        from (irb):11
```

What if it terminated normally? This time, print out the numbers from 0 to 9 and end with 'complete' immediately without sleep. Once the main thread is created, call th.join to wait for the end of the thread execution.

```
>> th = Thread.new { 10.times { |x| p x} ; 'complete' }
>> th.join
0
1
2
3
4
5
6
7
8
9
=> #<Thread:0x..... dead>
>> th.status
=> false
>> th.alive?
=> false
>> th.stop?
=> true
```

th.join usually waits for the thread to end. Since it already ended in this case, it returns immediately if you run th.join again.

```
>> th.join
=> #<Thread:0x2ac4d35c dead>
```

th.value should return 'complete', which was evaluated by the thread right before it ended.

```
>> th.value
=> "complete"
```

This gives you basic control of threading; we've tried all the options in irb. In the next section, we'll go through how to safely pass objects among threads.

5.3 Thread-Safe Communication Using Locking, Mutex, and MonitorMixin

So far, we've seen how to generate and operate threads. When using multiple resources (file, network, GUI) or time-consuming processes, threading helps you write programs easily. However, if you don't have a way to communicate and pass objects among threads, then you aren't able to work with the results of thread operations. In this section, you'll learn a few ways for threads to communicate with each other safely.

Exclusive Locking

When multiple threads try to operate on the same object at the same time, the object sometimes ends up in a "broken" state.

"Broken" in this case doesn't mean that its memory space is broken but that the value of an instance variable is changed in an unexpected way. To avoid multiple threads operating at the same time, you need to have some sort of exclusive locking mechanism.

Prohibiting Switching with Thread.exclusive

The simplest way to do exclusive locking is to prohibit threads from switching. Let's look into this strategy first, using Thread.exclusive. To use Thread.exclusive, you first wrap the operation that you don't want to switch to another thread into a block of Thread.exclusive.

```
Thread.exclusive do
  # some operation you want to protect
end
```

Let's try an example of prohibiting threads from switching using Thread.exclusive. This example prints out a character twenty times using multiple threads:

```
% irb --prompt simple
>> def foo(name)
>>   20.times do
?>     print name
>>     print ' '
>>   end
>> end
=> nil
>> foo('a')
a a a a a a a a a a a a a a a a a a a a => 20
```

Let's call foo using multiple threads.

```
>> def test1
>>   t1 = Thread.new { foo('a') }
>>   t2 = Thread.new { foo('b') }
>>   t1.join
>>   t2.join
>> end
=> nil
>> test1
ab ab a ba ba ba ba ba ba ba ba ba ba ba ba b ab ab ab ab ab
=> #<Thread:0x2ac2b9ec dead>
```

You should see that a and b (and whitespace) are mixed randomly. This is because the t1 and t2 threads switch while running foo.

Let's rewrite this using Thread.exclusive.

```
>> def test2
>>   t1 = Thread.new { Thread.exclusive { foo('a') } }
>>   t2 = Thread.new { Thread.exclusive { foo('b') } }
>>   t1.join
>>   t2.join
>> end
=> nil
>> test2
a a a a a a a a a a a a a a a a a a a a b b b b b b b b b b b b b b b b b b b b
=> #<Thread:0x2ac0df8c dead>
```

With Thread.exclusive { foo('a') }, foo('a') doesn't switch while executing, so it will print out a without mixing with b.

Thread has critical and critical= class methods to control the state of whether you can switch threading. Setting Thread.critical = true prohibits thread switching. While in this state, execution in the running thread can't move into another thread. To stop this, you have to set Thread.critical = false. You can check whether thread switching is allowed via Thread.critical. To turn on and off thread switching via Thread.critical, it's common practice to record the previous value before doing Thread.critical = true and then put it back once the critical section is processed. Thread.exclusive does exactly that. In fact, the only exclusive locking mechanism in Ruby is Thread.critical. All other locking libraries we are going to learn next, such as Mutex and Queue, are built on top of Thread.critical.

Locking Single Resources with Mutex

Thread.exclusive halts all threads except the current thread. This isn't natural and also a bit of a waste of resource usage. It would be more efficient if you could acquire an exclusive lock only on the resource you are accessing and leave other threads running.

Mutex offers such a mechanism. Mutex is an acronym for *mutual exclusion*. A mutex has a lock state. A mutex can be locked by only one thread at a time and can be unlocked only by that thread. While a mutex is locked, any thread that attempts to acquire a lock will block until the mutex is unlocked. (In Ruby 1.8, any thread was able to unlock.) If a thread is trying to lock while being blocked, then it will block until the lock is unlocked.

Mutex has lock and unlock methods, but you usually don't use them directly. Instead, you use the synchronize method, which wraps these methods. Let's experiment with using Mutex with dRuby. First fire up irb in two terminals. Terminal 1 acts as a server with a Mutex object, and terminal 2 acts as a client.

```
# [Terminal 1]
% irb --prompt simple -r drb/drb
>> m = Mutex.new
>> DRb.start_service('druby://localhost:12345', m)
>> m.locked?
=> false
```

```
# [Terminal 2]
% irb --prompt simple -r drb/drb
>> DRb.start_service
>> m = DRbObject.new_with_uri('druby://localhost:12345')
>> m.locked?
=> false
```

Each variable of irb refers to the Mutex of terminal 1. You can use locked? to check their locking status. They should return false in both terminals. Let's try to acquire a lock at terminal 1 and then try to lock at terminal 2.

```
# [Terminal 1]
>> m.lock
=> #<Mutex:0x2ad9bcc0 @locked=true, @waiting=[]>
>> m.locked?
=> true
```

```
# [Terminal 2]
>> m.lock
```

Did you notice that there is no prompt coming back at terminal 2? This is because we acquired a Mutex lock at terminal 1, so the next lock is blocked by the previous lock. Let's try to unlock at terminal 1 and check the lock status.

```
# [Terminal 1]
>> m.unlock
=> #<Mutex:0x2ad9bcc0 @locked=true, @waiting=[]>
>> m.locked?
=> true
```

locked? still returns true. This is because the previous locks at terminal 2 were unlocked, and terminal 2 acquired a new lock. Did you see a prompt from terminal 2?

```
# [Terminal 2]
>> m.lock           # <= Statement you typed earlier
=> #<DRb::DRbObject:0x2ad9bcc0 @ref=nil, @uri="druby://localhost:12345">
>> m.locked?
=> true
```

Now let's try try_lock. This should return false immediately instead of blocking your terminal.

```
# [Terminal 1]
>> m.try_lock
=> false
```

Right now, a lock is held at terminal 2. Can we unlock from terminal 1?

```
# [Terminal 1]
>> m.unlock
ThreadError: Attempt to unlock a mutex which is locked by another thread
        from (irb):9:in `unlock'
        from (irb):9
        from /usr/local/bin/irb19:12:in `<main>'
```

In Ruby 1.8, you can unlock it even from the session that didn't acquire the lock. The behavior of Mutex changed in Ruby 1.9, and now it raises ThreadError.

You have to bear in mind that Mutex is just a gentlemen's agreement, and it won't actually protect the resource. It is similar to how a traffic light works. A traffic light tells you when is the right time to cross street, but it will not protect you if a car ignores the traffic light signal.

You may sometimes forget to unlock the resource you locked earlier. To avoid this situation, synchronize provides the "lock -> executing the block -> unlock" sequence within the method so that you can write a critical operation within the synchronize block.

Let's see this method in action. You'll need to do this next experiment quickly. Write the sample code in terminal 2 while the code of terminal 1 is still running (it finishes within ten seconds). Let's enter exactly the same statement into both terminals. (Make sure you unlock the lock you acquired in the previous example at terminal 2 before you start this experiment.)

```
# [Terminal 1]
>> m.synchronize { puts('lock'); sleep(10); puts('unlock') }
```

```
# [Terminal 2]
>> m.synchronize { puts('lock'); sleep(10); puts('unlock') }
```

The following should be the printing order:

```
(Terminal1) lock
10 sec
(Terminal1) unlock
(Terminal2) lock
 10 sec
(Terminal2) unlock
```

Next, what will happen if you `unlock` when it isn't actually locked?

```
# [Terminal 1]
>> m.unlock
ThreadError: Attempt to unlock a mutex which is not locked
>> m.locked?
=> false
```

Let's try `try_lock` again. It should return `true` because nothing has been locked.

```
# [Terminal 1]
>> m.try_lock
=> true
>> m.locked?
=> true
```

Next, let's write a simple counter.

counter0.rb

```
class Counter
 def initialize
   @value = 0
 end
 attr_reader :value

 def up
   @value = @value + 1
 end
end
```

The Counter class implements a basic counter. A value is incremented by one with the up method.

However, this script has a problem.

```
@value = @value + 1
```

The code first takes a value from @value, adds 1, and then assigns the value back to @value. This will cause trouble if another thread takes the value while one thread is taking the value and assigning the incremented value. The following shows the flow of this example. This explains the situation when the value is incremented by 1 even when the up method is called by two different threads.

1. Initial value: @value is 5.
2. Thread A takes 5 from @value.
3. Thread B takes 5 from @value.
4. Thread A assigns the calculated result (6) into @value.
5. Thread B assigns the calculated result (6) into @value.
6. The result of @value becomes 6, even though the expected value is 7.

The problem is that multiple threads try to operate @value at the same time. You need a way to restrict the operation of @value to be allowed by only one thread.

When you want to manage shared resources, you should prepare Mutex to protect the resource.

counter1.rb

```
class Counter
 def initialize
   @mutex = Mutex.new
   @value = 0
 end
 attr_reader :value

 def up
   @mutex.synchronize do
     @value = @value + 1
   end
 end
end
```

counter1.rb is a modified version of counter0.rb where it adds a Mutex exclusive lock. When one thread is updating @value, Mutex prevents other threads from updating @value.

```
def up
  @mutex.synchronize do
    @value = @value + 1
  end
end
```

The preceding Mutex#synchronize takes care of the following:

1. Locking by Mutex(lock)
2. Executing a given block (yield)
3. Unlocking Mutex(unlock)

unlock happens inside the ensure block so that the unlocking operation will happen even if an error happens inside the block.

The up method locks Mutex, executes (@value = @value + 1), and then unlocks the lock.

Because only one thread can acquire a Mutex lock, it guarantees that multiple threads won't be able to control @value.

The Reminder program that we wrote in Section 1.2, *Building the Reminder Application*, on page 7 is actually not multithread safe. Let's review reminder0.rb and modify the dangerous part.

reminder01.rb

```
class Reminder
  def initialize
    @item = {}
    @serial = 0
  end
  def [](key)
    @item[key]
  end
  def add(str)
    @serial += 1
    @item[@serial] = str
    @serial
  end
  def delete(key)
    @item.delete(key)
  end
  def to_a
    @item.keys.sort.collect do |k|
      [k, @item[k]]
    end
  end
end
```

add method increments a key at @serial, but @serial isn't multithread safe, just as you saw in the up method in the Counter class.

The to_a method generates an array from @item, which could also return some data that another thread removed.

Let's protect each method one at a time. First we generate a Mutex object in initialize and keep it in a @mutex variable.

```
def initialize
  @mutex = Mutex.new
  @item = {}
  @serial = 0
end
```

The [](key) method only reads a value and doesn't need to acquire exclusive locks, so we'll leave it as is. (Here's a question for you to ponder on your own: is this really true? If Hash#[](key) is multithread safe, then it should be OK—but what if someone redefines the method?)

The add method adds an item, but incrementing a value in the @serial part could become a problem, so let's protect the entire add method using Mutex. This is easy.

```
def add(str)
  @mutex.synchronize do
    @serial += 1
    @item[@serial] = str
    @serial
  end
end
```

The smaller the area Mutex protects, the more areas multiple threads could run at the same time. You can say that it's more efficient if you can minimize the code protected by synchronize. So, let's think about which area you really need to protect for the add method. The following shows the flow of the add method:

1. Generate a key for the new item.
2. Register the item to hash.
3. Return the key.

If we assume that the []=(key, value) method is multithread safe, then we only need to protect the key generation part. This is because if the key generation is atomic, the key used is unique, and assigning a value is safe. The following is the modified add method using this tactic. We separated the key generation part as a serial method, and we protect only this part via Mutex. You may even want to make the serial method a private method.

```
def serial
  @mutex.synchronize do
    @serial += 1
    return @serial
  end
end

def add(str)
  key = serial
  @item[key] = str
  key
end
```

If the lock method is called while Mutex is locked, the thread that called the lock method will be locked until the first lock is unlocked. If both the serial method and the add method call @mutex.synchronize, this will cause a deadlock because each method tries to lock the other.

```
def serial
  @mutex.synchronize do
    @serial += 1
    return @serial
  end
end

def add(str)
  @mutex.synchronize do
    key = serial
    @item[key] = str
    return key
  end
end
```

This is the deadlock scenario (see Figure 26, *Deadlock caused by nested synchronize*, on page 95). First the synchronize method inside add will acquire a Mutex lock. Then it calls the serial method. The synchronize method inside the serial method tries to acquire the Mutex lock again, so it will cause a deadlock.

You have to be careful not to cause a deadlock when using Mutex. You'll find out more about MonitorMixin in *Monitoring with MonitorMixin*, on page 96, which allows you to avoid these problems.

I've already mentioned that the Mutex#synchronize method is a wrapper of Thread.critical. The serial method does only simple operations, but is it worth using the synchronize method of Mutex? Can we just use Thread.exclusive?

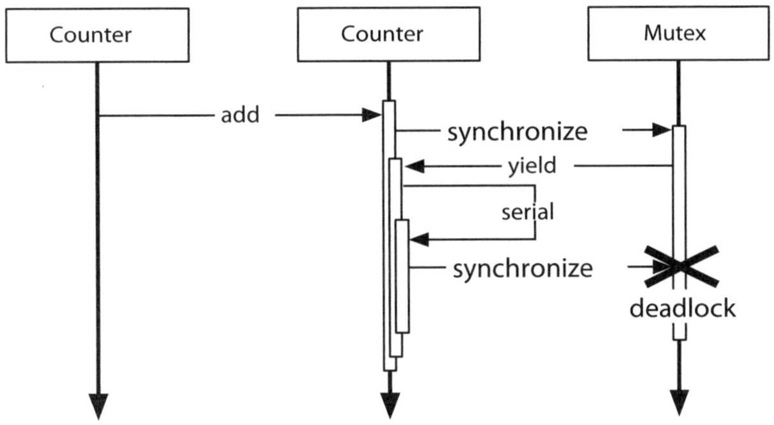

Figure 26—Deadlock caused by nested synchronize

```
def serial
  Thread.exclusive do
    @serial += 1
    return @serial
  end
end
```

This serial method is rewritten using Thread.exclusive. This version of serial works fine, and it won't sacrifice the ability to run concurrently. How about readability? Thread.exclusive clearly means that it executes exclusively, but it looks a bit arbitrary to use Thread.exclusive when other methods inside the Counter class already use Mutex. It's better to code in a consistent way, rather than using an arbitrary method in exchange for a slight performance gain.

The following script is a modified version of the delete and to_a methods with Mutex. These two methods protect their entire methods.

```
def delete(key)
  @mutex.synchronize do
    @item.delete(key)
  end
end

def to_a
  @mutex.synchronize do
    @item.keys.sort.collect do |k|
      [k, @item[k]]
    end
  end
end
```

Monitoring with MonitorMixin

MonitorMixin is one of my favorite libraries. It is an advanced thread coordination mechanism that uses ConditionVariable (a status variable), similar to Mutex. This is very good for writing complex synchronization logic that's hard to write using a simple exclusive locking mechanism. The MonitorMixin#synchronize also lets you write a nested lock, so you can use it as a more convenient version of Mutex without using a status variable.

First we'll see how this works as a convenient version of Mutex, and then we'll use ConditionVariable.

Using Monitor

To use Monitor, you first need to require monitor. It provides a mixin module called MonitorMixin and an independent class called Monitor.

Let's use MonitorMixin to make Reminder multithread safe, as we did with Mutex. Let's load MonitorMixin with require 'monitor'.

```
require 'monitor'

class Reminder
  include MonitorMixin
  def initialize
    super
    @item = {}
    @serial = 0
  end
```

In the preceding code, MonitorMixin is included inside Reminder. To initialize MonitorMixin, call the super method inside the initialize method of Reminder.

Now let's add a synchronize method inside each method. Because MonitorMixin is already included, we'll call its own method, unlike @mutex.synchronize of the Mutex version.

```
def add(str)
  synchronize do
    @serial += 1
    @item[@serial] = str
    @serial
  end
end

def delete(key)
  synchronize do
    @item.delete(key)
  end
end
```

```
def to_a
  synchronize do
    @item.keys.sort.collect do |k|
      [k, @item[k]]
    end
  end
end
```

Because the synchronize method of MonitorMixin can handle nested locks, you don't have to worry about having a deadlock, unlike in the Mutex version.

```
def serial
  synchronize do
    @serial += 1
    return @serial
  end
end

def add(str)
  synchronize do
    key = serial
    @item[key] = str
    return key
  end
end
```

It may look a bit thoughtless, but you can systematically wrap any method that needs thread safety with the synchronize method because MonitorMixin#synchronize handles a nested lock. It's similar to the synchronized keyword in Java. It can be a good tactic to first put synchronize into every method and investigate only the part that's causing a bottleneck.

Monitor has two methods—mon_enter and mon_exit—for locking and unlocking. These methods are named in this way with the idea that critical code *enters* and *exits* the Monitor class.

```
% irb --prompt simple
>> require 'drb/drb'
>> require 'monitor'
>> m = Monitor.new
>> DRb.start_service('druby://localhost:12345', m)
>> m.mon_enter
=> 1
>> m.mon_enter
=> 2
>> m.mon_exit
=> nil
>> m.mon_exit
=> #<Mutex:0x007fdb7c802528>
```

```
>> m.mon_exit
ThreadError: current thread not owner
        from /usr/local/lib/ruby/1.9/monitor.rb:249:in `mon_exit'
        from (irb):16
```

As you can see, this doesn't lock mon_enter from the same thread. This also raises a ThreadError exception if there are more mon_exit methods than mon_enter methods.

Let's experiment with mon_enter using multiple terminals. First, a thread in terminal 1 (the one you started) enters a monitor with the mon_enter method.

```
>> m.mon_enter
=> 1
```

Now let's try to synchronize from terminal 2.

```
% irb --prompt simple
>> require 'drb/drb'
>> DRb.start_service
>> m = DRbObject.new_with_uri('druby://localhost:12345')
>> m.synchronize { puts('hello') }
```

It should be blocked because terminal 1 is already in the monitor. The block at terminal 2 should be executed when the thread in terminal 1 exits with the mon_exit command.

```
>> m.mon_exit
hello
=> nil
```

Did you get the prompt back at terminal 2? This means you can enter a monitor from the same thread but not from a different thread when using the synchronize method of Monitor and MonitorMixin.

The next example shows the different behavior between Ruby and dRuby. The nested synchronize doesn't work properly in dRuby. Let's try to operate a local object at terminal 1.

```
>> m.synchronize { m.synchronize { puts('nest') } }
nest
=> nil
```

Monitor lets the same thread enter, so this kind of nested synchronize will work without being blocked.

What will happen if we run similar code from terminal 2? Because m at terminal 2 is referencing Monitor at terminal 1, this is remote method invocation via dRuby. Try exactly the same command from terminal 2.

Ummm, the prompt doesn't come back. It looks like it's being blocked. This is because the thread that ran synchronize first and the thread that ran synchronize inside the thread are different, which causes a deadlock at terminal 2.

Let's try again from terminal 1.

```
>> m.synchronize { m.synchronize { puts('nest') } }
```

This should be stopped, because the first synchronize at terminal 2 has not finished yet.

Let's stop irb at terminal 2 using Ctrl-C; then type exit to completely quit irb.

```
# Continued from previous session.
>  m.synchronize { m.synchronize { puts('nest') } }
^CIRB::Abort: abort then interrupt!!
  from /usr/local/lib/ruby/1.9/drb/drb.rb:566:in `call'
>> exit
```

When irb finishes, synchronize at terminal 2 ends, and the thread at terminal 1 starts.

You usually won't use Monitor in this way, but I wanted to show that the thread that calls the block and the thread that runs the block are different in dRuby.

Using ConditionVariable

Let's see how to use the condition variable. ConditionVariable is a synchronization mechanism used with Monitor. You can generate the variable using the new_cond method of Monitor. ConditionVariable is used when a thread enters a monitor (when a thread acquires a lock and releases it when certain conditions are met).

In typical usage, an application consists of two roles. One is to wait until certain conditions are met, and another is to notify of state change. Let's first look at the pseudocode that awaits the state.

```
def foo
  synchronize do
    until some_condition()
      @cond.wait
    end
    do_foo()
  end
end
```

This acquires a lock, waits until a certain condition (some_condition()) is satisfied by running the wait method of the @cond instance, and then returns the lock. The wait method will block until the signal or broadcast method is called. When @cond.wait unblocks the control, a thread will acquire the lock again.

```
until some_condition()
  @cond.wait
end

while some_condition()
  @cond.wait
end
```

This is a frequently used idiom to deal with condition variables. ConditionVariable has some utility methods to handle this kind of loop. The following is an extract of the monitor.rb code:

```
class ConditionVariable
  ...
  def wait_while
    while yield
      wait
    end
  end

  def wait_until
    until yield
      wait
    end
  end
end
```

You use the code like this:

```
@cond.wait_until { some_condition() }
```

Let's now look at the pseudocode that notifies of the status change.

```
def bar
  synchronize do
    do_bar()
    @cond.broadcast
  end
end
```

The signal method restarts only the one waiting thread (wakeup). broadcast restarts all the waiting threads. The restarted threads from these methods try to acquire new locks. Only the thread that manages to acquire the lock can complete wait mode and go back to its operation, so not all the threads that were called by signal or broadcast complete the wait method. It's also worth mentioning that there is only one thread that runs the monitor.

This pseudocode opens up all threads using broadcast. You should use signal only when you know that there is just one thread to wakeup. For example, if a method that did wakeup was killed before starting its operation, it may cause a deadlock. If you aren't sure, it's safe to use broadcast.

Synchronization Example with Rendezvous

Let's write a simple synchronization mechanism using Monitor. We'll write a message exchange mechanism called Rendezvous. Here's the specification (see Figure 27, *Rendezvous synchronization*, on page 102):

- Rendezvous has two operations, send and recv.
- One thread performs the send operation, and another thread performs the recv operation.
- When send is called, the calling thread will be blocked and wait until recv is called.
- When recv is called first, the calling thread will be blocked and wait until send is called.
- If another send is called while the previous one is still running, then both get blocked. If recv is called, one of the threads gets unlocked.
- If another recv is called while the previous one is still running, then both get blocked. If recv is called, one of the threads gets unlocked.

You can also consider this as a SizedQueue with default size 0.

Let's first load the library.

```
require 'monitor'

class Rendezvous
  include MonitorMixin
  def initialize
    super
    @arrived_cond = new_cond
    @removed_cond = new_cond
    @box = nil
    @arrived = false
  end
```

There are two condition variables, @arrived_cond and @removed_cond. @box stores the newly arrived messages, and @arrived is a flag to indicate that the new message has arrived. @arrived_cond is a condition variable to notify when a new message has arrived when the send method is called. @removed_cond is a condition variable to notify when a message is removed. This is called when @box receives data.

Let's look at the send code:

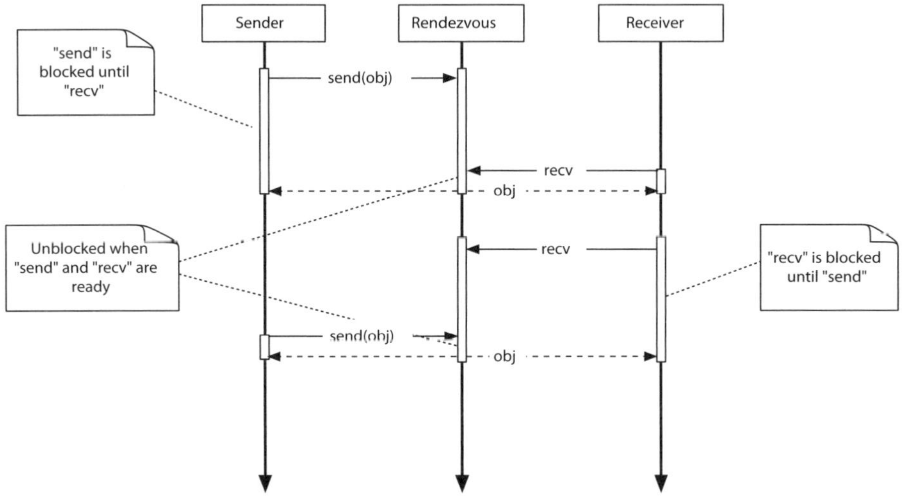

Figure 27—Rendezvous synchronization

```
def send(obj)
  synchronize do
①   while @arrived
      @removed_cond.wait
    end
②   @arrived = true
    @box = obj
③   @arrived_cond.broadcast
④   @removed_cond.wait
  end
end
```

Here's the flow of the send method:

① Wait until all messages are received. This means that it waits while @arrived is true.

② Change @arrived to true, and assign obj to @box.

③ Notify that messages have arrived.

④ Wait until messages are received.

Can you see how the script flows like this?

The most important point for the monitor and condition variable is at the while loop (we are using while rather than if because we are awaiting multiple conditions using broadcast rather than awaiting a single event with signal). Without the monitor, another thread may change the state of @arrived even when one thread goes through the loop. The monitor and condition variable provide a way to safely acquire the status change.

Let's now follow the flow of the recv code.

```
def recv
  synchronize do
①   until @arrived
      @arrived_cond.wait
    end
②   @arrived = false
③   @removed_cond.broadcast
④   return @box
  end
end
```

① Wait until all messages are received. This means that it waits until @arrived becomes true.

② Change @arrived to false.

③ Notify that messages have arrived.

④ Return @box.

You may think that send becomes activated when notified and changes @box, but it won't. Another thread won't change @box when notification is received at (3), because other threads can't enter into the monitor unless either wait is called or the code completes the synchronize block.

The following is the final version of Rendezvous. We replaced the wait loop with wait_until.

rendezvous.rb

```
require 'monitor'
class Rendezvous
  include MonitorMixin
  def initialize
    super
    @arrived_cond = new_cond
    @removed_cond = new_cond
    @box = nil
    @arrived = false
  end

  def send(obj)
    synchronize do
      @removed_cond.wait_while { @arrived }
      @arrived = true
      @box = obj
      @arrived_cond.broadcast
```

```
      @removed_cond.wait
    end
  end

  def recv
    synchronize do
      @arrived_cond.wait_until { @arrived }
      @arrived = false
      @removed_cond.broadcast
      return @box
    end
  end
end
```

5.4 Passing Objects via Queue

So far, we've discussed various exclusive locking mechanisms to "protect something." In this section, we'll focus more on a messaging layer that passes objects among threads.

Using Queue

Queue provides first in, first out (FIFO) buffering (see Figure 28, *How the queue mechanism works*, on page 105). Queue is one of the most common ways to act as a messaging layer.

To put data into Queue, you can use the enq method or the push method. Queue doesn't have any upper limit. To take out data from Queue, you can use either the deq method or the pop method. If you deq when Queue is empty, then the thread gets blocked. This will be unblocked when data gets enq. enq and deq are atomic operations, and therefore multiple threads will not deq the same data at the same time.

Let's open two terminals to experiment with Queue. To use Queue, require 'thread'. On the first terminal, create a Queue object, publish via DRb, and then call the enq method to put integer 1.

```
% irb --prompt simple -r drb/drb
>> require 'thread'
>> q = Queue.new
>> DRb.start_service('druby://localhost:12345', q)
>> q.enq(1)
```

On the second terminal, create a reference object to the published Queue object, and call deq. When deq is called for the first time, it should return 1, because 1 was enq earlier. If you deq for the second time, it should be blocked because there is no data.

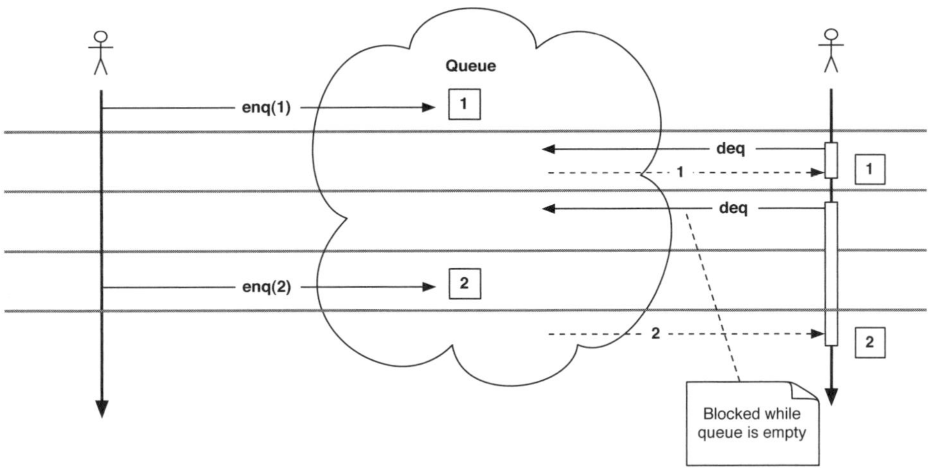

Figure 28—How the queue mechanism works

```
% irb --prompt simple -r drb/drb
>> DRb.start_service
>> q = DRbObject.new_with_uri('druby://localhost:12345')
>> q.deq
=>1
>> q.deq
```

Go to terminal 1 and do enq again. This unblocks deq at terminal 2.

```
>> q.enq(2)
```

Using SizedQueue

SizedQueue is a subclass of Queue, and it is a Queue with an upper limit (see Figure 29, *SizedQueue mechanism*, on page 106). Queue doesn't have any upper limit, so it never blocks enq, but SizedQueue will block enq if called over the limit. When deq decreases the number of objects below the upper limit, then the enq block will be unblocked. Let's try it.

First create a SizedQueue with a length of 4 at terminal 1 and then publish it at 'druby://localhost:12345'.

```
% irb --prompt simple -r drb/drb
>> require 'thread'
>> q = SizedQueue.new(4)
>> DRb.start_service('druby://localhost:12345', q)
```

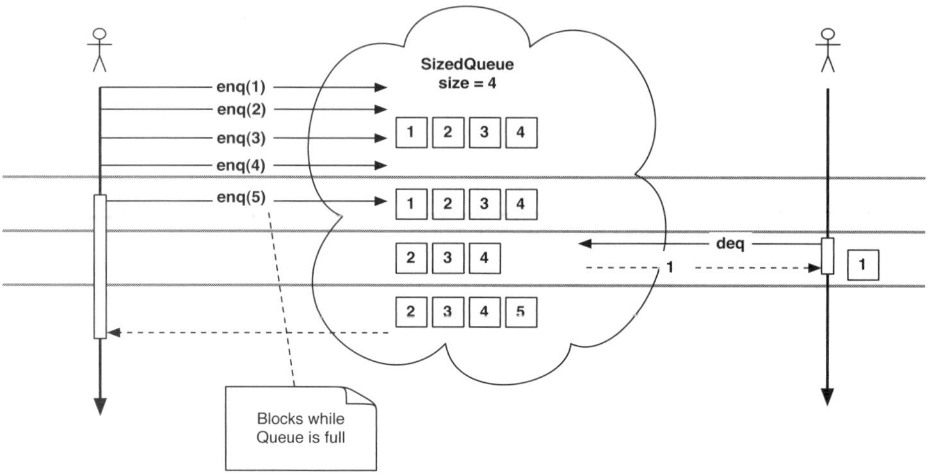

Figure 29—SizedQueue mechanism

At terminal 2, connect to the dRuby server you just started at terminal 1 and assign the remote object to q and then enq four objects into SizedQueue. When it's finished, we'll check the length of SizedQueue with the length method.

```
% irb --prompt simple -r drb/drb
>> DRb.start_service
>> q = DRbObject.new_with_uri('druby://localhost:12345')
>> q.enq(1)
>> q.enq(2)
>> q.enq(3)
>> q.enq(4)
>> q.length
=> 4
```

If you enq again, the enq should get blocked because it already reached the limit. Let's try it from terminal 1.

```
# [Terminal 1]
>> q.enq(5)
```

Your enq should be blocked. Now, let's unblock by doing deq at terminal 2.

```
# [Terminal 2]
>> q.deq
=> 1
```

You should have received 1, which you enq in the very beginning. When this happens, it should have unblocked your terminal 1.

Like we did for Queue, let's check how it blocks using deq. This time, it loops until nil arrives. Go back to terminal 1 and type the following loop command:

```
>> loop do
?>   puts "length: #{q.length}"
>>   it = q.deq
>>   puts "deq: #{it}"
>>   break if it.nil?
>> end
length: 4
deq: 2
length: 3
deq: 3
length: 2
deq: 4
length: 1
deq: 5
length: 0
```

When q.length becomes 0, deq gets blocked. Let's unblock using enq at terminal 2.

```
>> q.enq(6)
```

It first gets unblocked, goes to the next loop, and gets blocked again at the next deq. To finish the loop, enq nil at terminal 2.

```
>> q.enq(nil)
```

The loop at terminal 1 should complete because it received nil from terminal 2.

Rewriting Rendezvous with SizedQueue

Before we finish this chapter, let's reimplement Rendezvous, which we created using Monitor in *Synchronization Example with Rendezvous*, on page 101. We'll use SizedQueue this time. Exclusive locking and "messaging layer" are two sides of the same coin. If you have one implementation, you can create another implementation. This time, the SizedQueue version is a lot shorter. It's probably because SizedQueue is the more abstracted method but also because it's more suited for this problem.

rendezvous_q.rb

```
require 'thread'
class Rendezvous
  def initialize
    super
    @send_queue = SizedQueue.new(1)
    @recv_queue = SizedQueue.new(1)
  end
```

```
  def send(obj)
    @send_queue.enq(obj)
    @recv_queue.deq
  end

  def recv
    @send_queue.deq
  ensure
    @recv_queue.enq(nil)
  end
end
```

To pass objects among threads, you can use another mechanism called Rinda::TupleSpace. Rinda::TupleSpace is a Ruby implementation of the Linda tuplespace. We'll talk about Rinda::TupleSpace in Chapter 6, *Coordinating Processes Using Rinda*, on page 111.

As we have seen in this chapter, you can use the majority of threading coordination mechanisms in dRuby. It's a common practice to use Monitor and Queue in dRuby like you do in Ruby to ensure thread safety.

5.5 Moving Ahead

In this chapter, we learned the following:

- How important multithreading is when dealing with dRuby
- How to use the Thread class and its different states.
- How to safely communicate among threads without causing data corruption or deadlock. There are various ways, such as Thread.exclusive, Mutex, Monitor, and Queue.

In the next chapter, I'll introduce another Ruby standard library that I created called Rinda. Rinda is built on top of dRuby and will be very useful when you want to communicate across different applications.

Part III

Process Coordination

By the end of the previous part, you saw how difficult it can be to exchange information safely among multiple processes. In this part, you'll find out about a library called Rinda that provides a framework to make process coordination seamless, and you'll learn about additional libraries, too.

CHAPTER 6

Coordinating Processes Using Rinda

As your system grows more complex, you need a way for multiple processes to talk to each other. This might include background image processing, parallel web crawlers, or different systems exchanging data. You may have used various non-Ruby solutions such as queuing systems or messaging systems that were written in C, Java, or Erlang. Or perhaps you've built a similar structure on top of relational databases, but there is another way. This chapter introduces Rinda, a distributed shared memory space. Like dRuby and ERB, Rinda is written in pure Ruby and comes as part of the Ruby standard library, so it's highly portable, and you can start using it immediately.

6.1 Introducing Linda and Rinda

Rinda is a Ruby implementation of the Linda tuple space, which is a distributed processing system. To use Linda, you need to understand two concepts: *tuples* and *tuplespaces*. A tuple is data, and a tuplespace is a distributed shared memory. Each task can communicate with the other by writing into or reading from the tuplespace.

The concept of a tuple is similar to a memo in the real world. As you pass around a memo in your office to relay some information regarding your business, you send it from one person to the other. In the world of Rinda, the "memorandum" tuple walks from process to process via `TupleSpace`.

Linda is fairly simple; it allows you to do complex interprocess communication easily.

Linda

When you write parallel programs, you usually need two kinds of programs: one to describe how to process computation and another to coordinate the processing programs. The coordination language acts as a glue that holds together individually written programs. Linda is one of the coordination languages and was developed by David Gelernter and other contributors.

Linda has six different operations to access tuple space (see Figure 30, *How Linda's in and out operations work*, on page 113). Linda is usually provided as an extension of existing languages, such as C (the C extension version of Linda is called C-Linda) and Fortran. Linda allows you to coordinate across different programming languages or operating systems.

out
: Puts a tuple into the tuplespace.

in
: Takes out a tuple that matches a given pattern from tuplespace. If there's no matching tuple, it blocks the operation.

rd
: Copies a tuple that matches a given pattern from tuplespace. If there's no matching tuple, it blocks the operation.

inp
: Nonblocking version of `in`. If there's no matching tuple, it returns an error message.

rdp
: Nonblocking version of `rd`. If there's no matching tuple, it returns an error message.

eval
: Starts a new process and evaluates it.

Rinda

Rinda is a library to coordinate Ruby programs among different threads or different processes. It's similar to Linda in the sense that it can communicate across different operating systems as long as Ruby runs on it.

Rinda implements some important concepts of Linda, such as "tuple," "tuplespace ," "in," and "out" operations. "in" and "out" in Linda are renamed to `take` and `write`. These names came from a Java version of Linda called JavaSpaces. "eval" is not implemented as part of the standard library, but you can add it (we'll discuss this more in Chapter 8, *Parallel Computing and Persistence with Rinda*, on page 165).

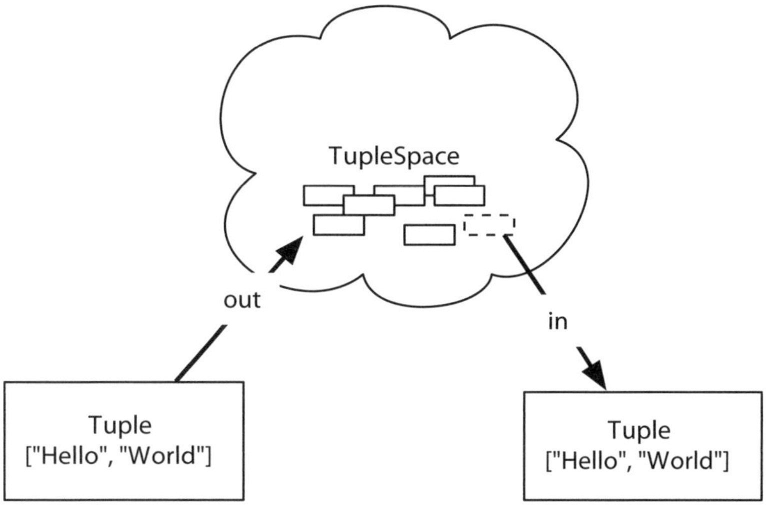

Figure 30—How Linda's in and out operations work

Those are the only differences between Rinda and Linda. You can apply the majority of Linda's concepts to Rinda.

6.2 How Rinda Works

OK, we've discussed the high-level concepts. Let's try them by writing some code.

Creating TupleSpace

In Linda, the tuplespace isn't visible and is accessible only through six operations. In Rinda, the tuplespace is implemented as a class that is called `Rinda::TupleSpace`.

The following is an example of starting up a tuplespace under the `druby://:12345` URI. dRuby automatically supplements the hostname, so the service will be provided under `druby://[hostname]:12345`. If you're going to use the service under the same machine, you can also specify `druby://localhost:12345`.

ts01.rb

```
require 'rinda/tuplespace'
$ts = Rinda::TupleSpace.new
DRb.start_service('druby://localhost:12345', $ts)
puts DRb.uri
DRb.thread.join
```

To use Rinda::TupleSpace, require rinda/tuplespace.

TupleSpace.new(timeout=60) creates the tuplespace. It takes timeout as an argument in seconds. When it reaches the timeout, it invokes a keeper thread to remove out-of-date tuples or raise an exception for out-of-date operations. The default is set to 60 seconds.

You can use Rinda::TupleSpace to synchronize among threads like Queue or Mutex. You can also publish it via dRuby.

Next you'll find out about the basic operations of TupleSpace.

Writing to and Taking from TupleSpace

In Rinda, a tuple is an array of multiple values. You can put any objects into a tuple. You can even put Thread objects and Proc objects, but they are passed only by reference, so this may not be practical (for an interesting way to pass Proc, refer to Chapter 8, *Parallel Computing and Persistence with Rinda*, on page 165).

Here are some examples of a tuple as an array:

```
['abc', 2, 5]
[:matrix, 1,6, 3.14]
['family', 'is-sister', 'Carolyn', 'Elinor']
```

write (equivalent to the "out" operation in Linda) writes tuples into tuplespace. take (equivalent to the "in" operation in Linda) reads a tuple by these arrays but also takes wildcard pattern matching. In C-Linda, a wildcard is expressed as *. In Rinda, it is expressed as nil. If you specify nil, it matches all elements of the object.

Let's try a write and take operation for Rinda::TupleSpace (see Figure 31, *Experimenting with the write and read operation*, on page 115).

Begin by using the previous example, ts01.rb, to start up tuplespace under the druby://localhost:12345 URI in terminal 1.

```
% ruby ts01.rb
```

Start up irb in terminal 2, put the ["take-test", 1] tuple, and then retrieve the same tuple with the ["take-test", nil] wildcard.

```
% irb -r drb --prompt simple
>> DRb.start_service
>> $ts = DRbObject.new_with_uri('druby://localhost:12345')
>> $ts.write(["take-test", 1])
>> $ts.take(["take-test", nil])
["take-test", 1]
```

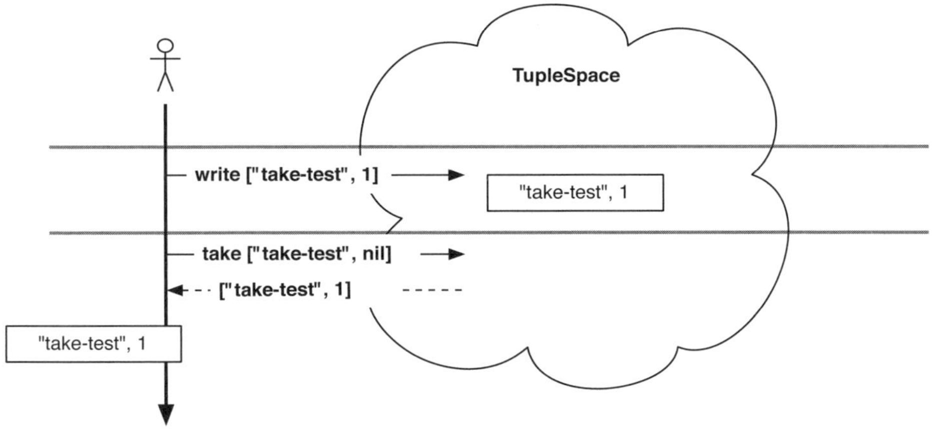

Figure 31—Experimenting with the write and read operation. A tuple is stored into and retrieved from tuplespace.

The next take operation should be blocked because you took out all tuples in $ts (see Figure 32, *The take is blocked when there is no tuple to take*, on page 116).

```
>> $ts.take(["take-test", nil])
```

Let's open terminal 3 and put a tuple into $ts.

```
% irb -r drb --prompt simple
>> DRb.start_service
>> $ts = DRbObject.new_with_uri('druby://localhost:12345')
>> $ts.write(["take-test", 2])
```

Now that you put a tuple that matches the pattern in terminal 2, terminal 2 should be unblocked, and you should get the prompt back.

```
$ts.take(["take-test", nil])
=> ["take-test", 2]
>>
```

A tuple doesn't have to be unique. You can write many duplicate tuples into tuplespace. Let's try to write ["take-test", 3] twice and then take them twice.

```
>> $ts.write(["take-test", 3])
>> $ts.write(["take-test", 3])
>> $ts.take(["take-test", nil])
["take-test", 3]
>> $ts.take(["take-test", nil])
["take-test", 3]
```

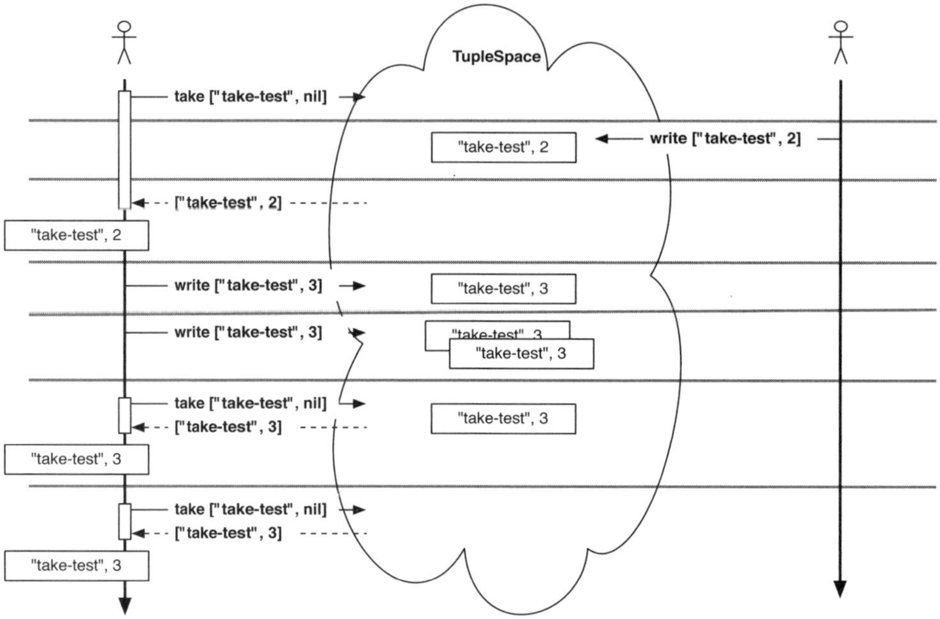

Figure 32—The take is blocked when there is no tuple to take.

Did it work as expected?

As a next example, let's write a service and a client program to calculate factorials (see Figure 33, *Expressing the factorial request tuple and the result tuple as a service*, on page 117).

We'll use terminal 2 as a client and terminal 3 as a server.

```
#[Terminal 2]

>> $ts.write(['fact', 1, 5])
>> res = $ts.take(['fact-answer', 1, 5, nil])
```

The client writes a tuple to request the factorial of 5 and takes the result. The client waits until the answer returns.

```
#[Terminal 3]
>> tmp, m, n = $ts.take(['fact', Integer, Integer])
>> value = (m..n).inject(1){|a, b| a * b}
>> $ts.write(['fact-answer', m, n, value])
```

The server takes ['fact', Integer, Integer] and writes its factorial result into a tuple. This tuple unblocks terminal 2.

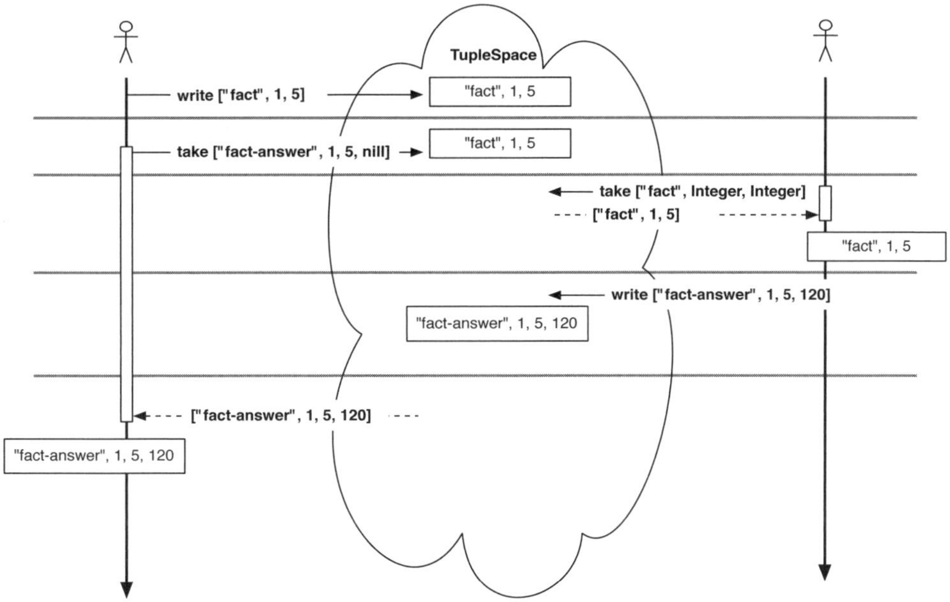

Figure 33—Expressing the factorial request tuple and the result tuple as a service

```
>> res = $ts.take(['fact-answer', 1, 5, nil])
["fact-answer", 1, 5, 120]
>> puts res[3]
120
```

Here is the script version of what we've just done:

ts01s.rb

```
require 'drb/drb'
class FactServer
  def initialize(ts)
    @ts = ts
  end

  def main_loop
    loop do
      tuple = @ts.take(['fact', Integer, Integer])
      m = tuple[1]
      n = tuple[2]
      value = (m..n).inject(1) { |a, b| a * b }
      @ts.write(['fact-answer', m, n, value])
    end
  end
end
```

```
ts_uri = ARGV.shift || 'druby://localhost:12345'
DRb.start_service
$ts = DRbObject.new_with_uri(ts_uri)
FactServer.new($ts).main_loop
```

ts01c.rb

```
require 'drb/drb'

def fact_client(ts, a, b)
  ts.write(['fact', a, b])
  tuple = ts.take(['fact-answer', a, b, nil])
  return tuple[3]
end

ts_uri = ARGV.shift || 'druby://localhost:12345'
DRb.start_service
$ts = DRbObject.new_with_uri(ts_uri)
p fact_client($ts, 1, 5)
```

Let's run the program. Make sure that your TupleSpace is up on terminal 1. If not, run ts01.rb again.

Next is the factorial client program in terminal 2. You may wonder why you have to start up the client program first rather than the server program (good question!). The client program will halt until the server program comes up.

```
% ruby ts01c.rb
```

Finally is the factorial server in terminal 3:

```
#[Terminal 3]
% ruby ts01s.rb
```

The client in terminal 2 should return an answer (120) once the server starts. Start the client again. This time, it returns the answer immediately.

```
% ruby ts01c.rb
120
```

The factorial server and the client communicate with each other via tuplespace. The client puts the request tuple and waits for the result tuple. The server takes out the request tuple and puts the result tuple. The processes are coordinated by exchanging tuples via tuplespace. Thanks to tuplespace as a central location, you can write a coordination program easily without worrying about the timing. Let's change the client program to split a request with a large factorial request into multiple requests divided by a certain range (see Figure 34, *Splitting a factorial service request into multiple requests*, on page 119).

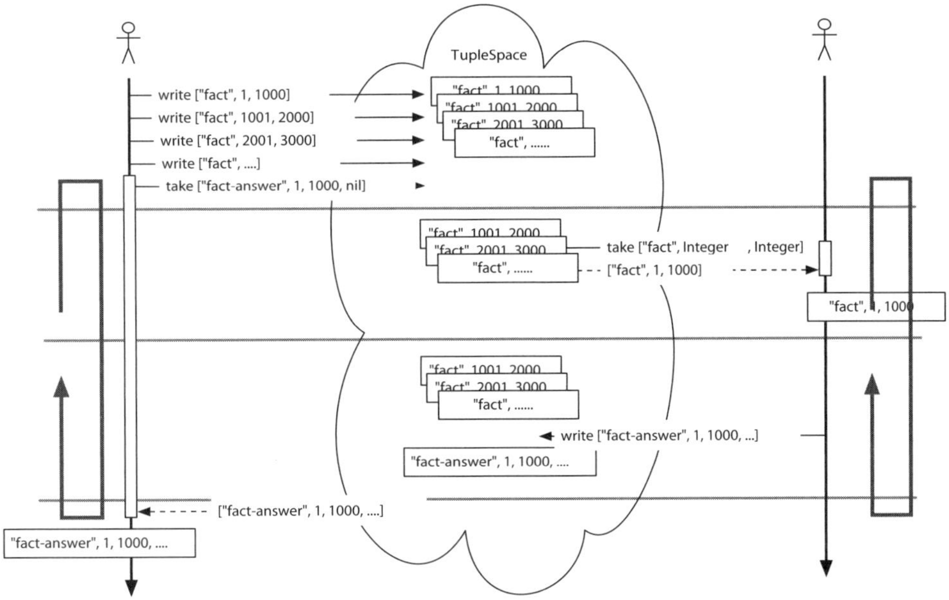

Figure 34—Splitting a factorial service request into multiple requests

ts01c2.rb

```
require 'drb/drb'

def fact_client(ts, a, b, n=1000)
  req = []
  a.step(b, n) { |head|
    tail = [b, head + n - 1].min
    req.push([head, tail])
    ts.write(['fact', head, tail])
  }

  req.inject(1) { |value, range|
    tuple = ts.take(['fact-answer', range[0], range[1], nil])
    value * tuple[3]
  }
end

ts_uri = ARGV.shift || 'druby://localhost:12345'
DRb.start_service
$ts = DRbObject.new_with_uri(ts_uri)
# p fact_client($ts, 1, 20000)
fact_client($ts, 1, 20000)
```

This program splits a request of 20,000 factorials per range of 1,000. It writes all the requests as (['fact'], head, tail), takes all the results, and sums them up. Here is an example output of the actual write request and the take response:

```
$ts.write(['fact', 1, 1000])
$ts.write(['fact', 1001, 2000])
$ts.write(['fact', 2001, 3000])
....
$ts.take(['fact-answer', 1, 1000, nil])
$ts.take(['fact-answer', 1001, 2000, nil])
$ts.take(['fact-answer', 2001, 3000, nil])
....
```

When there is only one server, the response speed doesn't change much. It does take a bit more time because of the additional network overhead. However, what will happen if you increase the number of servers? You could start a server in different hosts. If you have a machine with a multicore CPU, then you can start multiple servers in the same machine and can distribute its computation power. This will speed up processing time. The following is an example of starting a factorial server in a different host:

```
#[Terminal 4 in different host]
% ruby ts01s.rb druby://yourhost:12345

#[Terminal 2]
% ruby ts01c2.rb druby://yourhost:12345
```

By the way, did you notice that I commented out the p statement at the bottom of ts01c2.rb? I noticed that it takes more time to convert a huge Bignum into a string than to do the actual computation when I was benchmarking the result with various servers. If you're interested only in computation speed, you should comment it out like I did. You want to uncomment and print the result only when you want to see the result set. Thanks to the tuplespace, the client doesn't know whether the number of servers increases. It's worth noting that you don't have to change anything on the client side when you change the number of servers. This is one of the interesting aspects of Linda.

Let's sum up the features of Rinda's write and take operations (they're the same for Linda):

- Expresses data as a tuple
- Puts the tuple into tuplespace
- Takes the tuple from tuplespace

In the next section, we'll see how to use the read method.

Reading from TupleSpace

read is similar to take. It's equivalent to Linda's rd operation, and it returns the copy without removing the tuple from tuplespace. Let's try it. (See Figure 35, *Read operation*, on page 122.)

Make sure your tuplespace is up with ts01.rb. Then connect to the tuplespace via irb.

```
% irb -r drb --prompt simple
>>  DRb.start_service
>> $ts = DRbObject.new_with_uri('druby://localhost:12345')
>>  $ts.write(["read-test"])
>>  $ts.read(["read-test"])
=> ["read-test"]
```

The read method only reads a tuple; it doesn't delete it from tuplespace. Let's try it again.

```
>>  $ts.read(["read-test"])
=> ["read-test"]
```

It worked again. This is because the read method doesn't take out a tuple. If you do take and read, it will be blocked.

```
>> $ts.take(["read-test"])
=> ["read-test"]
>>  $ts.read(["read-test"])
```

As in the previous example, let's try to see whether writing a tuple from terminal 3 unblocks this. Open a new terminal and write a tuple.

```
$ irb -r drb -r rinda/tuplespace --prompt simple
>> DRb.start_service
>> $ts = DRbObject.new_with_uri('druby://localhost:12345')
>> $ts.write(["read-test"])
```

This should have unblocked the terminal 2 you had open earlier.

```
>> $ts.read(["read-test"])
=> ["read-test"]
>>
```

Unlike Linda, Rinda has a method called read_all. read_all returns copies of all matching tuples as arrays of arrays. If there are no matching tuples, it returns an empty array ([]).

```
>> $ts.read_all(["read-test"])
=> [["read-test"]]
>> $ts.take(["read-test"])
=> ["read-test"]
```

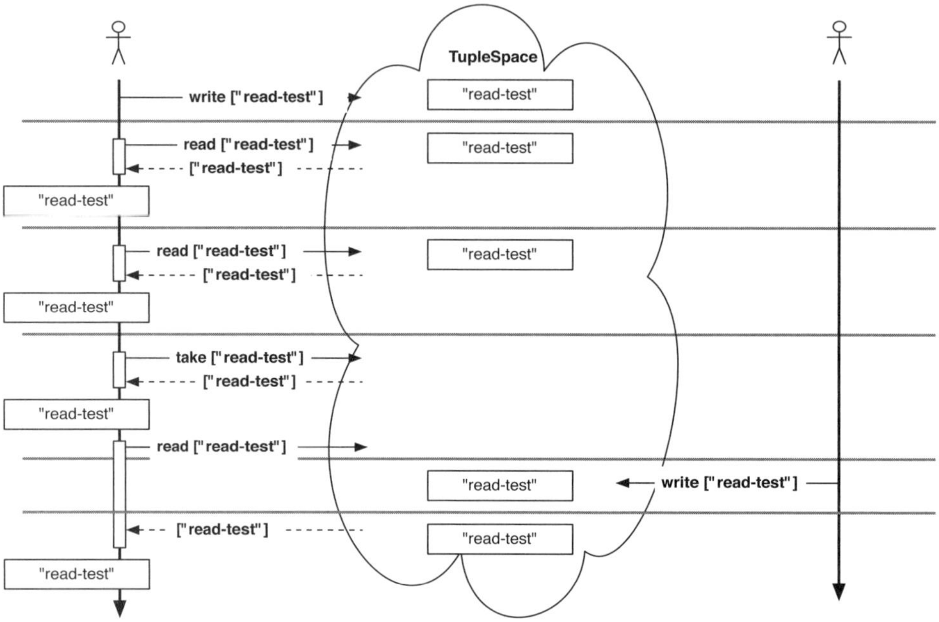

Figure 35—Read operation. Like take, read will be blocked if there is no tuple.

```
>> $ts.read_all(["read-test"])
=> []
>> $ts.write(["read-test", 1])
>> $ts.write(["read-test", 2])
>> $ts.read_all(["read-test"])
=> []
>> $ts.read_all(["read-test", nil])
=> [["read-test", 1], ["read-test", 2]]
>>
```

This will be handy for debugging purposes.

Taking and Writing with timeout

"inp" and "rdp" are nonblocking versions of "in" and "rd" in Linda. While "in" waits for matching tuples to be in tuplespace, "inp" returns an error if there are no matching tuples. Even though Rinda doesn't have "inp" and "rdp," you can get the same effect by setting a timeout.

take(pattern, sec=nil)
: Returns a matching tuple. Takes the timeout as a second argument in seconds. If nil is passed, it never times out. The default is set to nil.

read(pattern, sec=nil)
: Returns a copy of the matching tuple. Takes the timeout as a second argument in seconds. If nil is passed, it never times out. The default is set to nil.

If you set the timeout to 0, then it returns immediately, like the "inp" operation in Linda. When take times out, it raises Rinda::RequestExpiredError. (Make sure you require rinda/tuplespace. Otherwise, you will get a DRb::DRbUnknownError: Rinda:: message.)

```
#[Terminal 2]
>>  $ts.take(["timeout-test"], 0)
Rinda::RequestExpiredError: Rinda::RequestExpiredError
>> $ts.write(["timeout-test"])
>> $ts.take(["timeout-test"], 0)
=> ["timeout-test"]
```

The read method also has a timeout as a second argument in seconds. When 0 is specified, it becomes the same as the "rdp" operation in Linda.

```
#[Terminal 2]
>>  $ts.read(["timeout-test"], 0)
Rinda::RequestExpiredError: Rinda::RequestExpiredError
```

You need to be aware of a certain behavior of timeout timing. The "keeper" thread is in charge of checking and clearing up expired operations, and it's set to run every 60 seconds by default. This means expiration will not happen until the next time the keeper thread runs (except for 0—it gets executed immediately).

```
>>  $ts.take(["timeout-test"], 5)
```

This doesn't block for exactly five seconds but raises an exception within the next sixty seconds. You can adjust the timing by changing the keeper thread interval. You can also set the interval in the TupleSpace generation parameter. If you set the interval too soon, it may cause performance problems, so don't set it too short.

```
>> $ts2 = Rinda::TupleSpace.new(5)
>> $ts2.take(["timeout-test"], 5)
```

The preceding example generates TupleSpace with a five-second timeout and then runs $ts.take with the same timeout period.

Pattern Matching in TupleSpace

In Rinda, pattern matching of a tuple is done by comparing each element of an array using ===. The tuple and the pattern match when the number of elements of both are the same and the comparison of each element returns true on ===. This lets you match not only a simple nil wildcard but also complex patterns, such as regular expressions, classes, and instances.

Let's take the tuple whose first element includes add or sub (regexp /add|sub/) and the second and the third element are integers (Integer). Let's try this from terminal 2.

```
>> $ts.take([/add|sub/, Integer, Integer])
```

Next, we'll write a tuple. If you write a tuple whose second element is Float (['add', 2.5, 5]), it won't match the take method you ran in terminal 2 because their classes are different and === doesn't return true.

```
>> $ts.write(['add', 2.5, 5])
```

Your take operation in terminal 2 should be still blocked. Next, write ['add', 2, 5]. Now take should complete because it matches the request.

```
# At terminal 1
>> $ts.write(['add', 2, 5])

..........

# At terminal 2
>> $ts.take([/add|sub/, Integer, Integer])
=> ["add", 2, 5]
```

By using Regexp, Range, and Class, you can describe very complex patterns. You could use it as a database if performance isn't a major concern (Rinda::TupleSpace searches groups of tuples linearly, so it will cause scalability issues).

6.3 Basic Distributed Data Structures

Linda's tuple space is a type of "set" that can hold duplicate elements, also known as a *bag* or *multiset*. Tuplespace can, however, be used to implement data structures other than bags by adjusting the structure of tuples and tuple operations.

How to Write Parallel Programs: A First Course [CG90][1] describes various distributed data structures that can be implemented with tuple space. The three main categories described are as follows:

Bag
: Data structures whose elements can be identified only by their value

1. http://www.lindaspaces.com/book/

Struct, hash
: Data structures whose elements can be identified by name

Array, stream
: Data structures whose elements can be identified by position

The following sections explain these basic distributed data structures. These basic structures contain lots of hints for using TupleSpace.

Expressing the Bag Data Structure

A bag is a variation of a set and allows duplicate elements. Like a set, its elements are unordered. This is the most natural way to use TupleSpace. A bag has two operations: addition and deletion of an element. In TupleSpace, they are equivalent to write and take.

This is an example of adding an element:

```
$ts.write(['fact', 1, 5])
```

And this is an example of deleting an element:

```
$ts.take(['fact', Integer, Integer])
```

Combining write and take enables you to manage tasks among multiple servers, as described in Figure 33, *Expressing the factorial request tuple and the result tuple as a service*, on page 117. Here's an example:

```
$ts.write(['fact', 1, 1000])
$ts.write(['fact', 1001, 2000])
$ts.write(['fact', 2001, 3000])

....

$ts.take(['fact-answer', 1, 1000, nil])
$ts.take(['fact-answer', 1001, 2000, nil])
$ts.take(['fact-answer', 2001, 3000, nil])

....
```

As an example of bag usage, let's implement a semaphore class called Sem (see Figure 36, *The implementation of a semaphore using TupleSpace*, on page 126). In a semaphore, there are two operations: down and up. down takes a resource, and up releases the resource. If you think of a tuple in TupleSpace as a resource, you can express a semaphore by writing and taking a tuple. Counting semaphores (there are *n* number of resources in semaphores) can also be expressed using *n* number of tuples.

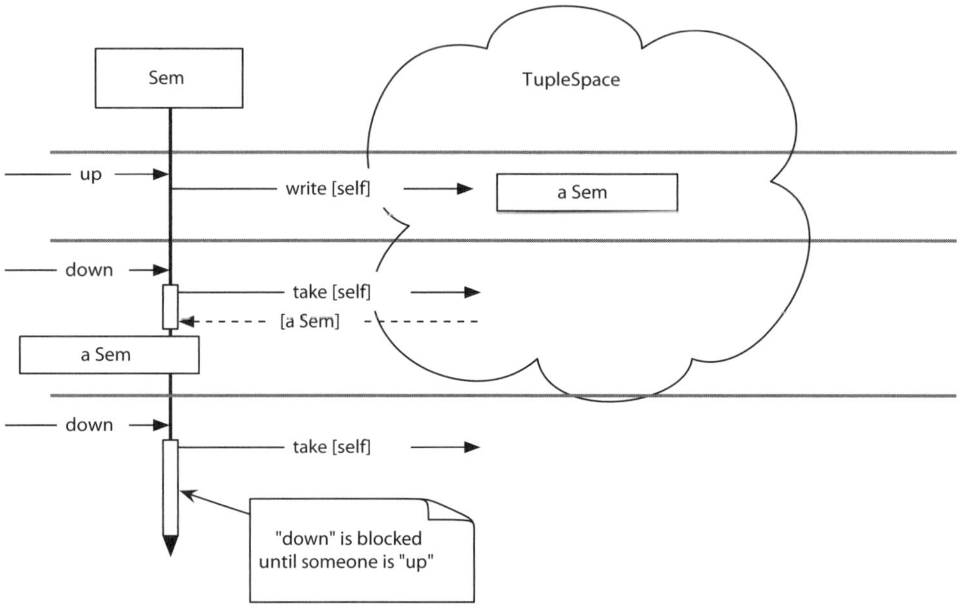

Figure 36—The implementation of a semaphore using TupleSpace. The down method is equivalent to write, and the up method is equivalent to take.

sem.rb

```
class Sem
  include DRbUndumped

  def initialize(ts, n, name=nil)
    @ts = ts
    @name = name || self
    n.times { up }
  end

  attr_reader :name
  def synchronize
    succ = down
    yield
  ensure
    up if succ
  end

private
  def up
    @ts.write(key)
  end
```

```
  def down
    @ts.take(key)
    return true
  end

  def key
    [@name]
  end
end
```

Here is a simple usage example of Sem:

```
require './sem'
require 'rinda/tuplespace'
sem = Sem.new(Rinda::TupleSpace.new, 1)
sem.synchronize do
  ....
end
```

key is a method to generate a tuple for each Sem object, and it returns a tuple that only contains @name as an element.

```
[@name]
```

Anyone can specify @name, but the value has to be unique within a system. The default is set to Sem itself to guarantee consistency. If @ts tuplespace and Sem share the same process, then the instance of Sem is included within a tuple. If the @ts tuplespace is a remote object, then DRbObject becomes an element to refer to the Sem instance.

The tuplespace implementation of a semaphore is less convenient than SemQ because it requires a tuplespace to be supplied to the constructor. (If we just want the properties of a semaphore, the Queue implementation is preferable to the tuplespace implementation.)

semq.rb

```
require 'thread'
class SemQ
  def initialize(n)
    @queue = Queue.new
    n.times { up }
  end

  def synchronize
    succ = down
    yield
    up if succ
  end

private
```

```
  def up
    @queue.push(true)
  end
  def down
    @queue.pop
  end
end
```

The TupleSpace version has more lines than the Queue version because it has to prepare TupleSpace. If you want to use it only as a queue, Queue may suit you better.

Structs and Hashes

Structs and hashes are structures with a key and a value. This is similar to Struct and Hash in Ruby. The basic structure is to use a tuple with a key and a value as a pair.

[key, value]

The following is an example of initializing a guid field with a 0 value:

```
ts.write(['guid', 0])
```

To update the value, use take and write.

```
key, value = ts.take(['guid', nil])
ts.write(['guid', name + 1])
```

The key part doesn't have to be one element of a tuple. You can use multiple elements as a key. An example is expressing an attribute of an object.

[object, attr_name, value]

The preceding example shows that you can use the combination of the object and the attribute name as a key. In Ruby, you can define a struct with Struct.new.

```
>> S = Struct.new(:foo, :bar)
>> s = S.new(1, 'bar')
>> s.foo = s.foo + 1
>> s.foo
=> 2
```

And the equivalent with TupleSpace is as follows:

```
>> s = Object.new
>> ts = Rinda::TupleSpace.new
>> ts.write([s, 'foo', 1])
>> ts.write([s, 'bar', 'bar'])
>> tuple = ts.take([s, 'foo',nil])
>> ts.write([s, 'foo', tuple[2] + 1])
```

To perform an update, it is important to perform a take before the write. The take operation is effectively an exclusive lock on the value, preventing other processes from changing the value during the update operation.

As a next example, let's implement a "barrier synchronization" mechanism using this data structure. Consider a program with multiple processes or threads running in parallel. Barrier synchronization is a mechanism that prevents the program from starting phase n+1 until after all processes have completed phase n. You can implement a barrier using a [key, n] tuple, where key is the barrier name and n is the number of processes to wait for. To initialize the barrier, all you do is write the [key, n] tuple into tuplespace.

Consider a program with multiple processes or threads running in parallel. Barrier synchronization is a mechanism that prevents the program from starting phase n+1 until after all processes have completed phase n.

barrier.rb

```
class Barrier
  def initialize(ts, n, name=nil)
    @ts = ts
    @name = name || self
    @ts.write([key, n])
  end
  def key
    @name
  end
end
```

When a process reaches a barrier, it performs a take on [key, nil], decrements the value, and writes the result to tuplespace. It then performs a read on [key, 0], which will block until the number of processes to wait for becomes 0. When all n processes reach the barrier, [key, 0] gets written, and all of the waiting read operations are unblocked. That all the processes can synchronize their wait just by reading [key, 0] is one of the coolest things about tuplespace.

barrier_sync.rb

```
class Barrier
  def sync
    tmp, val = @ts.take([key, nil])
    @ts.write([key, val - 1])
    @ts.read([key, 0])
  end
end
```

You may wonder how you can achieve an atomic operation without using any exclusive locking mechanism such as the Mutex#synchronize method. Now that the barrier tuple is temporarily removed from tuplespace by take([key, nil]), no other processes can take the tuple until you do write([key, val-1]). You can modify the value safely while take([key, nil]) operations from other processes are being blocked. This technique is very handy.

Last, let's abstract this process into methods without worrying too much about its practicality. Approach it as if you were solving a puzzle.

tsstruct.rb

```
class TSStruct
  def initialize(ts, name, struct=nil)
    @ts = ts
    @name = name || self
    return unless struct
    struct.each_pair do |key, value|
      @ts.write([@name, key, value])
    end
  end
  attr_reader :name
  def [](key)
    tuple = @ts.read([name, key, nil])
    tuple[2]
  end
  def []=(key, value)
    replace(key) { |old_value| value }
  end
  def replace(key)
    tuple = @ts.take([name, key, nil])
    tuple[2] = yield(tuple[2])
  ensure @ts.write(tuple) if tuple
  end
end
```

This class takes the tuplespace, assigns an object identifier, and then writes a struct into the tuplespace during its initialization. One nonpractical point about this TSStruct is that you can replace only an existing element, but you can't add a new element once instantiated.

Arrays and Streams

Arrays and streams contain order and position information. You can define them by making a tuple with index and value. This structure includes set structures such as matrixes, arrays, and streams.

Arrays, Matrixes, and Basic Streams

Each element is either a tuple of index and value...

```
[index, value]
```

or a tuple with object, index, and value.

```
[object, index, value]
```

A 2x2 matrix of an object a can be expressed as follows:

```
['a', 0, 0, 1.0]
['a', 1, 0, 0.0]
['a', 0, 1, 0.0]
['a', 1, 1, 1.0]
```

Even though you can express a matrix as in the preceding example, it may cause interprocess communication overhead if you leave this in tuplespace or if it requires synchronization between threads.

If you want to use Queue where only one process can append a value and only one process can push out a value, you can express it as an array with an index and a value.

```
['stream', 1, value1]
['stream', 2, value2]
['stream', 3, value3]
....
```

If you let a writing object manage @tail index information, then multiple writing objects can't append the same stream.

stream.rb

```
class Stream
  def initialize(ts, name)
    @ts = ts
    @name = name
    @tail = 0
  end
  attr_reader :name
  def push(value)
    @ts.write([name, @tail, value])
    @tail += 1
  end
end
```

The best way to let multiple processes append is to let the tuplespace manage the tailing index information. Do you remember the struct and hash data structures from *Structs and Hashes*, on page 128? You can create a tuple that consists of a name and its tail value as follows:

```
['stream', 'tail', tail index]
```

The following is the modified version of the Stream class that lets you append using multiple processes. You need to add more functionality to make this work for production use, but it's more important to understand the algorithm here.

stream_2.rb

```
class Stream
  def initialize(ts, name)
    @ts = ts
    @name = name
    @ts.write([name, 'tail', 0])
  end
  attr_reader :name
  def write(value)
    tuple = @ts.take([name, 'tail', nil])
    tail = tuple[2] + 1
    @ts.write([name, tail, value])
    @ts.write([name, 'tail', tail])
  end
end
```

So far, we've looked into the array, matrix, and stream data structures. There are some variations for streams, so let's talk about that next.

RDStream and InStream

There are two variants of streams, differing by the behavior of their read operations. The "in" stream consumes elements as they are read, while the "rd" (read) stream does not consume elements as they are read.

Let's discuss the "rd" stream first. The "rd" stream doesn't modify the stream itself. It uses a "read" operation to read out an element, and the position of the head information is managed by the reader object.

rdstream.rb

```
class RDStream
  def initialize(ts, name)
    @ts = ts
    @name = name
    @head = 0
  end

  def read
    tuple = @ts.read([@name, @head, nil])
    @head += 1
    return tuple[2]
  end
end
```

The `@head` instance variable represents the head of the stream for the reader. It reads an element and increments `@head` by one. When the `@head` value exceeds the index of the stream, it gets blocked until a new element is added to the stream.

Let's think about the "in" stream now. The "in" stream deletes each element as it is read from the stream. If only one process accesses a stream, all you need to do to change from the "rd" stream is to replace @ts.read with @ts.take.

instream.rb

```
class INStream
  def initialize(ts, name)
    @ts = ts
    @name = name
    @head = 0
  end

  def take
    tuple = @ts.take([@name, @head, nil])
    @head += 1
    return tuple[2]
  end
end
```

However, this doesn't work when multiple processes access the same stream. Each process manages @head information separately. Once a process takes out an element from the stream, no other processes can read from the stream.

How do we solve this problem? Do you remember how we managed appending elements to a stream by multiple processes in *Arrays, Matrixes, and Basic Streams*, on page 130? Like "tail" information, tuplespace can manage "head" information to share between multiple processes. Let's add the following tuple to manage @head information:

```
['stream', 'head', head index]
```

The following is the class definition:

instream_2.rb

```
class INStream

  def initialize(ts, name)
    @ts = ts
    @name = name
    @ts.write([@name, 'tail', 0])
    @ts.write([@name, 'head', 0])
  end

  def write(value)
    tuple = @ts.take([@name, 'tail', nil])
    tail = tuple[2] + 1
    @ts.write([@name, tail, value])
    @ts.write([@name, 'tail', tail])
  end
```

```
  def take
    tuple = @ts.take([@name, 'head', nil])
    head = tuple[2]
    tuple = @ts.take([@name, head, nil])
    @ts.write([@name, 'head', head + 1])
  end
end
```

You may have realized by now that INStream functionality is actually the same as the Queue library in Ruby.

6.4 Toward Applications

So far, we've looked into basic distributed data structures using tuplespace. The next step is to convert these data structures into classes that applications can easily reuse. As a starting point, let's extend TSStruct, which we created earlier.

TSStruct lets you read and write a field specified by Symbol. You can generate a new object by setting initialization values in the Struct or Hash instance as an object identifier. You can replace existing fields in TSStruct, but you can't add or delete new fields once initialized.

```
class TSStruct
  def initialize(ts, name, struct=nil)
    @ts = ts
    @name = name || self
    return unless struct
    struct.each_pair do |key, value|
      @ts.write([@name, key, value])
    end
  end
  attr_reader :name
  def [](key)
    tuple = @ts.read([name, key, nil])
    tuple[2]
  end
  def []=(key, value)
    replace(key) { |old_value| value }
  end
  def replace(key)
    tuple = @ts.take([name, key, nil])
    tuple[2] = yield(tuple[2])
  ensure @ts.write(tuple) if tuple
  end
end
```

Do you remember that each data structure requires a name that acts as an identifier?

Sem, Barrier, and RDStream require some sort of name. How would you generate such a unique name? There is no mechanism to check whether there are duplicate entities because the tuplespace is a bag and it allows duplicate entities. With this in mind, let's think about how we should generate a unique name. The first scenario is when tuplespace is used by only one process. The easiest way to obtain a unique identifier is to set an object itself as a value. Set it as follows:

```
key = Object.new
key2 = Object.new
p (key == keys2) # -> false
```

If there is only one process, you can easily use an object as an identifier. As long as an object exists in memory and until garbage collection (GC) wipes out the object, an object with the same ID won't be generated. As an alternative to using Object.new, you can use the object that manages the data structure. "@name = name || self" sets self as the default value.

```
class TSStruct
  def initialize(ts, name, struct)
    @ts = ts
    @name = name || self
    struct.each_pair do |key, value|
      @ts.write([@name, key, value])
    end
  end
  ...
end
```

This writes TSStruct itself as an element of a tuple into TupleSpace. What if multiple processes access the same object via dRuby? One strategy is to convert the object into a DRbObject object before name is sent to a remote location. You can include DRbUndumped to solve this problem.

```
class TSStruct
  include DRbUndumped
  ...
end
```

DRbObject consists of a URI of the process where an object exists (this is actually DRbServer, which starts up the process) and a unique object identifier within the process. Therefore, DRbObject can be unique within TupleSpace where TSStruct data exists.

When a process that generates TSStruct and a process that holds TupleSpace are different, then there are a few problems. One is a performance issue, and another is an object life span.

When a process accesses TSStruct, methods are invoked in both the process that generated the object and the process that holds TupleSpace where the TSStruct is stored.

There will be fewer RMI calls if the client process also holds TSStruct methods or invokes them at TupleSpace remotely. It shows off the great flexibility of dRuby if the client can hold TSStruct methods as well, but it will enhance performance if TupleSpace holds them.

The problem of object life span is trickier. If the process that generated the object dies, then the generated TSStruct becomes unavailable, and it leaves unused tuples in TupleSpace. This also causes problems with name identification. dRuby's URI is unique only while the process is up and running. Once the process that generated the object dies and a new dRuby service starts, then the same port number might be allocated.

The easier workaround to avoid the GC is that a process that holds TupleSpace should also hold TSStruct. (It's a bit sad to leave TupleSpace running on the back end, but you sometimes need a simpler solution for practical applications.)

6.5 Moving Ahead

In this chapter, we learned the following:

- Rinda's basic operations, such as write, take, and read
- Basic distributed data structures, such as bags, structs, hashes, arrays, and streams
- How to turn these structures into a class so that we can easily manage it from our application

If you want to learn more about tuplespace and Linda, read *How to Write Parallel Programs: A First Course*, which I mentioned in Section 6.3, *Basic Distributed Data Structures*, on page 124.

In the next chapter, we'll take a look at advanced uses of Rinda, such as adding timeouts, handling client disconnect, and using a service registration server call Ring. Not all these concepts existed in the original idea of Linda, but I added them while using Rinda in an actual application and found them useful.

CHAPTER 7

Extending Rinda

Most of the functionality you've seen so far has been ported from Linda. In this chapter, I'll introduce features that didn't exist in Linda's original conception but that I later added. You'll learn about some unique features and a unique way of using Rinda.

These include additional library features, such as adding expiration on a tuple, notifying newly added or deleted tuples, and expressing a tuple in a Hash. I added these features because I needed them while developing applications with Rinda. (I assume Linda doesn't have these extended features, because the author of Linda designed the minimum API that can comply with various applications. I hope that my extensions aren't diluting Linda's original design policy.)

However, the more I used Rinda in actual applications, the more features I thought I needed. For example, I had to handle situations where some application bugs left obsolete tuples. I wanted to be notified when other applications added or deleted tuples in the tuplespace. Expressing a tuple in a Hash may be more suitable than expressing it in an Array. And a naming server could be useful, too...and so on.

7.1 Adding a Timeout in a Tuple

We often make mistakes. Scripts contain bugs. While writing a script, we tend to rerun the same process again and again as we modify it. What happens if we leave a tuple in tuplespace that shouldn't be duplicated while we're developing? When both the tuplespace and the application run in one process, we won't leave obsolete tuples because both the tuplespace and the applications are restarted. However, the tuplespace process can contain old tuples only when the tuplespace and the application live in different processes and only the application process is restarted. In an ideal world, an application should clear the tuplespace before it stops, but this doesn't always happen.

Timeout and Renewer Class

You can set a timeout on a tuple (see Figure 37, *A tuple times out after thirty seconds and gets deleted automatically*, on page 139). When a tuple expires, it is automatically removed from the tuplespace. This avoids obsolete tuples left in tuplespace even when an application quits under unexpected circumstances. You can set the timeout in the second argument of the write method.

```
@ts.write(tuple, sec)
```

After it reaches the set period, the tuple is removed from tuplespace automatically. When nil is given, the timeout period becomes indefinite, and it doesn't get deleted automatically. The default is set to nil.

```
% irb -r rinda/tuplespace --prompt simple
>> ts = DRbObject.new_with_uri('druby://localhost:12345')
=> #<Rinda::TupleSpace:0x007ff99b03ba00>
>> ts.read_all(['test'])
=> []
>> ts.write(['test'], 30)
=> #<Rinda::TupleEntry:0x007ff99b889f90>
>> ts.read_all(['test'])
=> [["test"]]
>> sleep(30)
=> 30
>> ts.read_all(['test'])
=> []
```

We can specify not only Integer and nil but also an object called Renewer. Renewer has a renew instance method. The Renewer object returns how long it wants to extend once renew is called. Once the renew method returns true, the tuple is expired and removed from tuplespace immediately. An application can adjust how long it wants to extend a tuple's life span depending on its state by using Renewer.

Rinda has a class called Rinda::SimpleRenewer. You can define SimpleRenewer easily.

```
class SimpleRenewer
  include DRbUndumped
  def initialize(sec=180)
    @sec = sec
  end
  def renew
    @sec
  end
end
```

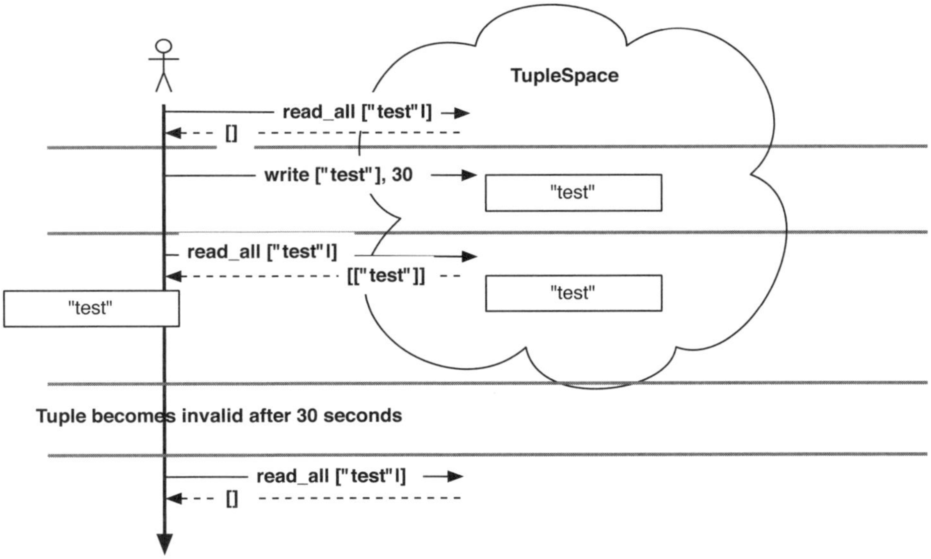

Figure 37—A tuple times out after thirty seconds and gets deleted automatically.

All this renew method does is return 180. The point is that this is being passed by reference because we included DRbUndumped. If you pass this SimpleRenewer as a second argument of the tuple's write method, the renew method will be called every time a tuple reaches the timeout period.

If an application finishes without leaving a tuple, the tuplespace calls the renew method in the next timeout period. However, it will fail to call the method because the application that puts SimpleRenewer has already finished. The tuplespace catches that it failed to call the renew method and deletes the tuple. By doing this, the tuplespace deletes the tuple for the next timeout period even when an application fails to clear up the tuple (see Figure 38, *When a process that holds SimpleRenewer finishes, it fails to update and the tuple is deleted*, on page 140).

The tuple expiration timing interval depends on the number that the renew method returns. In other words, it's possible for a tuple to stay on the tuplespace for a while after the application finishes. You can make this interval shorter, but making the interval too short may impact performance because Renewer requires dRuby method invocation for the periodic update.

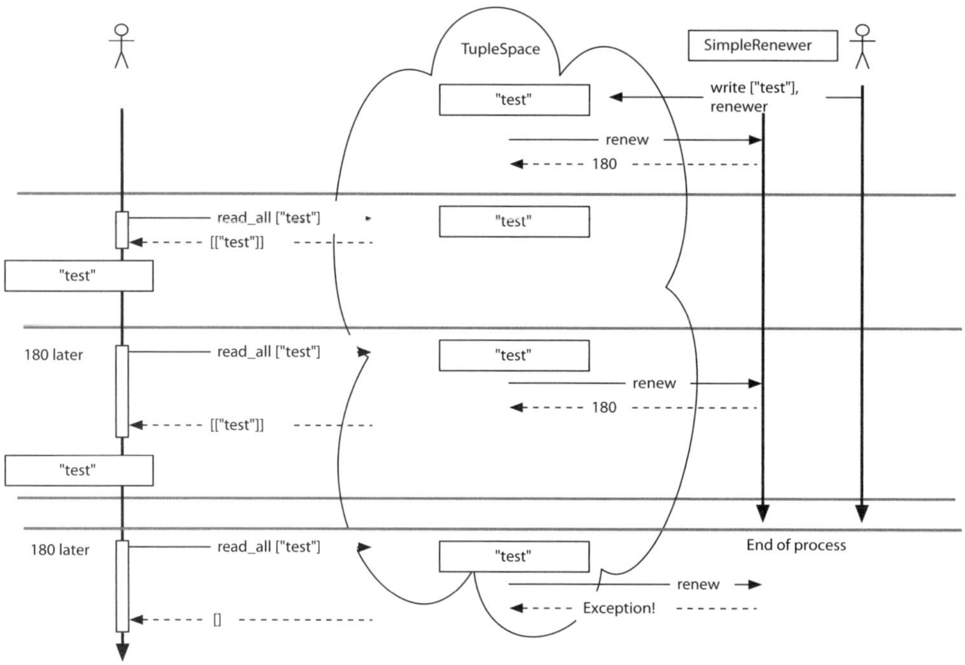

Figure 38—When a process that holds SimpleRenewer finishes, it fails to update and the tuple is deleted.

Invalidation Using TupleEntry

In addition to the Renewer method, there is a way to invalidate a tuple. However, this method is a little difficult to use when TupleSpace and an application are in different processes, so I recommend using Renewer. When you call the write method of TupleSpace, the method actually returns a value called TupleEntry. You can operate the tuple you put into tuplespace via TupleEntry. TupleEntry has the following methods:

cancel
: Set a tuple's timeout period to a past value and invalidate the tuple. The tuple is deleted from tuplespace.

renew(sec_or_renewer)
: Renew a tuple's timeout period. You can provide either a new time period value in seconds or a Renewer object. If you specify nil, it sets the timeout to indefinite.

Here are some examples:

```
@entry = @ts.write(['foo', 'bar])
@entry.cancel
```

The cancel operation doesn't fail even when the tuple is taken by some other process. TupleEntry is created inside TupleSpace during a write operation. If its associated tuple is taken, then TupleEntry is left and forgotten. One thing you have to be careful about is the life span of TupleEntry. This isn't an issue when the process that allocates TupleSpace and the process that writes the tuple are the same, but it will cause a GC problem if they are different. If another process has a returning value of a write operation, it holds only DRObject—which is referenced by TupleEntry—and it doesn't refer to TupleEntry itself. If take happens, then the object TupleEntry refers to doesn't exist anymore, and the object is wiped by GC. There are two workarounds to avoid this.

- Use TimerIdConv on the TupleSpace server to protect an object that dRuby refers to from GC (we'll discuss this in more detail in Chapter 11, *Handling Garbage Collection*, on page 221).
- Don't use take or don't count on TupleEntry for tuples that may not take.

You can accomplish the first workaround by putting the logic to control GC into a process that provides TupleSpace and avoids TupleEntry being garbage collected. You can accomplish the second at the application level by controlling TupleEntry only for the tuples that are less likely to be taken. However, both workarounds seem a bit cumbersome. If you know that multiple processes are to be involved, it's better to use Renewer.

7.2 Adding Notifications for New Events

Rinda has some additional features that don't exist in Linda. notify is a function to send a notification event when a tuple you're interested in is deleted or added. You can use it to monitor when some tuples are deleted, or you can use it for debugging purposes. There are three different events: write, take, and delete.

write
: Sends an event when a tuple is added to the tuplespace via a write operation

take
: Sends an event when a tuple is deleted from the tuplespace via a take operation

delete
: Sends an event when a tuple is deleted from the tuplespace, either when the tuple is deleted on expiration or by a cancel operation

Events are represented as a tuple in combination with the event name and the tuple itself. When the following tuple is written...

```
ts.write(["Hello", "World"])
```

then the following event gets notified:

```
["write", ["Hello", "World"]]
```

When the following tuple is taken...

```
ts.take(["Hello", nil])
```

then the following event gets notified:

```
["take", ["Hello", "World"]]
```

So, how do you write a script to actually receive these events? Use a notify event for this purpose. notify is a method to request event notifications, and you can specify an event name and tuple pattern.

notify(event, pattern, sec=nil)
: Requests to receive events in the tuplespace and receives events about tuples that match the pattern you specified. event is the type of event you are interested in. The element of a tuple is the same as normal tuple matching rules, so it notifies all tuples if nil is specified. The notify object returns a NotifyTemplateEntry object. When the time period specified in sec has passed, then the event notification terminates. When the termination happens, it generates a close event as the last event.

NotifyTemplateEntry is an object to retrieve the event you received from notify methods. Here are the major methods NotifyTemplateEntry provides:

each
: Calls a block when an event happens. The event tuples are passed to the block as follows:

```
["write", ["foo", "bar"]]
```

pop
: Takes out one event. Blocks if an event hasn't arrived yet.

cancel
: Cancels event notification requests. Once this is called, new events stop arriving.

If you call cancel after certain events have arrived, you can access them via pop. Once all events have arrived, it sends a close event to indicate the end of events.

The following is the code sequence to handle events:

```
# Request an event notification
notifier = ts.notify(nil, ['test', nil])

# Retrieve events
notifier.each do |event, tuple|
  ...
end
```

A NotifyTemplateEntry object is generated for each tuple pattern that the notify method requests. This means that multiple streams of event notifications are separated into their own queues and there is no way to guarantee the order among different queues. For example, if there are events for the ['test', nil] pattern and the ['name', 'rwiki',nil] pattern, they belong to different queues, and there are no methods to observe them at the same time. You could combine multiple queues to make them look like one by using a Queue object, but it doesn't guarantee the order in which they arrive. Here is a class to combine two notify events into one:

multiplenotify.rb

```
require 'drb/drb'
require 'rinda/rinda'
require 'rinda/tuplespace'
class MultipleNotify
  def initialize(ts, event, ary)
    @queue = Queue.new
    @entry = []
    ary.each do |pattern|
      make_listener(ts, event, pattern)
    end
  end
  def pop
    @queue.pop
  end
  def make_listener(ts, event, pattern)
    entry = ts.notify(event, pattern)
    @entry.push(entry)
    Thread.new do
      entry.each do |ev|
        @queue.push(ev)
      end
    end
  end
end
```

To use this class, try the following:

```
mn = MultipleNotify.new(ts, nil, [['test', nil], ['name', 'rwiki', nil]])
while true
  p mn.pop
end
```

The preceding example listens to two events and displays the tuples when notified.

7.3 Expressing a Tuple with Hash

All the tuples you've seen so far are based on Array, which is the same in Linda. I've also implemented Hash-based tuples. Contrary to an Array tuple, a Hash tuple offers an easier way to represent a tuple's semantics. In an Array tuple, the semantics of the tuple are represented by the order of its elements. In a Hash tuple, you can use a key for the purpose. All methods that write tuples into the tuplespace—such as write, read, and notify—provide a Hash tuple as well as an Array tuple. The pattern matching rule of a Hash-based tuple is almost the same as that of an Array-based tuple, but there are a few restrictions.

- A Hash key must be a String type.
- When nil is given as a wildcard, it only matches its key.

Here are some Hash tuple examples:

```
{"name" => "seki", "age" => 0x20}
{"kind" => "family", "name" => "Elinor", "sister" => "Carolyn"}
{"request" => "fact", "lower" => 1, "upper" => 10 }
{"answer" => "fact", "lower" => 1, "upper" => 10, "value" => 3628800 }
```

If a non-String key is given to a Hash tuple, a Rinda::InvalidHashTupleKey exception is raised. Here's a pattern matching example:

```
Pattern : {"name" => nil, "age" => Integer}
```

The preceding pattern has the following meanings:

- Contains the name key.
- The age key is an Integer.
- It has two keys.

Let's see which tuples match the preceding pattern:

```
1.{"name" => "m_seki", "age" => 32.5} # ×
2.{"name" => "seki", "age" => 0x20} # ○
3.{"name" => "seki", "age" => 0x20, "url" => "http://www.druby.org"} # ×
4.{"age" => 0x20 } # ×
```

Tuple 1 fails because it has correct keys, but age has a Float value, not Integer.

Tuple 2 succeeds because it has correct keys and because age has an Integer value.

Tuple 3 fails because it has a different number of keys.

Tuple 4 fails because it doesn't have a name key. Even when a wildcard pattern is passed, it at least has to have the key.

Let's rewrite the factorial service we wrote in Figure 33, *Expressing the factorial request tuple and the result tuple as a service*, on page 117 using a Hash tuple. Here are a request tuple and a response tuple:

```
{ "request" => "fact", "range" => Range }
{ "answer" => "fact", "range" => Range, "fact" => Integer }
```

The Hash tuple version has a more semantic meaning than the Array tuple version. The following is the client code:

ts01c2h.rb

```
require 'drb/drb'

def fact_client(ts, a, b, n=1000)
  req = []
  a.step(b, n) { |head|
    tail = [b, head + n - 1].min
    range = (head..tail)
    req.push(range)
    ts.write({"request"=>"fact", "range"=>range})
  }

  req.inject(1) { |value, range|
    tuple = ts.take({"answer"=>"fact", "range"=>range, "fact"=>Integer})
    value * tuple["fact"]
  }
end

ts_uri = ARGV.shift || 'druby://localhost:12345'
DRb.start_service
$ts = DRbObject.new_with_uri(ts_uri)
p fact_client($ts, 1, 20000)
```

And the following is the server code:

ts01sh.rb

```
require 'drb/drb'
class FactServer
  def initialize(ts)
    @ts = ts
  end
```

```
  def main_loop
    loop do
      tuple = @ts.take({"request"=>"fact", "range"=>Range})
      value = tuple["range"].inject(1) { |a, b| a * b }
      @ts.write({"answer"=>"fact", "range"=>tuple["range"], "fact"=>value})
    end
  end
end

ts_uri = ARGV.shift || 'druby://localhost:12345'
DRb.start_service
$ts = DRbObject.new_with_uri(ts_uri)
FactServer.new($ts).main_loop
```

Instead of calling tuple[3], now you can call it as tuple["range"], which is easier to understand.

7.4 Removing Tuples Safely with TupleSpaceProxy

In the previous example, processes may not finish properly if the client process quits abnormally.

```
[Terminal 1]
% ruby ts01.rb
[Terminal 2]
% ruby ts01shp.rb
## Ctrl-C
/usr/local/lib/ruby/1.9/drb/drb.rb:566:in `read': Interrupt
from /usr/local/lib/ruby/1.9/drb/drb.rb:566:in `load'
....
## Restart
[Terminal 2]
% ruby ts01shp.rb
[Terminal 3]
% ruby ts01c2h.rb
181920632023034513482764175686645876607l.........
```

In this example, we quit the process with Ctrl-C while FactServer at ts01.sh is calling take. We lose some tuples because the take method has not finished yet (see Figure 39, *Losing a tuple due to cancellation while calling the take method,* on page 147). This is a limitation of dRuby: it has no mechanism to notify when the calling process or thread terminated, so the remote method continues the process.

To avoid this problem, there is a method called move in TupleSpace. It's similar to the take method, but it does extra things to remove the tuple safely.

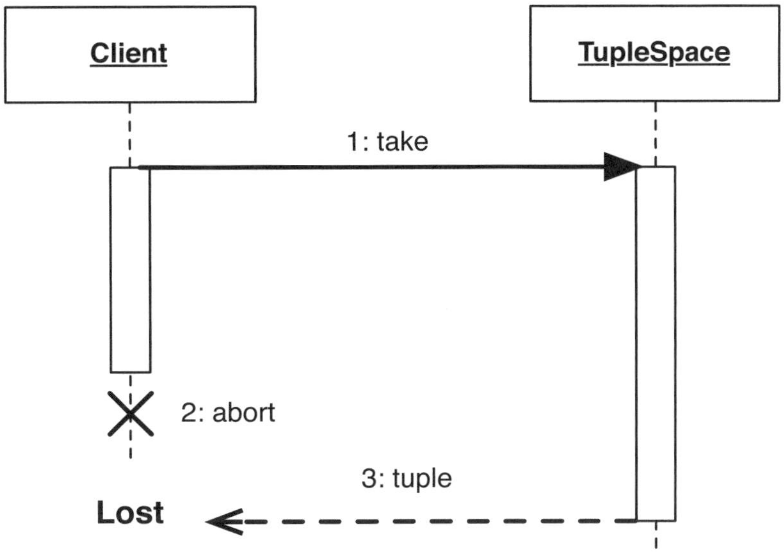

Figure 39—Losing a tuple due to cancellation while calling the take method

Using move(port, pattern, sec=nil, &block) moves a tuple to the specified port. It takes out a tuple like the take method does, but it first calls port.push(tuple) and then removes the tuple. If the port.push(tuple) operation fails, the operation becomes invalidated, and it doesn't delete the tuple. This catches the failure of a tuple move and therefore avoids missing tuples.

The move method is rarely used on its own. The TupleSpaceProxy class provides a take method that calls move internally. Here is the definition of TupleSpaceProxy#take:

```
class TupleSpaceProxy
  def take(tuple, sec=nil, &block)
    port = []
    @ts.move(DRbObject.new(port), tuple, sec, &block)
    port[0]
  end
end
```

All methods inside TupleSpaceProxy are pretty much the same as those in TupleSpace. Once a TupleSpaceProxy object is generated, you can use it in the same way as you use TupleSpace.

Here's an example usage of TupleSpaceProxy:

ts01shp.rb

```
require 'rinda/rinda'

class FactServer
  def initialize(ts)
    @ts = ts
  end

  def main_loop
    loop do
      tuple = @ts.take({"request"=>"fact", "range"=>Range})
      value = tuple["range"].inject(1) { |a, b| a * b }
      @ts.write({"answer"=>"fact", "range"=>tuple["range"], "fact"=>value})
    end
  end
end

ts_uri = ARGV.shift || 'druby://localhost:12345'
DRb.start_service
$ts = DRbObject.new_with_uri(ts_uri)
FactServer.new(Rinda::TupleSpaceProxy.new($ts)).main_loop
```

Let's try the same experiment that we did at the beginning of this section to compare the result. This time, ts01c2h.rb should return the value after terminating ts01sh.rb:

```
[Terminal 1]
% ruby ts01.rb
[Terminal 2]
% ruby ts01sh.rb
## Ctrl-C
/usr/local/lib/ruby/1.999999999/drb/drb.rb:554:in `read': Interrupt
from /usr/local/lib/ruby/1.9/drb/drb.rb:554:in `load'
....
## Restart
[Terminal 2] % ruby ts01sh.rb
[Terminal 3] % ruby ts01c2h.rb
181920632023034513482764175686645876 6071.........
```

Missing tuples will cause problems that are hard to debug. When you expect your subsystems to restart or halt, you should use TupleSpaceProxy#take.

7.5 Finding a Service with Ring

Ring is a name server, and it uses TupleSpace to publish your service on a local area network (LAN). The concept of Ring is close to Java's Jini. For those familiar with Jini, Ring is similar to Jini's discovery and lookup functionalities, but there are a few differences in terms of resource management. In Jini, a special service called a *lease* deletes objects if they haven't been used for a while, while Ring manages them by simply adding an expiration date on the tuplespace. A server needs to renew the tuplespace on its own. However, the code for the renewal will be minimal by using a callback from the tuplespace.

dRuby didn't have a default name server in the beginning, and I'll explain why later. So, why did I write Ring later? The answer is simple: it looked interesting to do. Ring provides you with a way to dynamically look up services. An application can connect to a Ring network, register itself, and search for other available services. Ring can also remove unavailable services periodically or notify when a new service is registered. These functionalities let you change the process architecture of your system dynamically (see Figure 40, *How RingService, a service, and an application work together*, on page 150).

Here are the advantages of Ring:

- There's no need to know the URI of services in advance.
- There's no need to know the URI of a name server in advance.
- When a service goes down, it will be removed from the name server periodically.
- The services can receive a notification when a new server joins Ring.

Ring consists of two elements:

- A structure to search `TupleSpace` within a LAN
- A name server that utilizes `TupleSpace`

Ring doesn't have a special class; it simply uses `TupleSpace` as a name server. Once you find a `TupleSpace`, you can use it for normal usage of `TupleSpace` (for example, for writing, reading, or deleting tuples).

When you ask Ring for a service, Ring searches in two steps, so it's not ideal for short-lived processes, such as CGI. It's more suited for long-running processes between web applications or between web applications and other back-end services.

Locating a Name Server

As mentioned earlier, I haven't provided a naming service, because you can just use `Hash` instead. Here is an example. First, you prepare a name server with a `URI` such as `'druby://localhost:12345'`.

```
require 'drb/drb'
DRb.start_service('druby://localhost:12345', Hash.new)
DRb.thread.join
```

Then, you can add an entry called `MyApp` as follows:

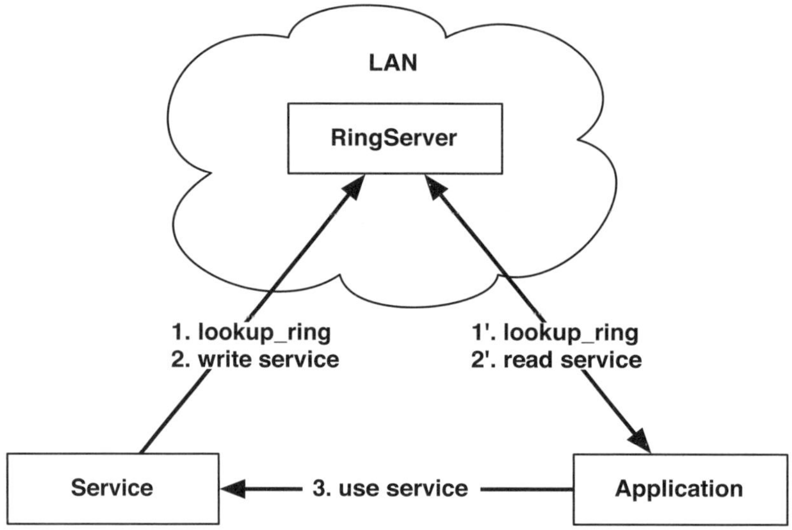

Figure 40—How RingService, a service, and an application work together

```
require 'drb/drb'
require 'myapp'
DRb.start_service(nil, MyApp.new)
ns = DRbObject.new_with_uri('druby://localhost:12345')
ns['MyApp'] = DRbObject.new(DRb.front)
DRb.thread.join
```

Once registered, you can use the object, like so:

```
require 'drb/drb'
DRb.start_service
ns = DRbObject.new_with_uri('druby://localhost:12345')
my_app = ns['MyApp']
my_app.do_it()
```

There's one thing I don't like about this approach: you have to know the location of the name server. Both the name server and the client have to know the URI of the name server before starting the server. In the preceding example, we hard-coded the URI inside the script. Even if you make it configurable, you still need to know the location of the URI.

This isn't a big problem if your system is relatively small (and the initial scope of dRuby use was for small systems), but I wanted to come up with a way to create a system without needing to know the name server's URI. This is how I started developing Ring.

Searching TupleSpace

In Ring, the name server functionality is built on top of TupleSpace. To use the TupleSpace, you need to search available services. In this section, we'll cover publishing and searching.

Publishing TupleSpace with RingServer

Ring uses UDP broadcasting to publish and search TupleSpace. RingServer is a class to support publishing TupleSpace via the User Datagram Protocol (UDP). RingServer monitors a UDP port and then returns references of TupleSpace requests. Here's a basic example of RingServer usage:

ring00.rb

```
require 'rinda/ring'
require 'rinda/tuplespace'

DRb.start_service

ts = Rinda::TupleSpace.new
place = Rinda::RingServer.new(ts)

DRb.thread.join
```

To use RingServer, instantiate an object by passing the tuplespace you want to publish as an argument.

RingServer.new(ts, port=7647) generates a RingServer with a tuplespace to publish. RingServer uses the UDP port number specified in the port argument. By default, it is 7647.

The internals of RingServer are a bit tricky. RingServer keeps waiting until DRbObject arrives at the UDP port of the RingServer. The object that gets sent via UDP is actually an Array tuple, as follows:

```
[:lookup_ring, DRbObject.new(block)]
```

RingServer executes a call method with the published tuple once the tuple arrives.

```
tuple[1].call(@ts)
```

UDP is used only to wait for DRbObject, and it isn't used to send replies. For replies, you use the remote method invocation of DRbObject. When a client receives the search result, it receives it with dRuby's RMI rather than writing code to wait for UDP.

Searching TupleSpace with RingFinger

RingFinger is a utility class that's published via RingServer to search a tuplespace. There are two ways to search; one way is a detailed search using the instance method, and another is a simple search using the class method.

RingFinger searches RingServer by broadcasting a reference (DRbObject) of proc via UDP first and then receiving a callback from RingServer (see Figure 41, *Searching by RingFinger using RingFinger#lookup_ring_any*, on page 153).

Use RingFinger.primary to find only one RingServer, and use RingFinger.to_a to find all RingServers in a network. Make sure you start the dRuby service before using RingFinger. Here's an example of searching one RingServer:

```
require 'rinda/ring'
DRb.start_service
ts = RingFinger.primary
```

Here's a list of all the RingFinger methods:

RingFinger.finger
: Returns an instance of RingFinger. When first called, it searches RingServer using lookup_ring.

RingFinger.primary
: Returns a reference to the TupleSpace of RingServer found by RingFinger.finger.

RingFinger.to_a
: Returns all references to the TupleSpace of RingServer found by RingFinger.finger.

RingFinger.new(broadcast_list=['<broadcast>', 'localhost'], port=7647)
: Generates RingFinger. Can specify broadcast range and port number.

RingFinger#lookup_ring(timeout=5, &block)
: Awaits callback for the timeout period after a search packet is broadcast via UDP. RingServer yields the block given at RingFinger#lookup_ring with a reference to TupleSpace. You should specify an action you want to take once the TupleSpace is found in the code block.

RingFinger#lookup_ring_any(timeout=5)
: Simplified version of lookup_ring. Returns the TupleSpace that responded to the first callback. Raises RingNotFound if nothing is found.

Searching by instance of RingFinger gives you more flexibility, such as being able to specify the range of broadcasting. Searching by class method will cache the result of the first search, so you can't look up per request. It depends on the use case as to which one to use, but using class methods is enough for simple applications. To be precise, searching by the class method of

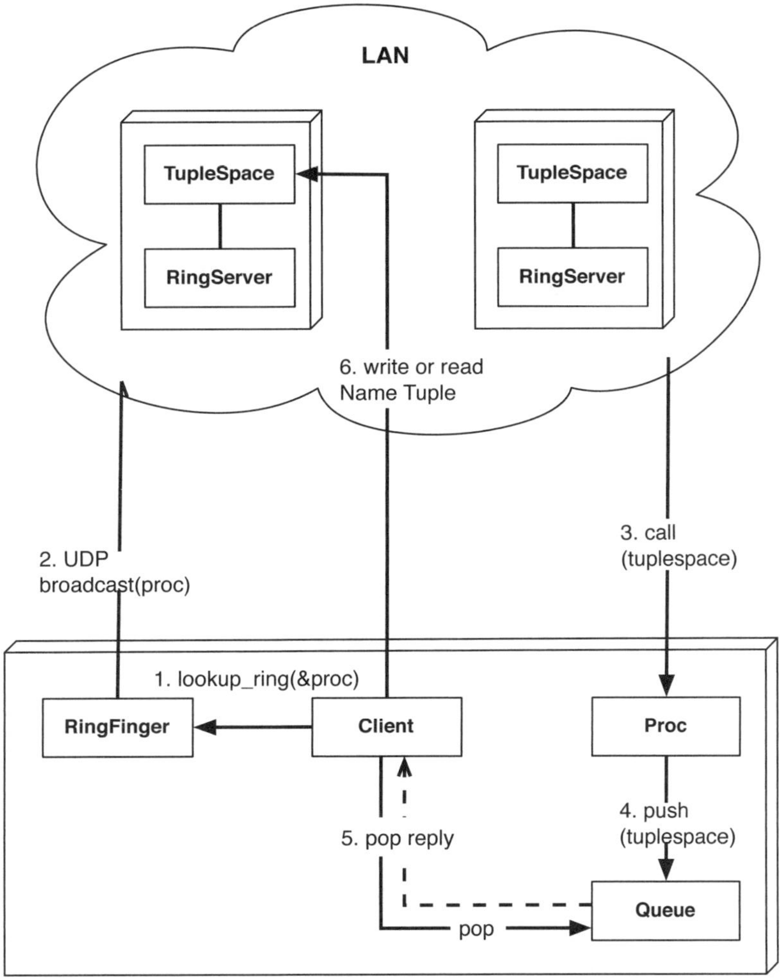

Figure 41—Searching by RingFinger using RingFinger#lookup_ring_any

RingFinger looks like a singleton, but I didn't implement it with class methods. This is because you don't have to limit the number of RingFingers to one, so it doesn't have to be a strict singleton.

Name Server Using TupleSpace

Ring uses TupleSpace to make a name server. This isn't a special TupleSpace, and it just uses the TupleSpace published by RingServer or RingFinger.

Here are the responsibilities of Ring's name server:

- Make a tuple consisting of name, type, and reference
- Publish the object via write to TupleSpace
- Search via read or all with pattern matching

This is the format of the tuple:

```
[:name, :type, a DRbObject, "comment"]
```

tuple[0]
: Symbol. Represents that this is a tuple representing a name server entry. The value is always :name.

tuple[1]
: Symbol. Represents a category (for example, :name_server, :place, :rwiki). This name should be decided per system.

tuple[2]
: DRbObject. A reference to the object to be published.

tuple[3]
: String. A comment to explain what this tuple is used for. If there's nothing to comment, use an empty string or nil.

Let's look at a few examples:

```
# Register a name valid for 600sec
ts.write([:name, :rwiki, book.front, "RWiki2 front"], 600)
# Search
tuple = ts.read([:name, :rwiki, DRbObject, nil])
rwiki = tuple[2]
```

There is a utility class to publish these objects. RingProvider supports publication of objects and has these responsibilities (you can still directly control tuples if you need more fine-grained control): it generates tuples and prepares renewer.

Here are the methods of RingProvider:

RingProvider.new(klass, front, desc, renewer = nil)
: Prepares [:name, klass, front, desc] tuple and renewer. If renewer is not specified, generates SimpleRenewer.

RingProvider#provide
: Searches tuplespace and writes the tuple and renewer into TupleSpace.

To publish a reference of your application to Ring, you need to instantiate RingProvider and then call provide. Here is the code:

ring01.rb

```
require 'rinda/ring'
class Hello
  def greeting
  "Hello, World."
  end
end

hello = Hello.new
DRb.start_service(nil, hello)
provider = Rinda::RingProvider.new(:Hello, DRbObject.new(hello), 'Hello')
provider.provide

DRb.thread.join
```

The last few lines of this script are key. It first generates Rinda::RingProvider and then calls provide to publish the object to the network. The argument of the new constructor is in the order of the type of the object to publish, the reference to the object, and the explanation of the object.

```
provider = Rinda::RingProvider.new(:Hello, DRbObject.new(hello), 'Hello')
provider.provide
```

provide adds an entry into the name server. When this is called, it writes the following tuple:

```
[:name, :Hello, DRbObject.new(hello), 'Hello']
```

You'll find out how to use this service within an application in the next section.

7.6 Examples of Ring Applications

In this section, we'll go through a simple example to explain how to use the Ring name server and then move to a more complex system that combines various components.

Various Ways to Wait

Let's use the "Hello" example we used in the previous section to understand how to use the name server. The easiest way to search is to use read.

ring02.rb

```
require 'rinda/ring'
DRb.start_service

ts = Rinda::RingFinger.primary
tuple = ts.read([:name, :Hello, DRbObject, nil])
hello = tuple[2]
puts hello.greeting
```

This example uses RingFinger to search a tuplespace and then read with pattern matching of [:name, :Hello, DRbObject, nil] (see Figure 42, *read will be blocked until a service is registered*, on page 157).

If a specific service isn't published, the process will be blocked until it becomes available. This is one of the advantages of utilizing TupleSpace as a name server. Let's do some experimentation. First, start RingServer.

```
# terminal1
% ruby ring00.rb
```

Next, start the client. This will be blocked because :Hello isn't registered yet.

```
# terminal2
% ruby ring02.rb
```

Next, start ring01.rb to publish :Hello. Once :Hello is published, the process at terminal 2 will be unblocked and continue its transaction.

```
# terminal3
% ruby ring01.rb
```

```
# continued from terminal2
% ruby ring02.rb
Hello, World.
```

Let's try ring02.rb again. This time, it should start the transaction immediately, because :Hello is already registered.

```
# terminal2
% ruby ring02.rb
Hello, World.
```

It's good if you can wait for a service to be available through Ring, but you may sometimes want to quit immediately if a service you're interested in isn't available. In such a case, just use read with a timeout or use read_all.

ring03.rb

```
require 'rinda/ring'

DRb.start_service

ts = Rinda::RingFinger.primary
begin
  tuple = ts.read([:name, :Hello, DRbObject, nil], 0)
rescue Rinda::RequestExpiredError
  puts "Hello: not found."
  exit(1)
end
hello = tuple[2]
puts hello.greeting
```

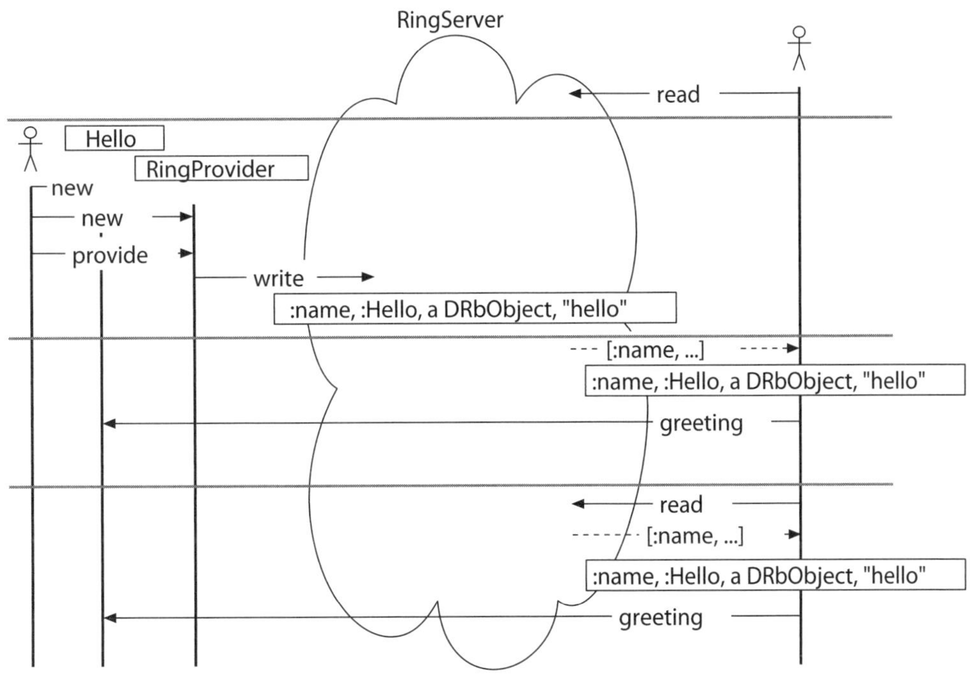

Figure 42—read will be blocked until a service is registered. The second read call receives a response immediately.

read_all may return multiple entries. In ring04.rb, it responds to all the returning entries.

ring04.rb
```
require 'rinda/ring'

DRb.start_service

ts = Rinda::RingFinger.primary
ary = ts.read_all([:name, :Hello, DRbObject, nil])
if ary.size == 0
  puts "Hello: not found."
  exit(1)
end
ary.each do |tuple|
  hello = tuple[2]
  puts hello.greeting
end
```

Let's see how it works:

```
# terminal1
% ruby ring00.rb
```

```
# terminal2
% ruby ring04.rb
Hello: not found.
```

It should fail immediately because the service is not up yet. Next, run ring04.rb after starting up two Hello services.

```
# terminal3
% ruby ring01.rb
```

```
# terminal4
% ruby ring01.rb
```

```
# terminal2
% ruby ring04.rb
Hello, World.
Hello, World.
```

You should see that "Hello, World." is displayed twice. This is because the service is registered to two different services. If you want to use only one service, then use first to take the first service, as shown in the following example, rather than iterating over using each. The following is the modified version using first:

ring05.rb

```
require 'rinda/ring'

DRb.start_service

ts = Rinda::RingFinger.primary
tuple = ts.read_all([:name, :Hello, DRbObject, nil]).first
if tuple.nil?
  puts "Hello: not found."
  exit(1)
end
hello = tuple[2]
puts hello.greeting
```

Next, let's think about how to deal with newly registered services. As explained earlier, you can use read_all to list all the registered services. However, what do you do when a new service is registered? The read method can wait for only one service, so it isn't a good way to keep track of all the new services. notify seems like a good way to get notification, because service registration is simply done by write to TupleSpace.

Let's write a class called RingNotify. This will read already registered services and newly registered services as each event happens. We can instantiate RingNotify by passing the type of services we want to watch and then take them out in the each block.

ringnotify.rb
```
require 'thread'
require 'rinda/ring'

class RingNotify
  def initialize(ts, kind, desc=nil)
    @queue = Queue.new
    pattern = [:name, kind, DRbObject, desc]
    open_stream(ts, pattern)
  end

  def pop
    @queue.pop
  end

  def each
    while tuple = @queue.pop
      yield(tuple)
    end
  end

  private
  def open_stream(ts, pattern)
    @notifier = ts.notify('write', pattern)
    ts.read_all(pattern).each do |tuple|
      @queue.push(tuple)
    end
    @writer = writer_thread
  end

  def writer_thread
    Thread.start do
      begin
        @notifier.each do |event, tuple|
          @queue.push(tuple)
        end
      rescue
        @queue.push(nil)
      end
    end
  end
end
```

The open_stream method calls notify first and then calls read_all. If it calls read_all first and then notify, you may miss the write method that happened between read_all and notify. If you notify first, then it won't miss the write method, even though there is a possibility of notifying twice.

ring06.rb is a revised Hello service client that handles both existing services and newly added services using RingNotify.

ring06.rb

```
require 'rinda/ring'
require './ringnotify'

DRb.start_service

ts = Rinda::RingFinger.primary
ns = RingNotify.new(ts, :Hello)
ns.each do |tuple|
  hello = tuple[2]
  puts hello.greeting
end
```

Let's experiment now. First, start RingServer.

```
# terminal1
% ruby ring00.rb
```

Next, start the Hello service.

```
# terminal2
% ruby ring01.rb
```

Next, start the client ring06.rb. Now that the Hello service is already registered, it should immediately print out "Hello, World." and then wait (being blocked) until the next Hello is registered.

```
# terminal3
% ruby ring06.rb
Hello, World.
```

Let's run another ring01.rb and publish Hello.

```
# terminal4
% ruby ring01.rb
```

The process at terminal 2 will be now unblocked, continue the transaction, and then wait until the next Hello is published.

```
# terminal2 (continues)
% ruby ring06.rb
Hello, World.
Hello, World.
```

As you just saw, you can write a script with read_all and notify to handle inter-service dependencies no matter how often the dependent services restart.

With this script, you aren't bound to the restart timing of dependent services, and the re-registration of the service will become easier. If you have a complex system with many subsystems, this script will simplify the management of the start-up.

What if registered services finish? If you register an object with the renewer option, then the timed-out service will be removed automatically. However, invalid tuples will remain in TupleSpace for several minutes until the next round of housekeeping work happens. Let's experiment with this.

```
# terminal1
% ruby ring00.rb

# terminal2
% ruby ring01.rb
## Halt this process with Ctrl-C

# terminal3
% ruby ring06.rb
/usr/local/lib/ruby/1.9/drb/drb.rb:706:in
`open': druby://localhost:52180 -
#<Errno::ECONNREFUSED: Connection refused - connect(2)> (DRb::DRbConnError)
....
```

With Ring's name service, an invalid entry will be deleted automatically, but this example shows that it will take a while until the invalid entry gets detected and deleted from the system. (Even if you can control it perfectly, a service could be terminated after you take out the service, so you still need to take special care.)

This is a common problem among dRuby systems. How to deal with referencing these invalid remote objects depends on each application.

ring07.rb

```ruby
require 'rinda/ring'
require './ringnotify'

DRb.start_service

ts = Rinda::RingFinger.primary
ns = RingNotify.new(ts, :Hello)
ns.each do |tuple|
  hello = tuple[2]
  begin
    puts hello.greeting
  rescue
  end
end
```

This time, we took a strategy of simply ignoring a failure to invoke methods.

In this section, we went through the following common patterns for registering and searching services:

- Waiting for available services using `read`
- Timing out, or searching services with `read_all`
- Using `read_all` to deal with multiple services
- Dealing with service re-registration using `read_all` and `notify`
- Handling invalid services

Next, you'll see subsets of complex systems actually in use.

Tiny "I Like Ruby"

"I like Ruby" is my Japanese website originally used to distribute dRuby and Rinda. It's also the first practical system to use Ring. Rwiki (a dRuby-powered wiki) maintains the content, and Div (another library written by me, similar to Rail's view helper) formats and indexes the content. It also has some sample applications.

For example, the following services are up and running:

- A process with the WEBrick HTTP server and a session management system called Tofu
- RWiki: A dRuby-powered wiki server
- RWiki: An editor-only Div
- RWiki: A formatting-only Div
- A dRuby-based game called Hako Iri Musume
- A simple database-backed expense reporting application called Saifu (meaning "wallet" in Japanese)

Multiple Div applications are running on top of a WEBrick-based HTTP server. Some of the Div applications are used outside WEBrick, such as within RWiki.

Thanks to Ring, you don't have to restart all the services when you want to deploy part of your system. This is very handy when you want to do minor upgrades or small bug fixes.

7.7 Moving Ahead

In this chapter, we learned the following:

- How to handle unexpected situations by adding timeout, invalidation, and notification
- How to handle things when client connections die, using `move` and `TupleSpaceProxy`
- How to use the Ring name server

In the next chapter, you'll find out about two additional features: `rinda_eval` and `PTupleSpace`. They are not included as part of the Ruby standard library, but they're easy to install and will help you understand parallelism and persistency in Rinda.

CHAPTER 8

Parallel Computing and Persistence with Rinda

In this chapter, you'll get acquainted with a library called *more_rinda*. The more_rinda library adds two additional features to Rinda. One enables you to do parallel computing in an interesting way (called rinda_eval), and the other is to add persistence in Rinda.

You can easily install these features with the following command:

```
gem install more_rinda
```

You can also download the source code at GitHub.[1] You'll find lots of sample code to try in the test or sample directory.

8.1 Computing in Parallel with rinda_eval

In the previous chapter, I mentioned that I didn't implement eval because I couldn't come up with a good way to implement it. Actually, it's possible to replicate similar functionality to eval for Portable Operating System Interface for Unix (POSIX)–compliant operating systems.[2] I didn't include this as part of the standard library, because this doesn't run on Windows machines and is also very difficult to unit test. Having said that, you should be able to use rinda_eval in environments such as Linux or OS X. We'll first review what eval in Linda is like and then move on to the usage of rinda_eval and its internals.

By the way, don't be fooled by the word *eval*. It doesn't use Ruby's eval.

1. https://github.com/seki/MoreRinda
2. http://en.wikipedia.org/wiki/POSIX

Using eval with Linda

In Linda, there are two operations to generate a tuple: "out" and "eval." The "out" operation is equivalent to Rinda's Rinda::TupleSpace#write.

Here's an example of generating a tuple that contains the result of a square root from 0 to 9 using the "out" operation:

```
for (i = 0; i < 10; i++)
    out("sqrt", i, sqrt(i));
```

The "eval" operation looks exactly the same as the "out" operation, but there is a big difference. The "eval" operation first generates processes while evaluating arguments and then puts the result into tuples. Here's an example of generating ten processes and returning the result in each tuple. It's important to understand that these newly generated processes evaluate the sqrt function, not the calling process.

```
for (i = 0; i < 10; i++)
    eval("sqrt", i, sqrt(i));
```

If you think in a normal way, this looks very strange—it should generate processes after each argument is evaluated. Apparently you can do this with C-Linda because it is some sort of preprocessor or language extension, rather than a library.

Rinda::rinda_eval

If you can use a fork system call in your OS, then you can generate a child process that inherits the entire environment of the Ruby runtime and then continue the process. Rinda::rinda_eval is implemented using this fork system call, so it won't work if your OS doesn't have fork. That's why Rinda::rinda_eval is targeted for POSIX-compliant systems. This module method creates a new process and then executes the block. You can also pass a reference to TupleSpace to the arguments so that the returning Array is added into the tuplespace.

The API isn't exactly the same as that of C-Linda, but nonetheless this is a practical API. As an example of a practical application, the next example generates worker processes and then stores the results of the calculation into tuples. It consists of two loops. The first loop creates ten worker processes that calculate Math.sqrt inside a rinda_eval block, and then the second loop receives the result sets.

```
10.times do |n|
  Rinda::rinda_eval($ts) do |ts|
    [:sqrt, n, Math.sqrt(n)]
  end
```

```
end
10.times do |n|
  p $ts.read([:sqrt, n, nil])
end
```

The block passed into rinda_eval gets executed inside the child processes generated by fork. The return value of the block will be written to TupleSpace.

8.2 Concurrency in rinda_eval

You can gain two benefits by splitting tasks into multiple processes. First, each task can have its own address space. Second (especially for MRI—the Matz Ruby Interpreter in Ruby), you can use the power of multicore CPUs. Let's see the latter benefit with some simple examples.

Rinda::rinda_eval and Thread

ruby-1.9 uses an OS-native thread that itself can make use of multicore CPUs. However, there is a limitation in which only one thread can run at a time, so you can't make use of multicore by just using Thread.

In the following example, we'll run a Fibonacci function as an example of a CPU-heavy task. Sure, you can run this code faster by using techniques such as memoization or by passing around an n-1 value, but we'll use a simple implementation because our intention here is to create a long-running task.

rinda_bench1.rb

```
require 'benchmark'
def fib(n)
  n < 2 ? n : fib(n - 2) + fib(n - 1)
end
def task(n)
  puts "fib(#{n}) = #{fib(n)}"
end

puts Benchmark.measure{
  [30, 30, 30].each{|x| task x}
}
```

First, let's call fibonacci three times with an argument of 30 and then measure the time it took to run.

```
$ ruby rinda_bench1.rb
fib(30) = 832040
fib(30) = 832040
fib(30) = 832040
  0.720000   0.000000   0.720000 (  0.737842)
```

Next, let's rewrite the code using Thread. I ran this on two-core machine (the result shouldn't change even if you run this on single-core machine).

rinda_bench2.rb
```
require 'benchmark'
def fib(n)
  n < 2 ? n : fib(n - 2) + fib(n - 1)
end
def task(n)
  puts "fib(#{n}) = #{fib(n)}"
end

puts Benchmark.measure{
  [30, 30, 30].map{|x| Thread.new{task x}}.map{|y| y.join}
}
```

```
$ ruby rinda_bench2.rb
fib(30) = 832040
fib(30) = 832040
fib(30) = 832040
  0.750000   0.010000   0.760000 (  0.767103)
```

The execution times were about the same. How disappointing. This is because of the limitation I mentioned earlier, in which a Ruby thread can run only one interpreter at a time. In Ruby 1.8, this is because Thread is implemented virtually at the user level (called *Green Thread*). Ruby 1.9 uses the native threading of the CPU, but it is restricted by the Global Interpreter Lock (GIL), and multiple threads can't run at the same time.

Next, let's rewrite this to the rinda_eval version. This time, we should be able to leverage the multicore.

rinda_bench3.rb
```
require 'benchmark'
require 'rinda/tuplespace'
require 'rinda/eval'
def fib(n)
  n < 2 ? n : fib(n - 2) + fib(n - 1)
end
def task(n)
  puts "fib(#{n}) = #{fib(n)}"
end

place = Rinda::TupleSpace.new
DRb.start_service

puts Benchmark.measure{
  [30, 30, 30].each {|x|
    Rinda::rinda_eval(place) {|ts| [:result, x, task(x)]}
  }.each {|x|
```

```
    place.take([:result, x, nil])
  }
}
```

```
$ ruby rinda_bench3.rb
fib(30) = 832040
fib(30) = 832040
fib(30) = 832040
  0.000000   0.000000   0.530000 (  0.477666)
```

The code became slightly bigger than the Thread version, but you should be able to experience a speed increase because this version creates a new process for each task and runs in multiple CPU cores.

By the way, you can work with multicores using Thread if you use JRuby, which runs on the Java Virtual Machine (JVM). Let's run the Thread example with JRuby.

```
$ jruby rinda_bench2.rb
fib(30) = 832040
fib(30) = 832040
fib(30) = 832040
  0.640000   0.000000   0.640000 (  0.492000)
```

The preceding code is an example of running the Thread version with JRuby. Notice the same speed increase as with the rinda_eval version. You can use just JRuby if your project allows it. If your Ruby environment depends on MRI, then rinda_eval can be a handy way to do concurrent computing, and you may want to add this into your toolbox.

By the way, there is a common misunderstanding about GIL. Some people may think that operations like read, write, and sleep will block other native threads and therefore Ruby threads can't switch operations from one thread to the other. The truth is that it is only the calling Ruby thread that gets blocked during the long system calls, and other Ruby threads will run without any problems (you need to be aware that there are actually some extension libraries that do block all the running threads). Therefore, Ruby threading is very effective for I/O and network operations that interact with external resources, such as web crawling.

Let's change the task from fibonacci to sleep. This swaps a CPU-intensive task with an external resource call.

rinda_bench4.rb

```
require 'benchmark'
def task(n)
  sleep(n * 0.1)
end
```

```
puts Benchmark.measure{
  [30,30,30].map{|x| Thread.new{task x}}.map{|y| y.join}
}
```

```
$ ruby rinda_bench4.rb
  0.010000   0.010000   0.020000 (  3.000341)
```

In the preceding example, we replaced fib(n) with sleep(n * 0.1). You can see that it finishes in three seconds. This will be the same if we replace fib with read or write. In the preceding example, multiple Ruby threads are dealing with multiple I/O, which is similar to how you handle multiple clients with one native thread in C with select and asynchronous read and write. Using Ruby Thread, you can easily write logic to receive chunks of packets from a TCP stream and return them to the higher layer. In fact, dRuby uses asynchronous I/O to handle multiple Ruby threads. Having said that, this model is useful for handling up to dozens of client connections with one process. If the number of clients increases to thousands or tens of thousands, then you may want to use other solutions, such as EventMachine.

Service with Rinda::rinda_eval

In the previous example, rinda_eval processed only one task at a time, but there is a better way. Not only can you communicate between processes one at a time through the end result of the rinda_eval block, but you also can directly communicate between parent and child processes, or even among child processes. This way, you can create a long-running service that behaves like the Actor model, explained in the next section.

Here's an example of a service to return a Fibonacci calculation:

rinda_eval_service.rb

```
require 'rinda/tuplespace'
require 'rinda/eval'

def fib(n)
  n < 2 ? n : fib(n - 2) + fib(n - 1)
end

def fib_daemon(place)
  Rinda::rinda_eval(place) do |ts|
    begin
      while true
        _, n = ts.take([:fib, Integer])
        ts.write([:fib_ans, n, fib(n)])
      end
      [:done]  # not reached
    rescue DRb::DRbConnError
      exit(0)
```

```
    end
  end
end

place = Rinda::TupleSpace.new
DRb.start_service

2.times { fib_daemon(place) }

[30, 20, 10, 30].each {|x|
  place.write([:fib, x])
}.each {|x|
  p place.take([:fib_ans, x, nil])
}
```

[:fib, Integer] represents a request for a new Fibonacci, and [:fib_ans, n, fib(n)] represents a response for the Fibonacci calculation result. The fib_daemon method generates a new process. Inside the rinda_eval block, a loop continues taking :fib and writing :fib_ans. Not only can the child processes return a single result, but they also keep processing multiple requests. If you treat :fib as an address and Integer as a message, then it looks similar to the *Actor model.*

Rinda::rinda_eval and the Actor Model

There is a concurrent computation model called the Actor model. The essence of this idea is that each process coordinates with one another by sending one-way messages. The primitive type of message passing goes only one way; it's not a "request and response" two-way cycle. When you send a message, you send an "address" and "message body" and send to the destination without caring about the state of the other end. The receiver takes messages one at a time when possible. You can avoid lots of shared resource–related problems in multithreaded programming if processes don't share objects or memory and each process reads its own message only when its own resource is not in a critical state. This exchange of messages in one direction is similar to Linda's process coordination model.

The key of the Actor model is the message passing and nonshared state. Erlang provides both functionalities as a pure Actor model, but implementations in most other languages are an afterthought. You can write it easily, even in Ruby. It's also easy to write in a message-passing style using a library, but it's difficult to create nonshared state.

If you really want to have nonshared state, you can leverage the power of the OS by just dividing actors into multiple processes. rinda_eval comes in handy in this situation because you can create real processes easily. You can have the entire copy of the object space of the parent process, such as the class definition and binding of the preprocessing state. At the same time, you can have completely nonshared space. You can use Rinda's tuplespace as message-passing middleware.

Looking Inside rinda_eval

So far, you've seen the power of rinda_eval; it's a handy way to create processes for concurrent computing. To see how this method is implemented, let's look inside the implementation of rinda_eval. [3]

```
require 'drb/drb'
require 'rinda/rinda'

module Rinda
  module_function
  def rinda_eval(ts)
    Thread.pass
    ts = DRbObject.new(ts) unless DRbObject === ts
    pid = fork do
      Thread.current['DRb'] = nil
      DRb.stop_service
      DRb.start_service
      place = TupleSpaceProxy.new(ts)
      tuple = yield(place)
      place.write(tuple) rescue nil
    end
    Process.detach(pid)
  end
end
```

Wow, it has fewer than twenty lines of code. The code looks complicated, but there are two key things in the code. It uses fork to generate a child process, and it passes a reference of TupleSpace into its child process.

fork

fork is a Unix system call that creates a new process by copying the memory space and resources of its parent process. Like Unix's fork, Ruby's fork method carries over the entire Ruby object space into the child process. This is useful to set up the initial state of the child process, by passing the state of the parent process right at the time of the fork method call. But how do you send information to a child process once fork is called? In traditional Unix programming, you use pipe or socketpair. Both functions use a stream between parent and child processes. rinda_eval uses TupleSpace to exchange information between processes.

3. https://github.com/seki/MoreRinda/blob/master/lib/rinda/eval.rb

This is a simple example of using fork:

fork.rb

```
result = 0
pid = fork do
result += 1
end
Process::waitpid(pid)
p result
```

The result of the preceding example returns 0. The result variable is redefined in the child process, so it won't change the state of the parent process.

Let's change the code to use the tuplespace to exchange values:

rinda_fork.rb

```
require 'drb'
proc = Proc.new {|x| x + 1}
parent = Rinda::TupleSpace.new
DRb.start_service
child = DRbObject.new(parent)
result = 0
pid = fork do
 DRb.stop_service
 child.write([:result, proc[result]])
end
Process.detach(pid)
_, result = parent.take([:result, nil])
p result
```

The result of the preceding example returns 1. You can pass the logic of the calculation using Proc because a child process inherits the entire context of its parent process. The difference between the two is shown in Figure 43, *Difference between passing the result via fork and via TupleSpace*, on page 174. Note that you can use Proc inside the fork block, because the child process has the entire context of the parent process. To run Ruby's block inside a different process, you need to pass the entire binding of the object space, not just the statement you want to execute. If your statement doesn't depend on the external environment, you can just pass the statement as a string and execute Ruby's eval method.

Remember, we created a distributed factorial service in Figure 33, *Expressing the factorial request tuple and the result tuple as a service*, on page 117. The downside of the service is that you had to define the algorithm of the computation (factorial logic) on the server side in advance. Using fork and TupleSpace, you can define anything in a parent process, distribute the computation into its child processes, and then receive the result afterward. rinda_eval abstracted the logic into twenty lines of code. The downside of rinda_eval compared to the

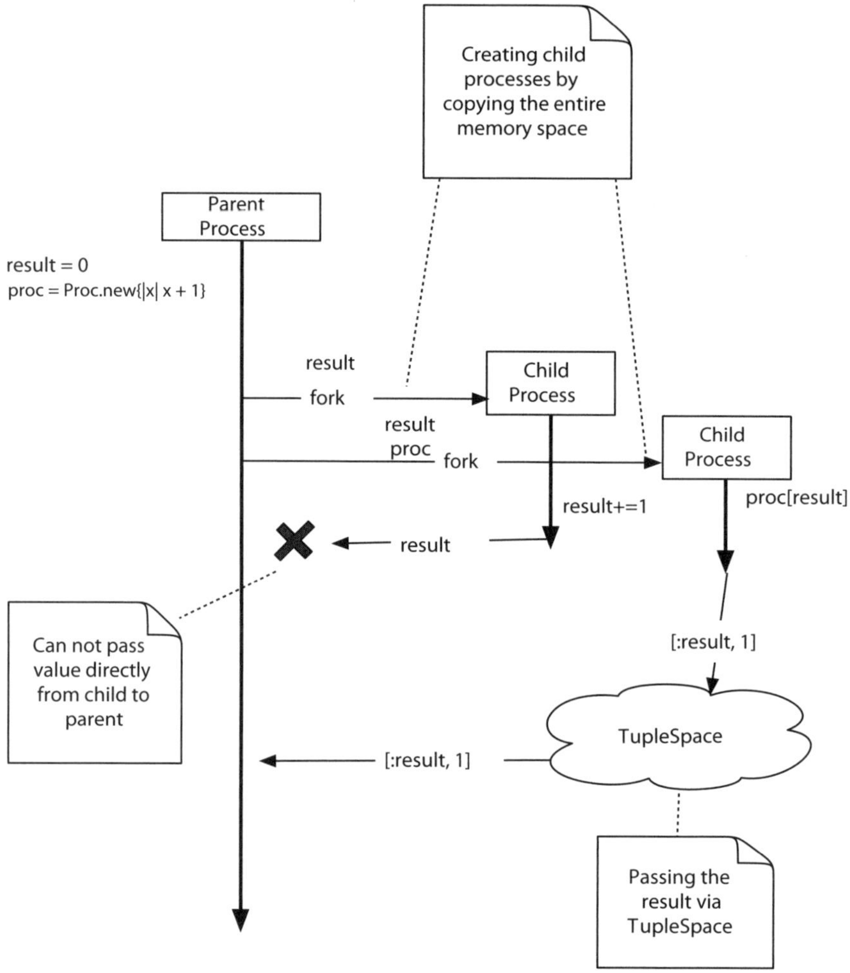

Figure 43—Difference between passing the result via fork and via TupleSpace

distributed factorial service is that you can't distribute to different machines, because rinda_eval depends on fork.

8.3 Persisting a Tuple with PTupleSpace

TupleSpace in Rinda makes complex interprocess communication very easy. However, the fact that the entire tuplespace is in volatile memory is worrisome —you could lose all your data when the system crashes. That's a bit frightening. To work around the problem, I created a persistency feature; let's discuss its architecture and limitations.

Persistency in TupleSpace

Let's get acquainted with the basic use of PTupleSpace while learning about its crash and recovery mechanism.

PTupleSpace is a subclass of TupleSpace. It keeps logging the change of the tuple state. When PTupleSpace is restarted, it recovers to the last state of the tuple.

Using PTupleSpace is easy; here's an example:

ptuple.rb

```
require 'rinda/ptuplespace'
store = Rinda::TupleStoreLog.new('ts_log')
Rinda::setup_tuple_store(store)

DRb.install_id_conv(Rinda::TupleStoreIdConv.new)
ts = Rinda::PTupleSpace.new
DRb.start_service('druby://localhost:23456', ts)
ts.restore

ts.write(['Hello', 'World'])
p ts.read_all(['Hello', nil])
p ts.take(['Hello', nil])

x = ts.write(['Hello', 'cancel'], 2)
p ts.read_all(['Hello', nil])
ref = DRbObject.new(x)
ref.cancel
p ts.read_all(['Hello', nil])
x = ts.write(['Hello', 'World'])

p DRbObject.new(x)
```

Running the script should show output like this:

```
$ ruby ptuple.rb
[["Hello", "World"]]
["Hello", "World"]
[["Hello", "cancel"]]
[]
#<Rinda::PTupleEntry:0x00000101392388>
```

Let's see what just happened. To use PTupleSpace, you need to prepare TupleStore first. This becomes the persistency layer of this PTupleSpace process. There are different kinds of TupleStore, so you can switch between them. In this example, I used a simple persistency layer using Marshal, called TupleStoreLog. To use it, you need to specify the directory name to save the TupleStoreLog logs.

```
store = Rinda::TupleStoreLog.new('ts_log')
Rinda::setup_tuple_store(store)
```

Once the persistency layer is set up, you can create a PTupleSpace and then recover to the previous state.

```
ts = Rinda::PTupleSpace.new
ts.restore
```

This will rebuild itself based on the information logged before you call the restore method.

Hmmm, this statement is unfamiliar to me. What does this do?

```
DRb.install_id_conv(Rinda::TupleStoreIdConv.new)
```

This is a trick to use when TupleSpace crashes so that the same DRbObject can refer to the same object after the recovery. With the default behavior of dRuby, DRbObject uses Object.object_id as reference information, and this will be lost when the process restarts. To work around this problem, this trick uses a static (nonvolatile) ID as reference information so that a process can refer to the same object after the process restarts.

You can set a timeout or cancel the timeout of the tuple in the same way as you use TupleSpace.

Comparing PTupleSpace and Key-Value Store

Now let's compare PTupleSpace with a key-value store and discuss their similarities and differences. We'll also discuss the pros and cons of its crash and recovery strategy, which is vital to any persistency layer.

Can We Use a Key-Value Store?

Let's think about what TupleSpace means from an API point of view. TupleSpace is a group of tuples. This is categorized as a Bag (see Section 6.3, *Basic Distributed Data Structures*, on page 124 for more details), because you can have duplicate keys.

The acronym KVS is popular nowadays as part of the NoSQL movement. The definition of KVS varies, but it is often common to have a similar API as Ruby's Hash. Hash is a "dictionary" that consists of a pair of unique keys and its value.

It isn't easy to represent a dictionary using TupleSpace. Let's consider what would happen if we represented a dictionary with a [key, value] tuple. Reading the data looks easy.

```
@ts.read([key, nil])
```

How about adding an element?

```
@ts.write([key, value])
```

This code doesn't prevent you from writing duplicate keys. To prevent that, you need to lock the entire TupleSpace, remove the tuple, and then write a new one.

```
def []=(key, value)
  lock = @ts.take([:global_lock])
  @ts.take([key, nil], 0) rescue nil
  @ts.write([key, value])
ensure
  @ts.write(lock) if lock
end
```

You need this global lock even when you read data. This is because the other thread may be updating the data while you are reading it.

```
def [](key)
  lock = @ts.take([:global_lock])
  _, value = @ts.read([key, nil], 0) rescue nil
  return value
ensure
  @ts.write(lock) if lock
end
```

You don't need a global lock if an element doesn't increase or decrease (as shown in *Structs and Hashes*, on page 128). You can't access the element if someone is updating an element. However, you can simply wait until you can read the element. This requires only a local lock.

How about each? There isn't a good way to go through the entire TupleSpace. You need to run read_all, generate an array of all the elements, and then delegate each to the array.

```
def each(blk)
  lock = @ts.take([:global_lock])
  @ts.read_all([nil, nil]).each(&blk)
ensure
  @ts.write(lock) if lock
end
```

This method works when the number of elements are relatively small, but the method call will become slower as the data size becomes bigger.

It's difficult to implement each and keys in a distributed hash table with a relatively low execution cost. Some of the currently popular storage options have a sequence of elements sorted by keys. If the storage option has a sorting functionality, it will be easier to browse a relatively large data space. You could even customize your key to include versioning information like this:

```
def []=(key, value)
  @rbtree[[key, Time.now]] = value
end
```

However, it's difficult to replicate this behavior using Rinda's TupleSpace, because Rinda doesn't provide sorted order functionality.

By the way, did you really want to use Hash as a data structure? In some cases, Bag may be sufficient.

Managing Crash and Recovery

As explained in Section 6.1, *Introducing Linda and Rinda*, on page 111, the concept of Tuple is similar to a memo in the real world. The "memorandum" tuple walks from process to process via TupleSpace.

PTupleSpace saves only the "memorandum" stored in the TupleSpace. When a process holds a "memorandum," it's out of the hands of PTupleSpace, and it won't be persisted. You can't save the state that you are waiting on for a tuple either. You can't recover the exact state of process coordination.

If you expect TupleSpace to be just a storage for a "memorandum," then this should be sufficient. You can restore any information once it is written to PTupleSpace. This is what most applications probably expect for persistency. How useful is TupleSpace compared to just exposing Array or Hash via dRuby then? The strong pattern matching of Rinda TupleSpace could be an advantage. In exchange for this strong pattern matching capability, however, I wasn't able to use a more efficient data structure when I implemented TupleSpace. It may become slow when the number of tuples increases because it does a linear search internally.

How about process coordination, which is the primary role of TupleSpace? Let's think about what happens when PTupleSpace crashes and you need to recover it. When a PTupleSpace process halts, any mutable RMI call to change the state of a tuple (such as write and take) will raise a dRuby exception. When PTupleSpace is restarted, it recovers to the last known state, and you have to write logic to retry any failed operations once the restart completes. These are difficult and time-consuming steps to write.

The use of RMI causes another problem. Let's think about some mutable operations to change the state of tuples, such as write or take. In a normal Ruby method call, the control flow goes back to the caller as soon as the work of the callee completes. On the other hand, there is one extra step between these two steps in RMI. RMI requires socket communication between the caller and the callee. From the caller's point of view, it won't be able to know whether the exception happened before the method call to the callee ended or before the result reached the caller. It could crash even when the tuple is logged into the secondary storage of PTupleSpace and right before the result reaches the client. If I change the implementation to write a log after all the operations complete, then it may crash after the client received the tuple but before saving to storage.

Not only can PTupleSpace crash, but its client application can also crash. It may be beyond the responsibility of PTupleSpace, but let's think about such a situation. If a process crashes after it took out a "memorandum," then there is no way to recover. Let's look at this short script:

```
def succ
  _, count = @ts.take([:count, nil])
  count += 1
  yield(count)
ensure
  @ts.write([:count, count) if count
end
```

This example takes [:count, Integer], increments the number, and then writes it back. While the "memorandum" is in our process, other processes can't read or take the same "memorandum," so we can safely increment the counter. But what if our process dies while we are manipulating the memorandum? Since PTupleSpace can recover only a memorandum inside PTupleSpace, we'll lose the memorandum forever. If other processes were also waiting to manipulate the counter, then all the other processes will halt. In such a situation, not only do you need to restart TupleSpace and all the other processes that depend on the TupleSpace (I guess you have to do it anyway when you are dealing with process coordination), but you also have to reset the counter. Saving the tuple in such a scenario misses the point.

PTupleSpace works to persist TupleSpace itself, but that isn't enough to recover all the process coordination state. You may feel a bit cheated if you expected TupleSpace to handle the entire crash and recovery scenario.

8.4 Moving Ahead

In this chapter, we learned about the following:

- rinda_eval as a way of concurrent computing
- PTupleSpace as a persistency layer and its limitations

We learned that there is a huge gap between the ability to persist and for the persistence to be useful. In the case of TupleSpace, just providing persistence isn't good enough; we need a few more tweaks. What would "persistable process coordination" look like? In the next chapter, you'll find out about Drip, which is one of my answers to this question.

CHAPTER 9

Drip: A Stream-Based Storage System

In this chapter, you'll get acquainted with Drip, a stream-based storage system that I'm really into. Drip is a storage as well as process coordination mechanism. It may sound somewhat similar to Rinda, but it is not a replacement. Drip is based on my experience with writing applications for Rinda. Drip is an object storage, and it started from several prototypes of mine, such as an object-oriented database, a key-value store, and a multidimensional list.

9.1 Introducing Drip

Drip is an "append-only" storage mechanism, in which you can log Ruby objects in chronological order. Drip only lets you insert new elements and doesn't provide update or delete functionality. It also provides a localized and inexpensive browsing API that's suitable for dRuby's RMI. For example, you can bulk transfer objects, and you can filter and seek using simple pattern matching.

Drip is also a process coordination mechanism. You can wait for new objects to arrive. Objects never change once stored in Drip. The data in Drip is immutable. Elements retrieved from multiple processes with different timing never change. You often see this characteristic in distributed file systems, because this architecture decreases the need to exclusively access information.

You can use Drip for simple object storage, process coordination, temporary storage for batch processing, and logging your day-to-day experiences. It's so simple that you can use it for pretty much anything—which is why it might be hard to imagine exactly what to use it for.

I've used Drip for the following applications:

- Middleware for batch processing
- Wiki system storage and full-text search system
- Twitter timeline archiving and its bot framework
- Memos while using irb

Is this still too vague? Starting with the next section, I'll introduce how to use Drip by comparing it with other familiar data structures: Queue as a process coordination structure and Hash as an object storage.

9.2 Drip Compared to Queue

Let's first compare Drip with Queue to understand how process coordination works differently.

We use the Queue class that comes with Ruby. Queue is a FIFO buffer in which you can put any object as an element. You can use push to add an object and pop to take it out. Multiple threads can pop at the same time, but an element goes to only one thread. The same element never goes to multiple threads with pop.

If you pop against an empty Queue, then pop will block. When a new object is added, then the object reaches to only the thread that acquired the object.

Drip has an equivalent method called read. read will return an element newer than the specified cursor. However, Drip doesn't delete the element. When multiple threads read with the same cursor, Drip returns the same element.

Both Drip and Queue can wait for the arrival of a new element. The key difference is whether the element is consumed.

Queue#pop will consume the element, but Drip#read doesn't consume elements. This means multiple people can read the same element repeatedly. In Rinda, if you lose a tuple because of an application bug or system crash, it means that the entire system could go down. In Drip, you never need to worry about the loss of an element.

Let's see how this works in Drip with code.

Basic Operations with Read and Write Methods

You can use two methods to compare with Queue.

```
Drip#write(obj, *tags)
```

Drip#write adds an element to Drip. This is the only operation to change the state of Drip. This operation stores an element obj into Drip and returns the key that you use to retrieve the object. You can also specify tags to make object access easier, which I'll explain in *Using Tags*, on page 187.

Another method is read.

```
Drip#read(key, n=1, at_least=1, timeout=nil)
```

This is the most basic operation for browsing Drip. key is a cursor, and this method returns n number of arrays that consist of key and value pairs added later than the requested key. n specifies the number of matched pairs to return. You can configure it so that the method is blocked until at_least number of elements arrive with timeout.

In short, you can specify "Give me n elements, but wait until at_least elements are there."

Installing and Starting Drip

Oops, we haven't installed Drip yet. Drip depends on an external library called RBTree. If you use gem, it should install the dependency as well.

```
gem install drip
```

Next, let's start the Drip server.

Drip uses a plain-text file as a default secondary storage. To create a Drip object, you need to specify a directory. The next script generates Drip and serves via dRuby.

drip_s.rb

```
require 'drip'
require 'drb'

class Drip
  def quit
    Thread.new do
      synchronize do |key|
        exit(0)
      end
    end
  end
end

drip = Drip.new('drip_dir')
DRb.start_service('druby://localhost:54321', drip)
DRb.thread.join
```

The quit method terminates the process via RMI. The script waits until Drip doesn't write to any secondary storage using synchronize (see *Locking Single Resources with Mutex*, on page 88 for more detail).

Start Drip like this:

```
% ruby drip_s.rb
```

It won't print out anything; it simply runs as a server.

MyDrip

I prepared a single-user Drip server called MyDrip. This works only for POSIX-compliant operating systems (such as Mac OS X), but it's very handy. It creates a .drip storage directory under your home directory and communicates with the Unix domain socket. Since this is just a normal Unix domain socket, you can restrict permission and ownership using the file system. Unlike TCP, a Unix socket is handy, because you can have your own socket file descriptor on your own path, and you don't have to worry about port conflict with other users. To use MyDrip, you need to require my_drip (my_drip.rb comes with Drip gem, so you don't have to download the file by yourself).

Let's invoke the server.

```
# terminal 1
% irb -r my_drip --prompt simple
>> MyDrip.invoke
=> 51252
>> MyDrip.class
=> DRb::DRbObject
```

MyDrip is actually a DRbObject pointing to the fixed Drip server port, but it also has a special invoke method. MyDrip.invoke forks a new process and starts a Drip daemon if necessary. If your own MyDrip server is already running, it finishes without doing anything. Use MyDrip.quit when you want to stop MyDrip.

MyDrip is a convenient daemon to store objects while running irb. In my environment, I always have MyDrip up and running to archive my Twitter timeline. I also use it to take notes or to use as middleware for a bot.

I always require my_drip so that I can write a memo to MyDrip while running irb. You can insert the following line in .irbrc to include it by default:

```
require 'my_drip'
```

Going forward, we'll use Drip for most of the exercises. If you can't use MyDrip in your environment, you can create the following client:

drip_d.rb

```
require 'drb/drb'
MyDrip = DRbObject.new_with_uri('druby://localhost:54321')
```

You can use drip_d.rb and drip_s.rb as an alternative to MyDrip.

Peeking at Ruby Internals Through Fixnum

Speaking of a Fixnum class in a 64-bit machine, let's find out the range of Fixnum. First let's find out the largest Fixnum. Let's start from 63 and make it smaller.

```
(2 ** 63).class   #=> Bignum
(2 ** 62).class   #=> Bignum
(2 ** 61).class   #=> Fixnum
```

It looks like the border of Bignum and Fixnum is somewhere between 2 ** 62 and 2 ** 61. Let's try it with 2 ** 62 – 1.

```
(2 ** 62 - 1).class #=> Fixnum
```

Found it! 2 ** 62 - 1 is the biggest number you can express with Fixnum. Let's convert this into Time using Drip's key generation rule.

```
Time.at(* (2 ** 62 - 1).divmod(1000000)) #=> 148108-07-06 23:00:27 +0900
```

How about the smallest Fixnum? As you may have guessed, it is -(2 ** 62). This is equivalent to a 63-bit signed integer, not 64-bit.

Fixnum in Ruby has a close relationship with object representation. Let's find out the object_id of an integer.

```
0.object_id #=> 1
1.object_id #=> 3
2.object_id #=> 5
(-1).object_id #=> -1
(-2).object_id #=> -3
```

The object_id of Fixnum n is always set to 2 * n + 1. Inside Ruby, objects are identified by pointer width. Most objects show the allocated area, but that won't be very efficient to allocate memory for Fixnum. To avoid the inefficiency, Ruby has a rule of treating objects as integers if the last 1 bit is 1. Because this rule takes up 1 bit, the range of Fixnum is a 63-bit signed char rather than 64-bit. By the way, it will be a 31-bit signed integer for a 32-bit machine.

There are also objects with a special object_id. Here's the list:

```
[false, true, nil].collect {|x| x.object_id} #=> [0, 2, 4]
```

And that's our quick look into the world of Ruby internals.

Comparing with Queue Again

Let's experiment while MyDrip (or the equivalent drip_s.rb) is up and running.

Let's add two new objects using the write method. As explained earlier, write is the only method to change the state of Drip. The response of write returns the key that's associated with the added element. The key is an integer generated from a timestamp (usec). The number will be a Fixnum class in a 64-bit machine.

```
# terminal 2
% irb -r my_drip --prompt simple
>> MyDrip.write('Hello')
=> 1312541947966187
>> MyDrip.write('world')
=> 1312541977245158
```

Next, let's read data from Drip.

```
# terminal 3
% irb -r my_drip --prompt simple
>> MyDrip.read(0, 1)
=> [[1312541947966187, "Hello"]]
```

`read` is a method to read `n` number of elements since the specified cursor, and it returns an array consisting of a key and value pair. To read elements in order, you can move the cursor as follows:

```
>> k = 0
=> 0
>> k, v = MyDrip.read(k, 1)[0]
=> [1312541947966187, "Hello"]
>> k, v = MyDrip.read(k, 1)[0]
=> [1312541977245158, "World"]
```

So far, you've read two elements. Let's try to read one more.

```
>> k, v = MyDrip.read(k, 1)[0]
```

It will be blocked since there are no elements newer than `k`. If you add a new element from terminal 2, it will unblock and be able to read the object.

```
# terminal 2
>> MyDrip.write('Hello, Again')
=> 1312542657718320
>> k, v = MyDrip.read(k, 1)[0]
=> [1312542657718320, "Hello, Again"]
```

How did it go? Were you able to simulate the waiting operation?

Let's increase the number of the listener and start reading from 0.

```
terminal 4
% irb -r my_drip --prompt simple
>> k = 0
=> 0
>> k, v = MyDrip.read(k, 1)[0]
=> [1312541947966187, "Hello"]
>> k, v = MyDrip.read(k, 1)[0]
=> [1312541977245158, "World"]
>> k, v = MyDrip.read(k, 1)[0]
=> [1312542657718320, "Hello, Again"]
```

You should be able to read the same element. Unlike Queue, Drip doesn't consume elements, so you can keep reading the same information. Instead, you need to specify where to read, every time you request.

Let's try to restart MyDrip. The quit method terminates the process when no one is writing. Call invoke to restart. MyDrip.invoke may take a while to start up if the log size is big.

```
# terminal 1
>> MyDrip.quit
=> #<Thread:...>
>> MyDrip.invoke
=> 61470
```

Let's call the read method to check whether you recovered the previous state.

```
# terminal 1
>> MyDrip.read(0, 3)
=> [[1312541947966187, "Hello"], [1312541977245158, "World"],
  [1312542657718320, "Hello, Again"]]
```

Phew, looks like it's working fine.

Let's recap what we've learned so far. Drip is similar to Queue, where you can retrieve data in a time order, and also you can wait for new data to arrive. It's different because data does not decrease. You can read the same elements from different processes, and the same process can read the same element again and again. You may have experienced that batch operations tend to stop often while developing them as well as running them in a production environment. With Drip, you can work around this if you make use of the functionality because you can restart from the middle many times.

So far, we've seen two basic operations, write and read, in comparison with Queue.

9.3 Drip Compared to Hash

In this section, you'll learn advanced usage of Drip by comparing it to KVS or Hash.

Using Tags

Drip#write will allow you to store an object with tags. The tags must be instances of String. You can specify multiple tags for one object. You can read with tag names, which lets you retrieve objects easily. By leveraging these tags, you can simulate the behavior of Hash with Drip.

Let's treat tags as Hash keys. "write with tags" in Drip is equivalent to "set a value to a key" in Hash. "read the latest value with the given tag" is equivalent to reading a value from Hash with the given tag. Since "the latest value" in Drip is equivalent to a value in Hash, "the older than the latest value" in Drip is similar to a Hash with version history.

Accessing Tags with head and read_tag Methods

In this section, we'll be using the head and read_tag methods.

```
Drip#head(n=1, tag=nil)
```

head returns an array of the first n elements. When you specify tags, then it returns n elements that have the specified tags. head doesn't block, even if Drip has fewer than n elements. It only views the first n elements.

```
Drip#read_tag(key, tag, n=1, at_least=1, timeout=nil)
```

read_tag has a similar operation to read, but it allows you to specify tags. It only reads elements with the specified tags. If elements newer than the specified keys don't have at_least elements, then it will block until enough elements arrive. This lets you wait until elements with certain tags are stored.

Experimenting with Tags

Let's emulate the behavior of Hash using head and read_tag. We'll keep using the MyDrip we invoked earlier.

First, let's set a value. This is how you usually set a value in a Hash.

```
hash['seki.age'] = 29
```

And here is the equivalent operation using Drip. You write a value 29 with the tag seki.age.

```
>> MyDrip.write(29, 'seki.age')
=> 1313358208178481
```

Let's use head to retrieve the value. Here is the command to take the first element with a seki.age tag.

```
>> MyDrip.head(1, 'seki.age')
=> [[1313358208178481, 29, "seki.age"]]
```

The element consists of [key, value, tags] as an array. If you're interested only in reading values, you can assign key and value into different variables as follows:

```
>> k, v = MyDrip.head(1, 'seki.age')[0]
=> [[1313358208178481, 29, "seki.age"]]
>> v
=> 29
```

Let's reset the value. Here is the equivalent operation in Hash:

```
hash['seki.age'] = 49
```

To change the value of seki.age to 49 in Drip, you do exactly the same as before. You write 49 with the tag seki.age. Let's try to check the value with head.

```
>> MyDrip.write(49, 'seki.age')
=> 1313358584380683
>> MyDrip.head(1, 'seki.age')
=> [[1313358584380683, 49, "seki.age"]]
```

You can check the version history by retrieving the history data. Let's use head to take the last ten versions.

```
>> MyDrip.head(10, 'seki.age')
=> [[1313358208178481, 29, "seki.age"], [1313358584380683, 49, "seki.age"]]
```

We asked for ten elements, but it returned an array with only two elements, because that's all Drip has for seki.age tags. Multiple results are ordered from older to newer.

What happens if you try to read a nonexistent tag (key in Hash)?

```
>> MyDrip.head(1, 'sora_h.age')
=> []
```

It returns an empty array. It doesn't block either. head is a nonblocking operation and returns an empty array if there are no matches.

If you want to wait for a new element of a specific tag, then you should use read_tag.

```
>> MyDrip.read_tag(0, 'sora_h.age')
```

It now blocks. Let's set up the value from a different terminal.

```
>> MyDrip.write(12, 'sora_h.age')
=> 1313359385886937
```

This will unblock the read_tag and return the value that you just set.

```
>> MyDrip.read_tag(0, 'sora_h.age')
=> [[1313359385886937, 12, "sora_h.age"]]
```

Let's recap again. In this section, we saw that with tags we can simulate the basic operation of setting and reading values from Hash.

The difference is as follows:

- You can't remove an element.
- It has a history of values.
- There are no keys/values.

You can't remove an element like you do in Hash, but you can work around by adding nil or another special object that represents the deleted status. As a side effect of not being able to remove elements, you can see the entire history of changes.

I didn't create keys and each methods on purpose. It's easy to create them, so I created them once but deleted them later. There are no APIs in Drip at this moment. To implement keys, you need to collect all elements first, but this won't scale when the number of elements becomes very big. I assume this is why many distributed hash tables don't have keys.

There are also some similarities with TupleSpace. You can wait for new elements or their changes with read_tag. This is a limited version of read pattern matching in Rinda TupleSpace. You can wait until elements with certain tags arrive. This pattern matching is a lot weaker than Rinda's pattern matching, but I expect that this is enough for the majority of applications.

When I created Drip, I tried to make the specification narrower than that of Rinda so that it's simple enough to optimize. Rinda represents an in-memory, Ruby-like luxurious world, whereas Drip represents a simple process coordination mechanism with persistency in mind.

To verify my design expectations, we need a lot more concrete applications.

In the previous two sections, we explored Drip in comparison with Queue and Hash. You can represent some interesting data structures using this simple append-only stream. You can stream the world using Drip because you can traverse most of the data structures one at a time.

9.4 Browsing Data with Key

In this section, we will learn multiple ways to browse the data stored in Drip. In Drip, all the elements are stored in the order they were added. Browsing data in Drip is like time traveling.

Most browsing APIs take the cursor as an argument. Let's first see how keys are constructed and then see how to browse the data.

How Key Works

Drip#write returns a key that corresponds to the element you stored. Keys are incremented integers, and the newly created key is always bigger than the older ones. Here's the current implementation of generating a key:

```
def time_to_key(time)
  time.tv_sec * 1000000 + time.tv_usec
end
```

Keys are integers generated from a timestamp. In a 64-bit machine, a key will be a Fixnum. The smallest unit of the key depends on µsec (microsecond), so it will collide if more than one element tries to run within the same µsec. When this happens, the new key will increment from the latest key by one.

```
# "last" is the last (and the largest) key
key = [time_to_key(at), last + 1].max
```

Zero becomes the oldest key. Specify this number as a key when you want to retrieve the oldest element.

Browsing the Timeline

So far, we've tried the read, read_tag, and head methods for browsing. There are other APIs:

read, read_tag, newer
: Browsing to the future

head, older
: Browsing to the past

In Drip, you can travel the timeline forward and backward using these APIs. You can even skip elements by using tags wisely.

In this section, you'll find out how to seek for certain elements using tags and then browse in order.

The following pseudocode takes out four elements at a time. k is the cursor. You can browse elements in order by repeatedly passing the key of the last element to the cursor.

```
while true
  ary = drip.read(k, 4, 1)
  ...
  k = ary[-1][0]
end
```

To emulate the preceding code, we'll manually replicate the operation using irb. Is your MyDrip up and running? We also use MyDrip for this experiment. Let's write some test data into Drip.

```
# terminal 1
% irb -r my_drip --prompt simple
>> MyDrip.write('sentinel', 'test1')
=> 1313573767321912
>> MyDrip.write(:orange, 'test1=orange')
=> 1313573806023712
>> MyDrip.write(:orange, 'test1=orange')
=> 1313573808504784
>> MyDrip.write(:blue, 'test1=blue')
=> 1313573823137557
>> MyDrip.write(:green, 'test1=green')
=> 1313573835145049
>> MyDrip.write(:orange, 'test1=orange')
=> 1313573840760815
>> MyDrip.write(:orange, 'test1=orange')
=> 1313573842988144
>> MyDrip.write(:green, 'test1=green')
=> 1313573844392779
```

The first element acts as an anchor to mark the time we started this experiment. Then, we wrote objects in the order of orange, orange, blue, green, orange, orange, and green. We added tags that corresponded with each color.

```
# terminal 2
% irb -r my_drip --prompt simple
>> k, = MyDrip.head(1, 'test1')[0]
=> [1313573767321912, "sentinel", "test1"]
>> k
=> 1313573767321912
```

We first got a key of the anchor element with the "test1" tag. This is the starting point of this experiment. It's a good idea to fetch this element with the fetch method.

Then, we read four elements after the anchor.

```
>> ary = MyDrip.read(k, 4)
=> [[1313573806023712, :orange, "test1=orange"],
[1313573808504784, :orange, "test1=orange"],
[1313573823137557, :blue, "test1=blue"],
[1313573835145049, :green, "test1=green"]]
```

Were you able to read as expected? Let's update the cursor and read the next four elements.

```
>> k = ary[-1][0]
=> 1313573835145049
>> ary = MyDrip.read(k, 4)
=> [[1313573840760815, :orange, "test1=orange"],
[1313573842988144, :orange, "test1=orange"],
[1313573844392779, :green, "test1=green"]]
```

It should return the next three elements. This is because there are only three elements newer than the cursor k. What will happen if you try to read further? It should block the read as you expect.

```
>> k = ary[-1][0]
=> 1313573844392779
>> ary = MyDrip.read(k, 4)
```

Let's write from another terminal and check whether the read gets unblocked.

```
# terminal 1
>> MyDrip.write('hello')
=> 1313574622814421
```

terminal 2 should be unblocked. Next, let's filter using read_tag. Let's rewind the cursor and try it again.

```
# terminal 2
>> k, = MyDrip.head(1, 'test1')[0]
=> [1313573767321912, "sentinel", "test1"]
```

We'll request to read two to four elements with the "test1=orange" tag.

```
>> ary = MyDrip.read_tag(k, 'test1=orange', 4, 2)
=> [[1313573806023712, :orange, "test1=orange"],
[1313573808504784, :orange, "test1=orange"],
[1313573840760815, :orange, "test1=orange"],
[1313573842988144, :orange, "test1=orange"]]
```

We get four oranges. Let's update the cursor and do the same operation again.

```
>> k = ary[-1][0]
=> 1313573842988144
>> ary = MyDrip.read_tag(k, 'test1=orange', 4, 2)
```

This blocks your terminal because there are no orange elements newer than the cursor. Let's write two oranges from another terminal, and read_tag should start working.

```
# terminal 1
>> MyDrip.write('more orange', 'test1=orange')
=> 1313575076451864
>> MyDrip.write('more orange', 'test1=orange')
=> 1313575077963911
```

```
# terminal 2
>> ary = MyDrip.read_tag(k, 'test1=orange', 4, 2)
=> [[1313575076451864, "more orange", "test1=orange"],
[1313575077963911, "more orange", "test1=orange"]]
```

You've just learned how to seek and read using tags, as well as filter using read_tag. These are basic idioms to browse through Drip.

There are also other utility methods.

```
Drip#newer(key, tag=nil)
```

This will return one element newer than the key. You can also specify a tag. newer is a wrapper method of read and read_tag. If there are no matching elements, it will return nil rather than block.

```
Drip#older(key, tag=nil)
```

This will return one element older than the key. You can also specify a tag. If there are no matching elements, it will return nil rather than block.

Oh, I almost forgot. There is an API to retrieve a value when you know the exact key.

```
Drip#[](key)
```

```
>> k, = MyDrip.head(1, 'test1')[0]
=> [1313573767321912, "sentinel", "test1"]
>> MyDrip[k]
=> ["sentinel", "test1"]
```

This returns an array of a value-tag pair. It won't return a key.

Those are all the major APIs. By the way, you haven't seen the each method often used in Ruby, have you? I'll explain the reason why in the next section.

9.5 Design Goals of the API

I designed the API of Drip to use with dRuby. dRuby has several weaknesses: it's hard to manage the life span of objects on the server side, it's hard to manage the mutex, and RMI is slow. It was important to design the API so that it doesn't create objects that keep state on the server side and also to decrease the number of RMI calls.

Let's think about the key of the read method once again. The key of read is equivalent to the concept of a cursor or pages inside a database. Often a database API hides a cursor inside the context.

For example, Ruby's File object remembers the current offset in a file, and you can read from or write to the specific point. On the other hand, Drip doesn't have any objects with state. A request to Drip is stateless just like a function is. It uses a cursor key instead of having an object to manage the context of the location. The reason I chose this API was to avoid creating a context-managing object inside the Drip server. Drip is designed to be used over RMI with dRuby in mind. If I introduce a context that generates and deletes an object (begin and end, open and close), then the server needs to manage the life span of the object. This will lead to the difficult problem of managing GC in a distributed environment. To avoid these problems, I designed the API such that you can interact only via Integer keys.

As shown in the preceding sections, you can simulate a recursive operation by using keys returned from read, instead of using an object to manage context. If you find this API interface cumbersome, then I suggest you write a wrapper to hide the key inside the context of the local process. Make sure you don't provide context on the Drip server side.

When using a read operation, you can specify the minimum and maximum number of elements to return. This batch operation will decrease the number of RMI calls compared to retrieving them one by one. This method is effective when processing batch operations that require throughput over response time. By specifying "at least n elements," you can avoid generating an RMI for every event. You can wait for the data to be accumulated in some amount before being transferred.

While creating prototypes prior to Drip, I learned the importance of not implementing too much. "Crafting" is such a fun thing that I tended to add more functionality whenever someone asked. When creating Drip, I made the concept of Drip very clear so that I could fight against the temptation of adding too much functionality.

9.6 Moving Ahead

In this chapter, we learned the following:

- Basic usage of Drip compared to Queue
- Basic usage of tags compared to Hash
- Design philosophy of Drip

In the next chapter, we will build a simple search system using Drip.

CHAPTER 10

Building a Simple Search System with Drip

In this chapter, we'll make a tiny search system. Making this miniature search system should give you some inspiration for creating other applications. This system consists of three processes: a crawler to search and register Ruby script files, an indexer to index the registered files, and the Drip server that sits in the middle.

10.1 Running the App

We'll use MyDrip again, so please make sure to run MyDrip.invoke or start a Drip server manually in a Windows environment.

```
$ irb -r drip -r my_drip
>> MyDrip.invoke
=> 45616
```

The sample code is included as part of the Drip source code. Let's download it first.

```
$ cd ~
$ git clone git://github.com/seki/Drip.git
$ cd Drip/sample/demo4book
```

Before running the crawler, please edit line 10 of crawl.rb and add the directory name you want to search. I suggest you choose a relatively small directory, because it will take a long time to experiment with a directory that has many files. About 500 files should be sufficient. In our experiment, I specified the root directory of the source code.

```
@root = File.expand_path('~/Drip/')
```

Now let's run crawl.rb. It will show the list of files.

```
$ ruby crawl.rb
["install.rb",
 "lib/drip/version.rb",
 "lib/drip.rb",
 "lib/my_drip.rb",
 "sample/copocopo.rb",
 "sample/demo4book/crawl.rb",
 "sample/demo4book/index.rb",
 "sample/drip_s.rb",
 "sample/drip_tw.rb",
 "sample/gca.rb",
 "sample/hello_tw.rb",
 "sample/my_status.rb",
 "sample/simple-oauth.rb",
 "sample/tw_markov.rb",
 "test/basic.rb"]
```

Next, start the indexer in a different terminal. Once started, type a word you want to search, and it will list the filenames that include the word. In the following example, we searched for the word *def*. It may not be fully indexed if you search right after starting up the indexer. If you repeat the search, you may be able to see the list of filenames grow.

```
$ ruby index.rb
def
["sample/demo4book/index.rb", "sample/demo4book/crawl.rb"]
2
def
["sample/drip_s.rb",
 "lib/drip.rb",
 "lib/my_drip.rb",
 "sample/copocopo.rb",
 "sample/demo4book/index.rb",
 "sample/demo4book/crawl.rb"]
6
```

The default crawling interval is set to sixty seconds. When you type something from standard input, the program will end once the crawling finishes. I designed this so that our crawler can rest from time to time to mimic how a crawler in a normal search system works. When the search range is very wide (for example, searching web pages), then it is impossible to keep crawling the update. You can update the indexing quickly if you shorten the crawling interval. If you modify this crawler, you may even be able to create your own real-time search tool. Some operating systems can notify about file changes, so integrating this as a trigger for crawling will be interesting, too.

In the following sections, we'll look in-depth at the source code.

10.2 Examining Each Component

The search system consists of three components, Crawler, Indexer, and Drip, as a messaging layer. In this section, we will examine each component.

How System Elements Are Structured

Let's start by looking at the objects and tags that this system writes to Drip. We'll mainly use Drip as the file update notification system.

- *File update notification*: Consists of an array of ['file name', 'content', 'timestamp']. We also use two tags: rbcrawl and rbcrawl-fname=file name. The crawler writes this information every time updated files are found. This not only archives the file content but also notifies the update event. The indexer updates the index every time it receives the notification.

There are also some optional tags:

- *Footprint of the crawler*: Writes the list of filenames and timestamp of the update. It uses the rbcrawl-footprint tag.
- *Anchor tag to declare the start of the experiment*: Uses the rbcrawl-begin tag. You can write anything with this tag when you repeat this experiment and you want to reset from scratch.

Next, let's see how to use these objects and tags.

How the Crawler Works

Here's the basic mechanism of this simple crawler:

```
class Crawler
  include MonitorMixin

  def initialize
    super()
    @root = File.expand_path('~/develop/git-repo/')
    @drip = MyDrip
    k, = @drip.head(1, 'rbcrawl-begin')[0]
    @fence = k || 0
  end

  def last_mtime(fname)
    k, v, = @drip.head(1, 'rbcrawl-fname=' + fname)[0]
    (v && k > @fence) ? v[1] : Time.at(1)
  end

  def do_crawl
    synchronize do
```

```
      ary = []
      Dir.chdir(@root)
      Dir.glob('**/*.rb').each do |fname|
        mtime = File.mtime(fname)
        next if last_mtime(fname) >= mtime
        @drip.write([fname, mtime, File.read(fname)],
                    'rbcrawl', 'rbcrawl-fname=' + fname)
        ary << fname
      end
      @drip.write(ary, 'rbcrawl-footprint')
      ary
    end
  end

  def quit
    synchronize do
      exit(0)
    end
  end
end
```

First the crawler tries to find files that match the *.rb wildcard under (@root). Once found, it checks the update time and writes the content and timestamp if the file has been updated since the last crawl. This will write the following data:

```
@drip.write(
  ["sample/demo4book/index.rb", 2011-08-23 23:50:44 +0100, "file content"],
  "rbcrawl", "rbcrawl-fname=sample/demo4book/index.rb"
)
```

The value is an array of a filename, timestamp, and file content. The value has two tags.

As explained earlier, the crawler runs every sixty seconds and ends after crawling if you type something from standard input. When the crawler terminates, it will write the list of filenames with an rbcrawl-footprint tag. Here's the example data:

```
@drip.write(["sample/demo4book/index.rb"], 'rbcrawl-footprint')
```

This version of the crawler doesn't update the file deletion information, but you may be able to add that functionality by using this information.

How do you find out if the file is updated? You can get the previous version with the head method and compare with it. Or, you can search the latest file version by passing rbcrawl-fname=file name into the head method.

```
k, v = @drip.head(1, "rbcrawl-fname=sample/demo4book/index.rb")[0]
```

Here is the complete crawler code:

crawl.rb

```
require 'pp'
require 'my_drip'
require 'monitor'

class Crawler
  include MonitorMixin

  def initialize
    super()
    @root = File.expand_path('~/develop/git-repo/')
    @drip = MyDrip
    k, = @drip.head(1, 'rbcrawl-begin')[0]
    @fence = k || 0
  end

  def last_mtime(fname)
    k, v, = @drip.head(1, 'rbcrawl-fname=' + fname)[0]
    (v && k > @fence) ? v[1] : Time.at(1)
  end

  def do_crawl
    synchronize do
      ary = []
      Dir.chdir(@root)
      Dir.glob('**/*.rb').each do |fname|
        mtime = File.mtime(fname)
        next if last_mtime(fname) >= mtime
        @drip.write([fname, mtime, File.read(fname)],
                    'rbcrawl', 'rbcrawl-fname=' + fname)
        ary << fname
      end
      @drip.write(ary, 'rbcrawl-footprint')
      ary
    end
  end

  def quit
    synchronize do
      exit(0)
    end
  end
end

if __FILE__ == $0
  crawler = Crawler.new
  Thread.new do
    while true
      pp crawler.do_crawl
```

```
      sleep 60
    end
  end

  gets
  crawler.quit
end
```

So far, we implemented the crawler script using write and head methods. Next, we will look into how to implement the indexer script.

How the Indexer Works

The indexer provides index creation, update, and searching. It returns the list of filenames that include the word you are searching for. Since this sample is a miniature version, it creates the index in memory using the RBTree library.

```
class Indexer
  def initialize(cursor=0)
    @drip = MyDrip
    @dict = Dict.new
    k, = @drip.head(1, 'rbcrawl-begin')[0]
    @fence = k || 0
    @cursor = [cursor, @fence].max
  end
  attr_reader :dict

①  def update_dict
    each_document do |cur, prev|
      @dict.delete(*prev) if prev
      @dict.push(*cur)
    end
  end

  def each_document
    while true
      ary = @drip.read_tag(@cursor, 'rbcrawl', 10, 1)
      ary.each do |k, v|
        prev = prev_version(k, v[0])
        yield(v, prev)
        @cursor = k
      end
    end
  end

②  def prev_version(cursor, fname)
    k, v = @drip.older(cursor, 'rbcrawl-fname=' + fname)
    (v && k > @fence) ? v : nil
  end
end
```

The indexer takes out objects with the rbcrawl tag and updates the index.

```
@drip.read_tag(@cursor, 'rbcrawl', 10, 1)
```

The fourth argument, 1, is very important. Do you remember that I said earlier if elements newer than the specified keys don't have at_least elements, then it will block until enough number of elements arrive? The preceding code requests ten elements at a time with a minimum of one element, so it will block if there are no elements to return. This enables the indexer to wait until the crawler writes data with an rbcrawl tag.

Objects with rbcrawl are notification events as well as documents on their own, containing the filename, the updated time, and their content. Unlike Queue, Drip lets you read the elements you already read repeatedly. You can check the previous version using the older method, as shown in ②.

If Indexer already has a previous document of the files that are updated, it will remove the old content first and then add an index with the new content, as shown in ①.

Once you start Indexer, the script will generate a thread and start creating an index under the subthread by dealing with data using Drip.read_tag.

```
indexer ||= Indexer.new(0)
Thread.new do
  indexer.update_dict
end
```

The main thread of the script awaits input from a user. It searches the word and prints out the result once the question is received from the input.

```
while line = gets
  ary = indexer.dict.query(line.chomp)
  pp ary
  pp ary.size
end
```

Here's the complete Indexer:

index.rb

```
require 'nkf'
require 'rbtree'
require 'my_drip'
require 'monitor'
require 'pp'

class Indexer
  def initialize(cursor=0)
    @drip = MyDrip
    @dict = Dict.new
```

```
    k, = @drip.head(1, 'rbcrawl-begin')[0]
    @fence = k || 0
    @cursor = [cursor, @fence].max
  end
  attr_reader :dict

  def update_dict
    each_document do |cur, prev|
      @dict.delete(*prev) if prev
      @dict.push(*cur)
    end
  end

  def each_document
    while true
      ary = @drip.read_tag(@cursor, 'rbcrawl', 10, 1)
      ary.each do |k, v|
        prev = prev_version(k, v[0])
        yield(v, prev)
        @cursor = k
      end
    end
  end

  def prev_version(cursor, fname)
    k, v = @drip.older(cursor, 'rbcrawl-fname=' + fname)
    (v && k > @fence) ? v : nil
  end
end

class Dict
  include MonitorMixin
  def initialize
    super()
    @tree = RBTree.new
  end

  def query(word)
    synchronize do
      @tree.bound([word, 0, ''], [word + "\0", 0, '']).collect {|k, v| k[2]}
    end
  end

  def delete(fname, mtime, src)
    synchronize do
      each_tree_key(fname, mtime, src) do |key|
        @tree.delete(key)
      end
    end
  end
```

```
  def push(fname, mtime, src)
    synchronize do
      each_tree_key(fname, mtime, src) do |key|
        @tree[key] = true
      end
    end
  end

  def intern(word)
    k, v = @tree.lower_bound([word, 0, ''])
    return k[0] if k && k[0] == word
    word
  end

  def each_tree_key(fname, mtime, src)
    NKF.nkf('-w', src).scan(/\w+/m).uniq.each do |word|
      yield([intern(word), mtime.to_i, fname])
    end
  end
end

if __FILE__ == $0
  indexer ||= Indexer.new(0)
  Thread.new do
    indexer.update_dict
  end

  while line = gets
    ary = indexer.dict.query(line.chomp)
    pp ary
    pp ary.size
  end
end
```

In the indexer script, we used `head`, `read_tag`, and `older` methods. So far, we've covered the core functionalities of this search system. Let's stop for a moment and discuss the architecture of this system.

10.3 Crawling Interval and Synchronization with Indexer

One thing I wanted to demonstrate with this sample application is that each program processes its own task at its own convenient timing.

The crawler starts the work periodically. The crawler doesn't worry about the status of the indexer. It just finds an update and writes to Drip. This applies to the indexer as well. The indexer doesn't worry about the status of the crawler. It reads documents stored in Drip in batches and updates the index.

Once all the documents are processed, then the indexer goes into sleep mode until a new document gets written.

If you draw the diagram of the flow of the data, it will look like Figure 44, *Crawler and indexer working independently through MyDrip*, on page 207. The data flow starts from the crawler, is stored in Drip, and then is taken out by the indexer for indexing. However, the indexer doesn't have direct dependency on the crawler. As a comparison, let's think about creating this search system using the Observer pattern. Imagine that indexing will all be done in the chain of the crawler and the various callback methods within the indexer using the Observer pattern. The speed of crawling has to be in line with the speed of indexing.

Drip doesn't receive notification passively. The listener actively goes and fetches the update information when it's convenient for the listener itself. This is similar to how the Actor model works (see *Rinda::rinda_eval and the Actor Model*, on page 171). The indexer will take out the next task only when all of the existing tasks complete and when it's ready for the next one. This is contrary to how dRuby works, because the dRuby server receives RMI calls under subthreads regardless of whether the server is busy.

Enough detail. It's important to understand that the crawler can work without waiting for the indexer to work and that the indexer can also work regardless of how often the crawling job happens. Drip loosely acts as messaging middleware.

10.4 Resetting Data

While you are repeating this experiment, you may want to start some of the exercises from scratch. The easiest way is to re-create the Drip database, but you may not want to delete all the data if you've already written some data into MyDrip.

In such a case, let's introduce a tag that indicates the start of the system. When we put an object with an `rbcrawl-begin` tag, we'll ignore any data prior to that so that we can treat it as if the system were empty.

In the example code, I used `fence` for both the crawler and the indexer. When the script calls the `older` or `head` method, it checks the key timestamp and ignores if the value is older than the one set in `fence`.

```
=> MyDrip.write('fence', 'rbcrawl-begin')
>> 1313573767321913
```

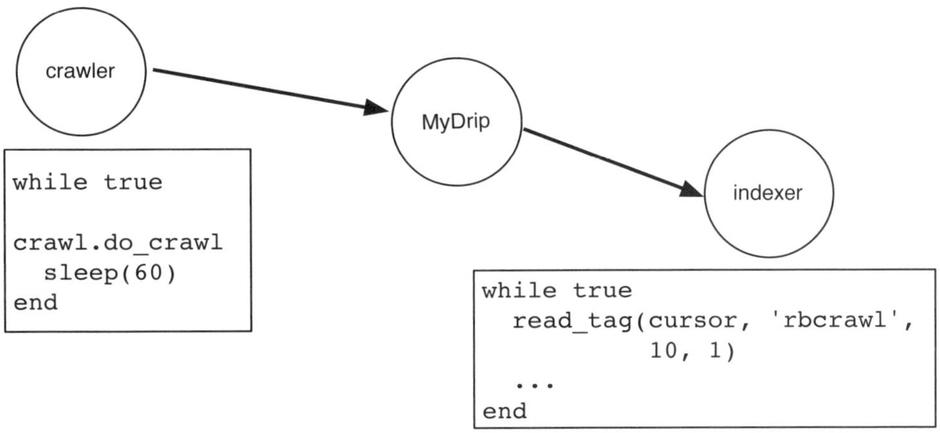

Figure 44—Crawler and indexer working independently through MyDrip

There is another use case for the fence pattern. Imagine you finish the search system after writing index information to disk. The next time you start the search system, the newly started search process needs to know up to where it has been indexed. In such a case, you can leave fence to indicate the progress of the indexing work so that the indexer can start from where it left off when it gets restarted. The earlier example uses the footprint to ignore any old data, but this situation uses the footprint to show the remaining tasks.

10.5 Using RBTree for Range Search

So far, we've seen how the crawler and the indexer use the tags and notification functionalities of Drip to update a document into the index. In this section, we'll look into how this indexing works internally.

The indexer uses a library called RBTree. RBTree provides a binary tree data structure and algorithm suited for a search. It's an acronym for "red-black tree," not "ruby-tree." Ruby's Hash class uses a magical function called a *hash function*. The function generates a hash value from a key object so that the value can be searched at a constant speed. RBTree prepares a sorted array (the underlying implementation uses a tree structure but doesn't provide an API to access the tree directly) and searches a value using binary search. You can do various interesting things using the sorting characteristics.

Let's try to implement a small indexing dictionary class. It lists the location of each word (equivalent to the page number of a book). You can easily implement this using Hash as follows:

dripdict1.rb
```
class Dict
  def initialize
    @hash = Hash.new {|h, k| h[k] = Array.new}
  end

  def push(fname, words)
    words.each {|w| @hash[w] << fname}
  end

  def query(word, &blk)
    @hash[word].each(&blk)
  end
end
dict = Dict.new
dict.push('lib/drip.rb', ['def', 'Drip'])
dict.push('lib/foo.rb', ['def'])
dict.push('lib/bar.rb', ['def', 'bar', 'Drip'])
dict.query('def') {|x| puts x}
# => ["lib/drip.rb", "lib/foo.rb", "lib/bar.rb"]
```

Let's assume that some files are updated so that we have to rebuild the index. To remove old indexes and add new indexes, you need to iterate over all Arrays inside the Hash. You can work around this problem by replacing the internal Array into Hash. Here's the revised version with Hash:

dripdict2.rb
```
class Dict2
  def initialize
    @hash = Hash.new {|h, k| h[k] = Hash.new}
  end

  def push(fname, words)
    words.each {|w| @hash[w][fname] = true}
  end

  def query(word)
    @hash[word].each {|k, v| yield(k)}
  end
end
dict = Dict2.new
dict.push('lib/drip.rb', ['def', 'Drip'])
dict.push('lib/foo.rb', ['def'])
dict.push('lib/bar.rb', ['def', 'bar', 'Drip'])
dict.query('def') {|x| puts x}
# => {"lib/drip.rb"=>true, "lib/foo.rb"=>true, "lib/bar.rb"=>true}
```

Hmmm, note that the value no longer has meaning. It only contains a value of true. The nested Hash looks almost like a tree structure. RBTree offers a similar API to Hash, so we can simply replace the preceding Hash with RBTree, but I'll introduce better ways of dealing with RBTree.

Let's expand the Hash version. This time, the key is the combination of the word and its location (filename). This is as if we flattened the previous nested Hash tree-like structure.

dripdict3.rb

```
require 'rbtree'

class Dict3
  def initialize
    @tree = RBTree.new
  end

  def push(fname, words)
    words.each {|w| @tree[[w, fname]] = true}
  end

①  def query(word)
    @tree.bound([word, ''], [word + "\0", '']) {|k, v| yield(k[1])}
  end
end
dict = Dict3.new
dict.push('lib/drip.rb', ['def', 'Drip'])
dict.push('lib/foo.rb', ['def'])
dict.push('lib/bar.rb', ['def', 'bar', 'Drip'])
dict.query('def') {|x| puts x}
# =>
# "lib/bar.rb"
# "lib/drip.rb"
# "lib/foo.rb"
```

The query method calls the bound method that looks up elements within the boundaries of two keys. The bound method takes lower and upper as arguments. You can obtain the index of a word if you specify the minimum and maximum values for the word as keys. The minimum value consists of an array of the word itself and a blank string (for example, [word, '']). What would the maximum value for the word be then? It's hard to come up with ideas when thinking this way. Instead, let's think about "the minimum value of the word that comes right next to the word you are looking for." Since Ruby's String can include \0, the maximum value of the word is the word itself plus \0. This looks a bit tricky. ① hides such a dirty trick in a method.

In this example, the location identifier of the word is its filename. The indexer used the combination of file update time and filename as the document ID. It can be fun to think about various key combinations such as the line number of the word in the document.

In addition to `bound`, there are `lower_bound` and `upper_bound` methods. You can move the cursor to the upper or lower boundary of the key you are searching for using these methods. You can use these methods to do an "and" or "or" search as well. For example, you can combine two cursors. If both cursors point to the same point, then your "and" search is successful. If not, then move the slower cursor to the faster cursor to match using `lower_bound`. By repeating this process, you can do an "and" search without iterating through all lines. This might sound a bit complicated, so let's try an example.

The following script is how you implement an "and" search using the `lower_bound` method. The script searches a line where both the words *def* and *initialize* appear. The filename and line number represent the location in this example.

query2.rb

```
require 'rbtree'
require 'nkf'

class Query2
  def initialize
    @tree = RBTree.new
  end

  def push(word, fname, lineno)
    @tree[[word, fname, lineno]] = true
  end

  def fwd(w1, fname, lineno)
    k, v = @tree.lower_bound([w1, fname, lineno])
    return nil unless k
    return nil unless k[0] == w1
    k[1..2]
  end

  def query2(w1, w2)
    f1 = fwd(w1, '', 0)
    f2 = fwd(w2, '', 0)
    while f1 && f2
      cmp = f1 <=> f2
      if cmp > 0
        f2 = fwd(w2, *f1)
      elsif cmp < 0
        f1 = fwd(w1, *f2)
      else
```

```
        yield(f1)
        f1 = fwd(w1, f1[0], f1[1] + 1)
        f2 = fwd(w2, f2[0], f2[1] + 1)
      end
    end
  end
end

if __FILE__ == $0
  q2 = Query2.new
  while line = ARGF.gets
    NKF.nkf('-w', line).scan(/\w+/) do |word|
      q2.push(word, ARGF.filename, ARGF.lineno)
    end
  end
  q2.query2('def', 'initialize') {|x| p x}
end
```

Imagine you have Ruby code like this:

query2_test.rb

```
class Foo
  # initialize foo
  def initialize(name)
    @foo = name
  end

  def foo; end
  def baz; end
end

class Bar < Foo
  # initialize bar and foo
  def initialize(name)
    super("bar #{name}")
  end
  def bar; end
end
```

This is the output when you run the script:

```
[demo4book (master)]$ ruby query2.rb query2_test.rb
["query2_test.rb", 3]
["query2_test.rb", 13]
```

When two cursors do the initial key lookup, both of the cursors move to the first matching lines:

```
first cursor ["query2_test.rb", 3] second cursor ["query2_test.rb", 2]
```

Then the cursor in the smaller number jumps to the same number.

```
# fwd(['initialize', fname, 3])
first cursor ["query2_test.rb", 3] second cursor ["query2_test.rb", 3]
```

Once matched, move both cursors one forward.

```
first cursor ["query2_test.rb", 7] second cursor ["query2_test.rb", 12]
```

Then move the smaller cursor. This time, it doesn't have the same number, so it jumps to the next largest number.

```
# fwd(['def', fname, 12])
first cursor ["query2_test.rb", 13] second cursor ["query2_test.rb", 12]
```

By repeating this, you can do a skipping "and" search (see Figure 45, *Skipping "and" search using rbtree*, on page 213 for the detailed diagram).

There is another reason for using lower_bound and upper_bound methods instead of bound. When you are dealing with a large number of elements, you need to put all of them into memory as an Array to use a bound method. If you move the scope of the range bit by bit using lower_bound, it will increase the frequency of method calls but can decrease the size of memory and the buffer of RMI for each method call. RBTree is in fact used inside Drip as an ordered data structure. It is used as a union of the Drip key (integer key). It is also used as a union of tags. This union consists of an array of a [tag(String), key(Integer)] collection as keys.

```
['rbcrawl-begin', 100030]
['rbcrawl-begin', 103030]
['rbcrawl-fname=a.rb', 1000000]
['rbcrawl-fname=a.rb', 1000020]
['rbcrawl-fname=a.rb', 1000028]
['rbcrawl-fname=a.rb', 1000100]
['rbcrawl-fname=b.rb', 1000005]
['rbcrawl-fname=b.rb', 1000019]
['rbcrawl-fname=b.rb', 1000111]
```

This will let you search the latest key with the rbcrawl-begin tag or the closest key to a cursor with rbcrawl-fname=a.rb with the cost of doing a binary search.

Rinda has strong pattern matching. However, its Array-based internal data structure had a scaling problem, because the search time increases linearly as data size grows (O(N)).[1] On the other hand, Drip uses RBTree internally so that you can access the starting point of the tag or key relatively quickly (O(log n)). Thanks to this data structure, you can program as if you don't have to worry about the data growth. The nonconsumable queue and resetting the data with rbcrawl-begin are examples of such a programming attitude.

1. http://en.wikipedia.org/wiki/Big_O_notation

Start

Word	Line number				
def	→ 3	7	8	13	16
initialize	→ 2	3	12	13	

fwd(['initialize', fname, 3])

Word	Line number				
def	→ 3	7	8	13	16
initialize	2	→ 3	12	13	

Forward Both

Word	Line number				
def	3	→ 7	8	13	16
initialize	2	3	→ 12	13	

fwd(['def', fname, 12])

Word	Line number				
def	3	7	8	→ 13	16
initialize	2	3	→ 12	13	

fwd(['initialize', fname, 13])

Word	Line number				
def	3	7	8	→ 13	16
initialize	2	3	12	→ 13	

Figure 45—Skipping "and" search using rbtree

10.6 Adding a Web UI

As a finale to this chapter, let's add a web UI on top of this small search system as we did in Chapter 3, *Integrating dRuby with eRuby*, on page 31. The system so far consists of a crawler, indexer, and Drip acting as middleware. We'll add WEBrick::HTTPServer and a servlet as a web UI component. We used WEBrick::CGI in *Reminder CGI interface*, on page 41 (remember?), but we will use the HTTPServer class this time.

Setting all these components as an independent process is a bit difficult to manage. We'll change their layout to put them all in one process. Changing the layout of process and objects is easy because the interface between processes is almost transparent for any dRuby system. They do just look like normal Ruby objects. Here is the entire script:

demo_ui.rb

```
require './index'
require './crawl'
require 'webrick/cgi'
require 'erb'

class DemoListView
  include ERB::Util
  extend ERB::DefMethod
  def_erb_method('to_html(word, list)', ERB.new(<<EOS))
<html><head><title>Demo UI</title></head><body>
<form method="post">
  <input type="text" name="w" value="<%=h word %>" />
</form>
<% if word %>
<p>search: <%=h word %></p>
<ul>
<%   list.each do |fname| %>
<li><%=h fname%></li>
<%   end %>
</ul>
<% end %>
</body></html>
EOS
end

class DemoUICGI < WEBrick::CGI
  def initialize(crawler, indexer, *args)
    super(*args)
    @crawler = crawler
    @indexer = indexer
    @list_view = DemoListView.new
  end

  def req_query(req, key)
    value ,= req.query[key]
    return nil unless value
    value.force_encoding('utf-8')
    value
  end

  def do_GET(req, res)
    if req.path_info == '/quit'
      Thread.new do
```

```
        @crawler.quit
      end
    end
    word = req_query(req, 'w') || ''
    list = word.empty? ? [] : @indexer.dict.query(word)
    res['content-type'] = 'text/html; charset=utf-8'
    res.body = @list_view.to_html(word, list)
  end

  alias do_POST do_GET
end

if __FILE__ == $0
  crawler = Crawler.new
  Thread.new do
    while true
      pp crawler.do_crawl
      sleep 60
    end
  end

  indexer = Indexer.new
  Thread.new do
    indexer.update_dict
  end

  cgi = DemoUICGI.new(crawler, indexer)
  DRb.start_service('druby://localhost:50830', cgi)
  DRb.thread.join
end
```

You can just use an HTTP server of WEBrick rather than using the actual web server and CGI. Here is the WebBrick version:

demo_ui_webrick.rb

```
require './index'
require './crawl'
require 'webrick'
require 'erb'

class DemoListView
  include ERB::Util
  extend ERB::DefMethod
  def_erb_method('to_html(word, list)', ERB.new(<<EOS))
<html><head><title>Demo UI</title></head><body>
<form method="post">
  <input type="text" name="w" value="<%=h word %>" />
</form>
<% if word %>
<p>search: <%=h word %></p>
<ul>
```

```
<%   list.each do |fname| %>
<li><%=h fname%></li>
<%   end %>
</ul>
<% end %>
</body></html>
EOS
end

class DemoUIServlet < WEBrick::HTTPServlet::AbstractServlet
  def initialize(server, crawler, indexer, list_view)
    super(server)
    @crawler = crawler
    @indexer = indexer
    @list_view = list_view
  end

  def req_query(req, key)
    value ,= req.query[key]
    return nil unless value
    value.force_encoding('utf-8')
    value
  end

  def do_GET(req, res)
    word = req_query(req, 'w') || ''
    list = word.empty? ? [] : @indexer.dict.query(word)
    res['content-type'] = 'text/html; charset=utf-8'
    res.body = @list_view.to_html(word, list)
  end

  alias do_POST do_GET
end

① if __FILE__ == $0
  crawler = Crawler.new
  Thread.new do
    while true
      pp crawler.do_crawl
      sleep 60
    end
  end

  indexer = Indexer.new
  Thread.new do
    indexer.update_dict
  end

  server = WEBrick::HTTPServer.new({:Port => 10080,
                                    :BindAddress => '127.0.0.1'})
```

```
  server.mount('/', DemoUIServlet, crawler, indexer, DemoListView.new)
  trap('INT') { server.shutdown }
  server.start
  crawler.quit
end
```

There are two new classes in this code. DemoUIServlet is in charge of the web UI. DemoListView is a View class to render the HTML.

Let's check a code block in ①. This starts the HTTP server after starting crawl.rb and index.rb under subthreads. You can stop crawling by sending a signal like Ctrl-C. The crawler will stop when it becomes idle.

You may wonder what the point is of using Drip if you run a crawler and indexer under one process. Having only one process lets you start the application easily, as if you were starting up a desktop application. It's easier to daemonize fewer processes.

10.7 Moving Ahead

In this chapter, we learned the following:

- How to create a simple search system using Drip
- How to use RBTree
- How to change the layout of processes flexibly

It's been a while since we last created a system using dRuby and ERB (access to dRuby is wrapped using the access to my_drip). dRuby, ERB, Rinda, Drip—each system is simple, and you can start using each one easily.

They may not be the best solutions to handle really big problems, such as handling data that doesn't fit into the main memory of one machine or handling many clients in real time, but they are best suited to handle your personal data on your machine or your network. I hope these libraries and the thought processes in this book diversify your design options.

Part IV

Running dRuby and Rinda in a Production Environment

When you start using dRuby and Rinda in a production environment, you may encounter problems that didn't show up during development. Also, you need to worry about how to secure your application from unauthorized access. This part covers these topics.

CHAPTER 11

Handling Garbage Collection

In Ruby, garbage collection (GC) automatically clears out unnecessary objects. GC collects clutter during process execution time, but this causes a bit of a problem when the system is composed of multiple processes, as happens when using dRuby. In this chapter, we'll discuss how dRuby handles GC.

11.1 Dealing with GC

While a script is running, there is a point when certain objects become not referenced anywhere. Once the object isn't referenced, then you aren't able to use it anymore. It is the responsibility of GC to clean up such unused objects. The Ruby interpreter looks up its own process object space from time to time and then cleans up unused objects to free up more memory space.

dRuby and GC

If an object is referenced anywhere, then the object must be in use. Normal Ruby never cleans up such objects, but it is a different story in dRuby.

DRbObject refers to an object in a different process, but the Ruby interpreter doesn't know about the existence of the other process, which causes some problems. Even when DRbObject retains a reference, if the object isn't referenced within its own process, then the object becomes the target of GC. Once an object becomes collected by GC, method calls to these objects are no longer guaranteed. You can't expect when CG will clean up objects, because the timing of GC cleanup depends on the Ruby interpreter, and accessing nonexistent objects will raise errors.

This is not necessarily a Ruby problem, but you do need to be prepared to avoid the problem. In this chapter, we'll look into how to deal with GC when using dRuby.

GC Workaround at the Application Level

The best way to handle GC is to create a workaround at the application level. Here are the general strategies:

- Manage lists of published objects.
- Don't publish references to objects that you can't control.

front objects and the return values of each method are examples of the preceding cases, so you have to be extra careful with them.

Some other long-running objects, such as global variables, class variables, and singletons, tend not to have these problems. They tend to live long and are less likely to be garbage collected, so you don't have to worry about them too much.

You may need some tricks when you are dealing with temporary objects. In most scenarios, you can simply pass by value, but there are times you have to pass by reference.

It's a common strategy to pass temporary objects via an iterator (block). Examples are open class methods in the File class or transactions in PStore.

```
File.open('foo.txt') do |fp|
  fp.gets
  ...
end
```

When you call File.open class methods with a block, you can pass a File object only while it is open. When it reaches the end of the block, then the object is closed automatically.

File.open is a convenient method, but notice in the sequential diagram that it's referencing the File object temporarily (see Figure 46, *Temporary File object stays referenced during an open block*, on page 223) while in a block.

The outer open method block wraps a File object, so this object is referenced within the stack of the memory space and won't become the target of garbage collection. You can use the temporal object without worrying about being garbage collected as long as you refer to it inside the open method block.

Next, a small class opens a file as read-only.

```
class DCP
  def open(fname, &block)
    File.open(fname, 'rb', &block)
  end
end
```

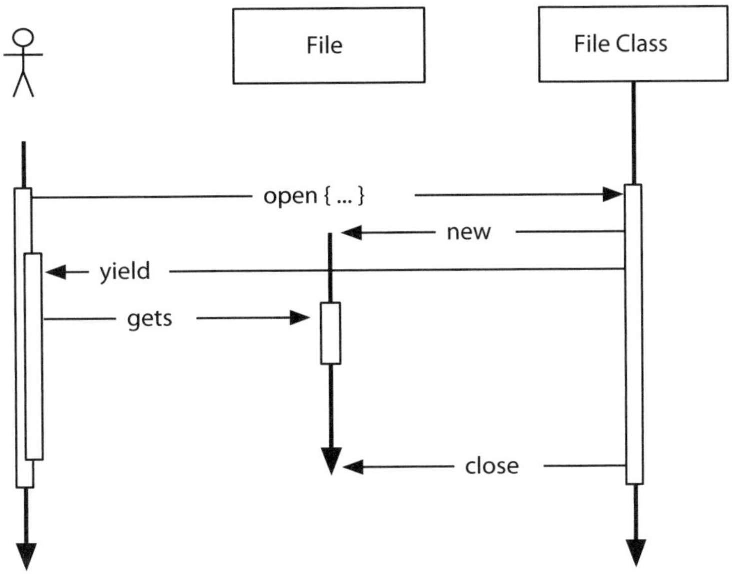

Figure 46—Temporary File object stays referenced during an open block

This strategy works not only to protect against GC but also to create a context inside the block and do some chunked operations. The next example is a class to transfer files. The DCP class defines both sending and receiving files.

dcp.rb

```
require 'drb/drb'

class DCP
  include DRbUndumped

  def size(fname)
    File.lstat(fname).size
  end

①  def fetch(fname)
    File.open(fname, 'rb') do |fp|
      while buf = fp.read(4096)
        yield(buf)
      end
    end
    nil
  end

②  def store_from(there, fname)
    size = there.size(fname)
    wrote = 0
```

```
    File.open(fname, 'wb') do |fp|
      there.fetch(fname) do |buf|
        wrote += fp.write(buf)
        yield([wrote, size]) if block_given?
        nil
      end
    end
    wrote
  end

  def copy(uri, fname)
    there = DRbObject.new_with_uri(uri)
    store_from(there, fname) do |wrote, size|
      puts "#{wrote * 100 / size}%"
    end
  end
end

if __FILE__ == $0
  if ARGV[0] == '-server'
    ARGV.shift
    DRb.start_service(ARGV.shift, DCP.new)
    puts DRb.uri
    DRb.thread.join
  else
    uri = ARGV.shift
    fname = ARGV.shift
    raise('usage: dcp.rb URI filename') if uri.nil? || fname.nil?
    DRb.start_service
    DCP.new.copy(uri, fname)
  end
end
```

The fetch method (①) and the store_from method (②) are the keys for the file transfer. They split large files into multiple parts and transfer them one by one, because reading a big file all at once will take up too much memory space. The fetch method yields a buffer of split files. The File object does multiple operations inside the fetch method.

To test the preceding example, run the script on one terminal with a -server option.

```
% mkdir s
% cd s
# This is a UNIX command to create a file with 10k size.
% mkfile 10k bigfile.txt
% ruby ../dcp.rb -server
druby://localhost:12345
```

Then run the same script in another terminal. This time, add the URI and filename as options.

```
% mkdir c
% cd c
% ruby ../dcp.rb druby://localhost:12345 bigfile.txt
  40%
  80%
  100%
```

You should see that a file is copied from server to client in a chunk. Next, we'll look into how to automatically avoid having objects be garbage collected.

11.2 Using DRbIdConv to Prevent GC

DRbObject consists of two parts. The URI is used to identify the remote server location, and the reference is used to identify the referencing object inside the remote server. DRbIdConv is used to exchange objects and their reference information. By default, DRbIdConv uses Object#__id__ as reference information. By exchanging these, you can protect objects against GC.

Let's first find out how to customize DRbIdConv and then talk about how to use it to protect against GC.

Customizing DRbIdConv

Let's look into the definition of DRbIdConv, which we use to exchange information.

```
class DRbIdConv
  def to_obj(ref)
    ObjectSpace._id2ref(ref)
  end

  def to_id(obj)
    obj.nil? ? nil : obj.__id__
  end
end
```

DRbIdConv has two methods: to_obj and to_id. The to_obj method is used to identify an object from its reference information, and to_id is used to identify a reference ID from the object.

By overwriting to_id, you can hook into each reference exchange. Let's write an example DRbIdConv class to convert everything into a Hash while converting objects into references.

dumbidconv.rb

```
require 'drb/drb'
class DumbIdConv < DRb::DRbIdConv
  def initialize
    @table = Hash.new
  end
  attr_reader :table
  def to_id(obj)
    ref = super(obj)
    @table[ref] = obj
    ref
  end
end
```

We made DumbIdConv a subclass of the DRbIdConv class. In the initialize method, we assign the @table instance variable, and the to_id method retains a reference as a key to the object.

To use DumbIdConv instead of DRbIdConv as the default, you need to configure it before DRb.start_service is called.

Once configured, this is how to use it:

```
DRb.install_id_conv(DumbIdConv.new)
```

You can also assign it as an argument in DRbServer.start_service.

```
DRb.start_service(uri, front, {:idconv => DumbIdConv.new})
```

Let's try to use DumbIdConv via irb.

First, start a service to publish Hash using DumbIdConv. Then add a Thread object into the Hash as follows:

```
% irb -r './dumbidconv' --prompt simple
>> $dumb = DumbIdConv.new
>> DRb.start_service('druby://localhost:12345', {}, {:idconv => $dumb})
>> DRb.front['main-thread'] = Thread.current
```

Let's open irb from another terminal and access the service you just started. Let's obtain a reference to the Thread object and call the method.

```
% irb -r drb --prompt simple
>> DRb.start_service
>> ro = DRbObject.new_with_uri('druby://localhost:12345')
>> ro.keys
=> ["main-thread"]
>> ro['main-thread']
=> #<DRb::DRbObject:0x2ad89598 @ref=358724596,
@uri="druby://localhost:12345">
>> ro['main-thread'].status
=> "sleep"
```

So far, Thread is the only reference published on the first terminal. Let's check table inside DumbIdConv there.

```
>> $dumb.table
=> {358724596=>#<Thread:0x2ac367e8 run>}
```

You should see that the Thread object is registered with an integer key. Any object passed by reference will be preserved on this table because any objects referenced in this table will be protected against GC. These objects won't be garbage collected while other processes are using them.

So far, we tried customizing DRbIdConv and preserving the reference of objects passed by reference.

DumbIdConv solves one problem by not garbage collecting objects, but it becomes a problem if all objects are preserved forever. DumbIdConv even preserves temporal objects that are actually not in use anymore.

To solve this problem, we have a class called TimerIdConv that sets a timer on objects to clear up. Though initially all objects are preserved, if methods on the registered objects have not been called for a certain period set by the timer, the objects will be removed from the table.

To use TimerIdConv, you need to require'drb/timeridconv'.

```
require 'drb/timeridconv'
DRb.install_id_conv(DRb::TimerIdConv.new)
```

With TimerIdConv, you can keep all referenced objects while releasing some temporal objects and reusing its memory space.

11.3 Moving Ahead

In this chapter, we learned the following:

- GC clears up nonaccessed objects in a process, so we need to take special care when accessing objects among processes using dRuby.
- The easiest workaround is to control at the application level by holding a list of referenced objects or not publishing objects that we can't control.
- We can also use DRbIdConv to keep all the object references.
- Keeping all remote objects causes another problem of memory bloat. TimerIdConv is a class to set a timer on all the referenced objects so that we can let GC clear some temporary objects while protecting other referenced objects against GC.

The next chapter is the last chapter of this book. We'll discuss dRuby's security options and how you can use dRuby safely. You'll also find out how to use dRuby across the network by using SSH.

CHAPTER 12

Security in dRuby

dRuby is powerful and dynamic. You can access remote objects without feeling that they are in different processes or different machines. This is a good thing but also a bad thing because anyone can potentially access your application without restrictions. In this chapter, you'll find out what dRuby offers (and what it doesn't offer) in terms of security. You'll also see how to use SSH for cross-network access.

12.1 dRuby's Attitude Toward Security

dRuby is a mechanism to extend Ruby's method invocation across processes or machines, and this applies to how it handles security, too. Here is dRuby's strategy toward security:

- No restriction on remote method invocation
- Retains restriction related to method invocations (for example, `private` method)
- Uses `$SAFE`, which is the security model for Ruby

I initially explored the possibility of maintaining the safety by restricting method invocation from dRuby. However, I quickly realized that this approach is too difficult because of the dynamic features of Ruby, so I ended up using `$SAFE`, the security model used in Ruby.

You need to be extra cautious with dRuby security, such as restricting access to the few trusted client machines or using dRuby only inside the trusted network. There are a few options to restrict client access, such as access control lists (ACLs) and Unix domain socket files.

Setting the Security Level with $SAFE

The Ruby security model consists of an object's *taint status* and $SAFE (safe level). $SAFE looks like a global variable, but you can set it per thread.

$SAFE takes a value between 0 and 4; the default is 0. The higher the number becomes, the more restrictive the security becomes. $SAFE is inherited to the subthread of the parent, and you can only increase the $SAFE value.

The state 0 doesn't have any restriction, but it marks as "tainted" if an object comes from I/O, an environment variable, or a command-line argument. This means that all parameters from remote method invocations are tainted. You can check the status via the tainted? method. You can use the taint method to explicitly mark it as tainted and use untainted methods to unmark it.

When $SAFE is set to 1, certain dangerous operations with tainted objects become prohibited, such as executing an external command or calling the eval method. When $SAFE is set to 2, more operations become restricted.

With dRuby, you can specify $SAFE on all method calls the server receives when starting DRbServer. Pass the $SAFE level to the third argument of DRb.start_service as a :safe_level hash value.

```
DRb.start_service(uri, front, { :safe_level => 1 })
```

You can also set the default $SAFE with DRbServer.default_safe_level. It becomes effective on any DRbServer after setting default_safe_level.

Here's an example of setting $SAFE to 2:

```
DRb::DRbServer.default_safe_level(2)
```

Alternatively, you can set $SAFE at the beginning of your script so that you can restrict all operations as well as remote method invocations.

```
$SAFE = 1
DRb.start_service(uri, front)
```

It's worth noting that you can't use iterators when $SAFE is set to 4, because an iterator is part of the I/O operation.

Let's experiment. The first example is to set $SAFE to 0. You can execute any code by sending the instance_eval method.

```
% irb --prompt simple -r drb
# [Terminal 1]
>> DRb.start_service('druby://localhost:12345', {})

# [Terminal 2]
% irb --prompt simple -r drb
```

```
>> DRb.start_service
>> ro = DRbObject.new_with_uri('druby://localhost:12345')
>> ro.instance_eval('undef :instance_eval')
```

First, undefine (undef) the instance_eval method of the ro instance so that you can send the method to the remote. Then, call the remote instance_eval.

```
>> ro.instance_eval('exit!')
```

irb at terminal 1 is terminated. Bummer!

Next, leave terminal 2 and retry the same operation in terminal 1, but set default_safe_level to 1.

```
# [Terminal 1]
% irb --prompt simple -r drb
>> DRb::DRbServer.default_safe_level(1)
>> DRb.start_service('druby://localhost:12345', {})

# [Terminal 2]
>> ro.instance_eval('exit!')
DRb::DRbConnError: connection closed
        ......
```

The connection at terminal 2 is closed and instance_eval fails. (It used to raise a SecurityError in Ruby 1.8.) Looking good.

Let's see whether the iterator works with a server of $SAFE level 1.

```
>> ro[:one] = 1
>> ro[:one] = 1
=> 1
>> ro.each {|k,v| p [k, v]}
[:one, 1]
=> {:one=>1}
```

Next, let's make sure that the iterator fails with a server of $SAFE 4.

```
# [Terminal 1]
>> DRb.start_service('druby://localhost:12346', {}, {:safe_level => 4})

# [Terminal 2]
>> r4 = DRbObject.new_with_uri('druby://localhost:12346')
>> r4[:four] = 4
 DRb::DRbConnError: connection closed
 ....
```

Hmmm, when $SAFE is set to level 4, even untainted objects can't be changed. Since the front object on terminal 1 is not tainted, it gets disconnected. Let's taint the object and try again.

```
# [Terminal 1]
>> DRb.front.taint

>> r4[:four] = 4
```

We were able to change Hash. How about calling an iterator?

```
# [Terminal 2]
>> r4.each {|k, v| p [k, v]}
 DRb::DRbConnError: DRb::DRbServerNotFound
 ....
```

At $SAFE 4, you can't use an iterator because it is restricted to call remote methods.

So far, you've seen how to configure Ruby's $SAFE mode. However, you may have a situation where you want to grant full access to a certain client. In the next section, you'll see how to set a security policy per client.

Setting IP-Level Security with ACL

With ACL, you can allow or prohibit client access per IP address.

```
require 'drb/acl'

acl = ACL.new(%w(deny all
                 allow 192.168.0.0/24
                 allow localhost))
DRb.install_acl(acl)

DRb.start_service(uri, front)
...
```

First, you generate an ACL object; then, you install it using DRb.install_acl.

Or, you can specify in the third argument of a Hash as a :tcp_acl key.

```
acl = ACL.new(%w(deny all
                 allow 192.168.0.0/24
                 allow localhost))
DRb.start_service(uri, front, {:tcp_acl => acl})
```

Create the ACL object by passing an array combining either the deny or allow keyword followed by the hostname or by IP addresses. It matches anything if you specify wildcards such as * or all. By default, ACL looks up in the order of allow and then deny and then allows anything if nothing matches. You can reverse it by specifying the ACL::ALLOW_DENY constant in the second argument of the ACL constructor. This denies any access unless specified in the ACL list.

The preceding example denies all entries except 192.168.0.0/24 and localhost.

Setting File-Level Security with a Unix Domain Socket

If you use Unix-origin operating systems, such as Linux POSIX, BSD, or Mac OS X, you can use a Unix domain socket. With a Unix domain socket, you can allow or deny access per client user ID by using file ownership.

To set up a Unix domain socket ownership or configuration, you need to specify it in the third argument of DRb.start_service.

:UNIXFileOwner
: Specifies Unix file ownership

:UNIXFileGroup
: Specifies Unix file group ownership

:UNIXFileMode
: Specifies file mode using numbers

Let's try access control using file mode.

```
# [Terminal 1]
% irb --prompt simple -r drb
>> DRb.start_service('drbunix:/tmp/drb000', {}, {:UNIXFileMode => 0600})
```

We just set permission to be accessible only by the file owner.

Let's try accessing now from the same user's terminal.

```
# [Terminal 2]
% irb --prompt simple -r drb
>> DRb.start_service
>> ro = DRbObject.new_with_uri('drbunix:/tmp/drb000')
>> ro.keys
=> []
```

Next, let's access from a different user's terminal. To simulate this, we use the sudo command, but you can do the same by login via a different user.

```
# [Terminal 3]
% sudo -u foo irb --prompt simple -r drb
>> DRb.start_service
>> ro = DRbObject.new_with_uri('drbunix:/tmp/drb000')
>> ro.keys
DRb::DRbConnError: drbunix:/tmp/drb000
- #<Errno::EACCES: Permission denied - /tmp/drb000>
 ....
```

You should receive an Errno::EACCES exception, and the method invocation should fail. You protected access from another user by setting ownership to

0600, which means only the owner can read and write. The preceding example showed that you can control access per user level by using Unix domain socket and file permission.

12.2 Accessing Remote Services via SSH Port Forwarding

Now that we've tightened our security level, let's find out how to extend dRuby's services across a network. We'll see how to connect across multiple networks via Secure Shell (SSH) port forwarding, as well as by using the dRuby gateway.

Experimenting with Port Forwarding with dRuby

SSH (OpenSSH) has a functionality called *port forwarding*, which transfers all communication to a specific TCP port on one machine to another using an encrypted channel. With port forwarding, you can use the services of other networks in a secure way.

You can use dRuby securely using this SSH port forwarding. Let's try it (see Figure 47, *Accessing objects on a different network using SSH port forwarding*, on page 235).

In this example, we connect to an iBook (10.0.1.2) and a Linux box (10.0.1.202) with SSH. A connection to port 12345 on the iBook is transferred to port 12345 on the Linux box and from port 23456 on the Linux box to the same port on the iBook. The iBook provides dRuby service on port 23456, and the Linux box does the same on port 12345.

In terminal 1, login to the Linux box via ssh with the -L and -R options specified. Once logged in, start the dRuby server. (I wanted to use localhost rather than the IP address, but it didn't work in my Mac OS X environment.)

```
# [Terminal 1]
osx% ssh -L 12345:localhost:12345 -R 23456:127.0.0.1:23456 10.0.1.202
Enter passphrase for key '/Users/mas/.ssh/id_rsa':
Last login: ....
linux% irb --prompt simple -r drb
>> DRb.start_service('druby://localhost:12345', {})
>> DRb.front.keys
=> []
```

In terminal 2, start the dRuby server (assuming you are on the iBook). It's important to specify localhost as the dRuby URI in terminals 1 and 2. Don't specify an actual hostname such as druby://hostname:12345. dRuby tries to connect hostname:12345 directly rather than using SSH when a remote procedure call refers to the local object, such as when using yield.

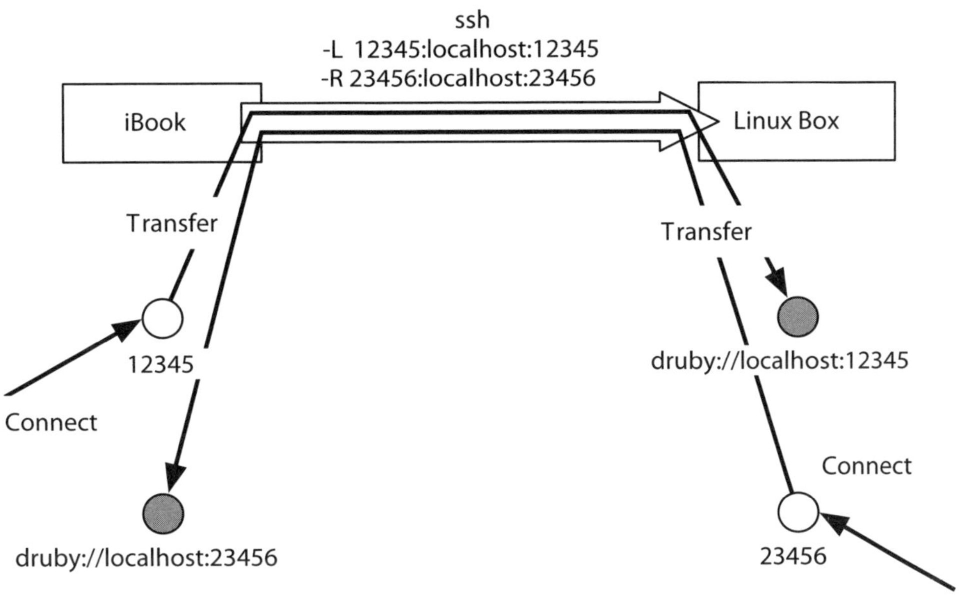

Figure 47—Accessing objects on a different network using SSH port forwarding

```
# [Terminal 2]
linux% irb --prompt simple -r drb
>> DRb.start_service('druby://localhost:23456', {})
>> DRb.front.keys
=> []
```

Next, let's try to assign some values to each other's front object (Hash).

```
# [Terminal 1]
>> osx = DRbObject.new_with_uri('druby://localhost:23456')
>> >osx[:msg] = 'linux box to osx'
>> osx.keys
=> [:msg]
>> osx.each { |kv| p kv }
[:msg, "linux box to osx"]
=> {:msg=>"linux box to osx"}
```

```
# [Terminal 2]
>> DRb.front
=> {:msg=>"linux box to osx"}
>> linux = DRbObject.new_with_uri('druby://localhost:12345')
>> linux[:msg] = 'osx to linux box'
>> linux.keys
=> [:msg]
=> linux.each { |kv| p kv }
[:msg, "osx to linux box"]
=> {:msg=>"osx to linux box"}
```

```
# [Terminal 1]
>> DRb.front
=> {:msg=>"osx to linux box"}
```

You can verify that the content of the front object changed. You can call methods of other machines since their ports are forwarded. You can use yield, too.

In this exercise, we connected services located in two different networks via SSH port forwarding. You can use this to provide simple services via SSH.

dRuby Gateway

In the previous examples, you could only access objects that are exposed via SSH port forwarding (see Figure 48, *Only the gateway object is accessible*, on page 237). You couldn't access other processes of the external network.

drb/gw.rb acts as a gateway so that you can access objects among other networks. GWIdConv replaces a reference object of the internal network with reference information for the gateway object. This replacement allows you to access objects that aren't accessible otherwise.

DRbObject consists of two components: a URI (@uri) for identifying the DRbServer location and reference information (@ref) that DRbServer uses to identify the object. drb/gw.rb wraps the original referenced objects. Once wrapped, the URI of the wrapping object contains the URI of the gateway object, and its reference points to the original DRbObject that contains both the original URI and the references (see Figure 49, *Wrapping the DRbObject*, on page 237).

```
@uri = Gateway URI
@ref = Source DRbObject
```

After this replacement, any following method invocation goes through the gateway.

DRbObject is referenced when Marshal#dump and Marshal#load are called. DRbObject is dumped when sending DRbObject to other processes, and it is loaded when DRbServer receives DRbObject from other processes.

The replacement action happens in the following order: it wraps when sending objects and unwraps when receiving objects.

When dumping

- When sending an object within the same process as the gateway, (= when DRb.uri and @uri are the same), it unwraps and sends the object. (It takes out the content of @ref and dump.)

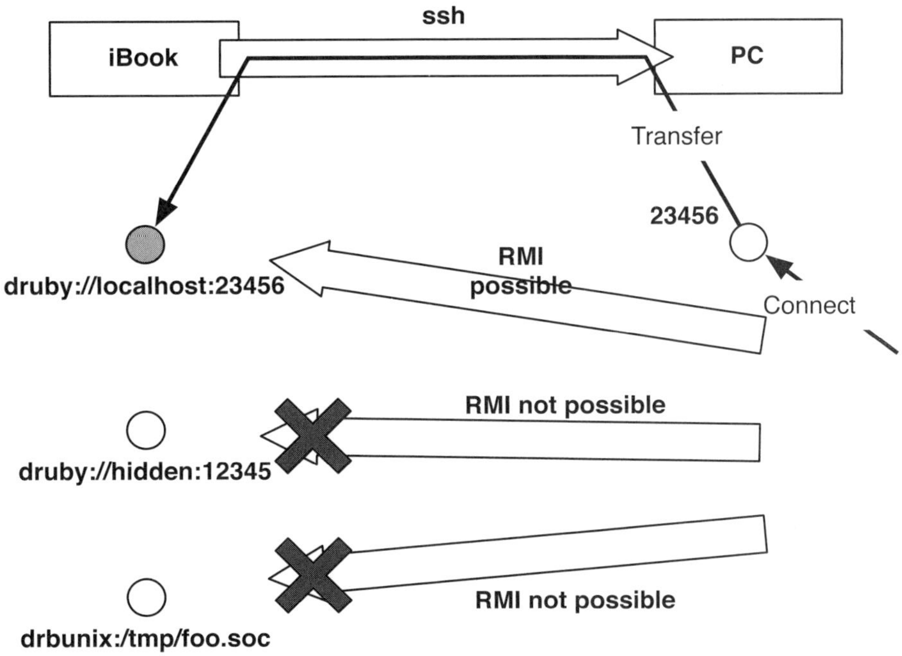

Figure 48—Only the gateway object is accessible.

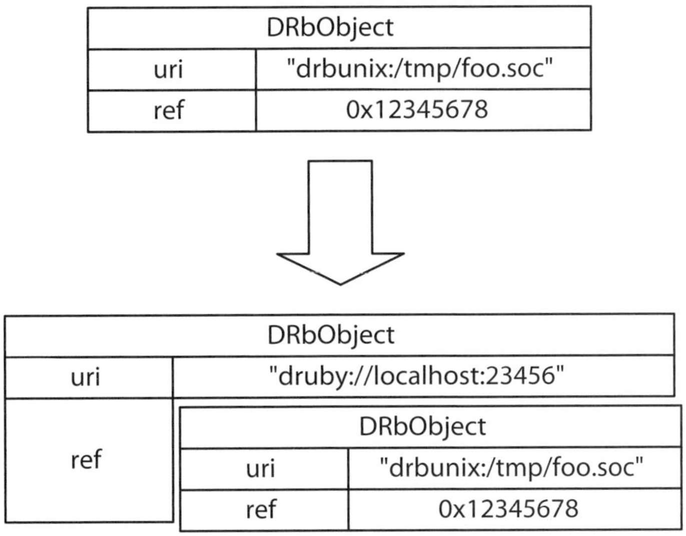

Figure 49—Wrapping the **DRbObject**

- When sending an object to other processes, it wraps the object and sends the wrapped object. @ref stores the @uri and @ref of the original and then gets loaded.

When loading

- When receiving an object within the same process, it uses @ref to regain the original object as usual. If @ref is DRbObject, it returns DRbObject itself.

- When receiving an object from different processes, it returns the reference by wrapping the reference to its own reference.

DRbObjects are wrapped into Array. Otherwise, DRbObjects will be recursively dumped forever (see Figure 50, *Wrapping the DRbObject and storing it into Array*, on page 239).

DRbObject
: Modified DRbObject with _load and _dump methods that are redefined to replace reference information.

GWIdConv
: Same as DRbIdConv, but this version handles the preceding modified DRbObject. You need to use this when using GW.

GW
: Specified as front objects of DRbServer on both sides. This is a Hash protected with MonitorMixin to work under a multithreading environment. GW is used as a utility class and is optional.

Now let's look at the actual gateway.

gw_s.rb

```
require 'drb/drb'
require 'drb/gw'
DRb.install_id_conv(DRb::GWIdConv.new)
gw = DRb::GW.new
s1 = DRb::DRbServer.new(ARGV.shift, gw)
s2 = DRb::DRbServer.new(ARGV.shift, gw)
s1.thread.join
s2.thread.join
```

First, let's install GWIdConv. Then, start two DRbServers. In a normal situation, you need to start only one DRbServer in DRb.start_service, but we need two DRbServers for gateway use.

You can invoke gw_s.rb as follows. Make sure to assign two different URIs.

```
% ruby gw_s.rb druby://localhost:12321 drbunix:/tmp/gw_s
```

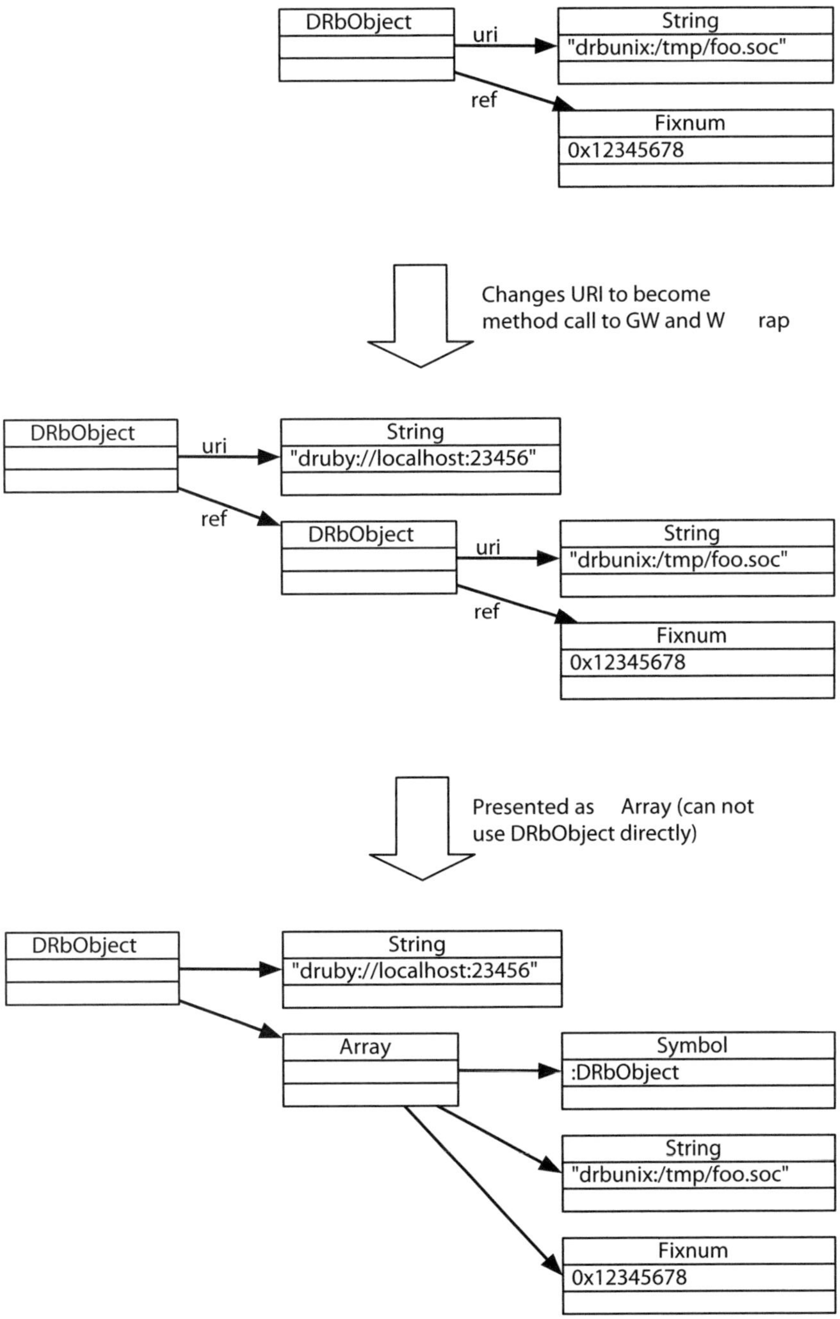

Figure 50—Wrapping the DRbObject and storing it into Array

In this example, we assign a TCP URI for other machines to be able to access and a Unix domain URI for different processes within the same machine to access.

Let's start a new terminal on the same machine where the gateway runs and start irb.

```
# [Terminal 1]
% irb --prompt simple -r drb/drb
>> DRb.start_service('drbunix:/tmp/gw_c')
>> ro = DRbObject.new_with_uri('drbunix:/tmp/gw_s')
>> require 'thread'
>> $q = Queue.new
>> ro[:unix] = DRbObject.new($q)
>> ro[:unix].push('test')
```

In this example, we specify the Unix domain to the URI for the same machine so that it can be accessed only within the same machine.

ro is a reference that's created by specifying the gateway Unix domain as the URI.

Let's generate a Queue object and assign it to ro[:unix]. We'll explicitly pass by reference, because a Queue object is passed by value by default.

Next, let's start irb from a different machine.

```
# [Terminal 2]
% irb --prompt simple -r drb/drb
>> DRb.start_service
>> ro = DRbObject.new_with_uri('druby://localhost:12321')
>> ro[:unix]
=> #<DRb::DRbObject:0x40300d18 @ref=[:DRbObject, "drbunix:/tmp/gw_s",
[:DRbObject, "drbunix:/tmp/gw_c", 2010008]], @uri="druby://localhost:12321">
>> ro[:unix].pop
=> 'test'
```

ro is a reference generated by specifying the URI of the gateway TCP. Notice that ro[:unix] is wrapped twice. You can see that ro[:unix].pop is actually calling an object on terminal 1.

What would happen if you registered an object on terminal 1 by using the TCP of the gateway? Both the Unix domain and TCP are the same DRb::GW object, but do they behave differently?

```
# [Terminal 1]
>> ro = DRbObject.new_with_uri('druby://localhost:12321')
>> ro[:tcp] = DRbObject.new($q)
>> ro[:tcp].push('test')
```

```
# [Terminal 2]
>> ro[:tcp]
=> #<DRb::DRbObject:0x40307c30 @ref=2010008, @uri="drbunix:/tmp/gw_c">
```

This does not look good.

```
>> ro[:tcp].pop
DRb::DRbConnError: drbunix:/tmp/gw_c -
 #<Errno::ENOENT: No such file or directory - /tmp/gw_c>
 ....
```

It raises an error, because it looked into the DRbServer on terminal 2, whose URI is drbunix:/tmp/gw_c, but it didn't find the URI.

The point of this gateway is to wrap the reference when a reference from one server goes to another. If you give a reference to DRbServer on the same side, it won't work as expected. As long as you're aware of this difference, you can publish objects across networks via the gateway easily.

12.3 Summary

In this chapter, we learned about the following:

- What dRuby offers (and doesn't offer) in terms of security
- Controlling the client access level with ACL and Unix domain sockets
- Accessing remote networks using SSH port forwarding and a gateway

This is the end of your journey with dRuby. I hope you've discovered many new things through this learning experience!

Bibliography

[CG90] Nicholas Carriero and David Gelernter. *How to Write Parallel Programs*. MIT Press, Cambridge, MA, 1990.

Index

N

O

P

Q

R

S

T

U

V

W

Y

Advanced Ruby and Rails

What used to be the realm of experts is fast becoming the stuff of day-to-day development. Jump to the head of the class in Ruby and Rails.

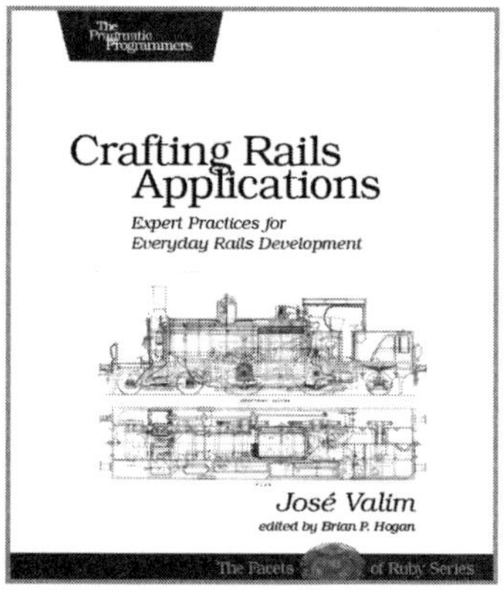

Rails 3 is a huge step forward. You can now easily extend the framework, change its behavior, and replace whole components to bend it to your will, all without messy hacks. This pioneering book is the first resource that deep dives into the new Rails 3 APIs and shows you how to use them to write better web applications and make your day-to-day work with Rails more productive.

José Valim
(184 pages) ISBN: 9781934356739. $33
http://pragprog.com/titles/jvrails

As a Ruby programmer, you already know how much fun it is. Now see how to unleash its power, digging under the surface and exploring the language's most advanced features: a collection of techniques and tricks known as *metaprogramming*. Once the domain of expert Rubyists, metaprogramming is now accessible to programmers of all levels—from beginner to expert. *Metaprogramming Ruby* explains metaprogramming concepts in a down-to-earth style and arms you with a practical toolbox that will help you write great Ruby code.

Paolo Perrotta
(296 pages) ISBN: 9781934356470. $32.95
http://pragprog.com/titles/ppmetr

Go Beyond with Rails and NoSQL

There's so much new to learn with Rails 3 and the latest crop of NoSQL databases. These titles will get you up to speed on the latest.

Thousands of developers have used the first edition of *Rails Recipes* to solve the hard problems. Now, five years later, it's time for the Rails 3.1 edition of this trusted collection of solutions, completely revised by Rails master Chad Fowler.

Chad Fowler
(350 pages) ISBN: 9781934356777. $35
http://pragprog.com/titles/rr2

Data is getting bigger and more complex by the day, and so are your choices in handling it. From traditional RDBMS to newer NoSQL approaches, *Seven Databases in Seven Weeks* takes you on a tour of some of the hottest open source databases today. In the tradition of Bruce A. Tate's *Seven Languages in Seven Weeks*, this book goes beyond a basic tutorial to explore the essential concepts at the core of each technology.

Eric Redmond and Jim Wilson
(330 pages) ISBN: 9781934356920. $35
http://pragprog.com/titles/rwdata

Pragmatic Guide Series

Get started quickly, with a minimum of fuss and hand-holding. The Pragmatic Guide Series features convenient, task-oriented two-page spreads. You'll find what you need fast, and get on with your work.

Need to learn how to wrap your head around Git, but don't need a lot of hand holding? Grab this book if you're new to Git, not to the world of programming. Git tasks displayed on two-page spreads provide all the context you need, without the extra fluff.

NEW: Part of the new *Pragmatic Guide* series

Travis Swicegood
(160 pages) ISBN: 9781934356722. $25
http://pragprog.com/titles/pg_git

JavaScript is everywhere. It's a key component of today's Web—a powerful, dynamic language with a rich ecosystem of professional-grade development tools, infrastructures, frameworks, and toolkits. This book will get you up to speed quickly and painlessly with the 35 key JavaScript tasks you need to know.

NEW: Part of the new *Pragmatic Guide* series

Christophe Porteneuve
(160 pages) ISBN: 9781934356678. $25
http://pragprog.com/titles/pg_js

Testing is only the beginning

Start with Test Driven Development, Domain Driven Design, and Acceptance Test Driven Planning in Ruby. Then add Shoulda, Cucumber, Factory Girl, and Rcov for the ultimate in Ruby and Rails development.

Behaviour-Driven Development (BDD) gives you the best of Test Driven Development, Domain Driven Design, and Acceptance Test Driven Planning techniques, so you can create better software with self-documenting, executable tests that bring users and developers together with a common language.

Get the most out of BDD in Ruby with *The RSpec Book*, written by the lead developer of RSpec, David Chelimsky.

David Chelimsky, Dave Astels, Zach Dennis, Aslak Hellesøy, Bryan Helmkamp, Dan North
(448 pages) ISBN: 9781934356371. $38.95
http://pragprog.com/titles/achbd

Rails Test Prescriptions is a comprehensive guide to testing Rails applications, covering Test-Driven Development from both a theoretical perspective (why to test) and from a practical perspective (how to test effectively). It covers the core Rails testing tools and procedures for Rails 2 and Rails 3, and introduces popular add-ons, including RSpec, Shoulda, Cucumber, Factory Girl, and Rcov.

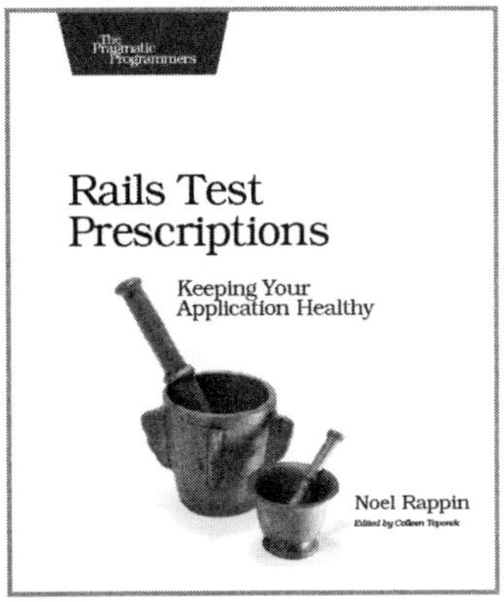

Noel Rappin
(368 pages) ISBN: 9781934356647. $34.95
http://pragprog.com/titles/nrtest

What you Need to Know

Each new version of the Web brings its own gold rush. Here are your tools.

HTML5 and CSS3 are the future of web development, but you don't have to wait to start using them. Even though the specification is still in development, many modern browsers and mobile devices already support HTML5 and CSS3. This book gets you up to speed on the new HTML5 elements and CSS3 features you can use right now, and backwards compatible solutions ensure that you don't leave users of older browsers behind.

Brian P. Hogan
(280 pages) ISBN: 9781934356685. $33
http://pragprog.com/titles/bhh5

Modern web development takes more than just HTML and CSS with a little JavaScript mixed in. Clients want more responsive sites with faster interfaces that work on multiple devices, and you need the latest tools and techniques to make that happen. This book gives you more than 40 concise, tried-and-true solutions to today's web development problems, and introduces new workflows that will expand your skillset.

Brian P. Hogan, Chris Warren, Mike Weber, Chris Johnson, Aaron Godin
(344 pages) ISBN: 9781934356838. $35
http://pragprog.com/titles/wbdev

Welcome to the Better Web

You need a better JavaScript and more expressive CSS and HTML today. Start here.

CoffeeScript is JavaScript done right. It provides all of JavaScript's functionality wrapped in a cleaner, more succinct syntax. In the first book on this exciting new language, CoffeeScript guru Trevor Burnham shows you how to hold onto all the power and flexibility of JavaScript while writing clearer, cleaner, and safer code.

Trevor Burnham
(160 pages) ISBN: 9781934356784. $29
http://pragprog.com/titles/tbcoffee

CSS is fundamental to the web, but it's a basic language and lacks many features. Sass is just like CSS, but with a whole lot of extra power so you can get more done, more quickly. Build better web pages today with *Pragmatic Guide to Sass*. These concise, easy-to-digest tips and techniques are the shortcuts experienced CSS developers need to start developing in Sass today.

Hampton Catlin and Michael Lintorn Catlin
(128 pages) ISBN: 9781934356845. $25
http://pragprog.com/titles/pg_sass

Be Agile

Don't just "do" agile; you want to *be* agile. We'll show you how.

The best agile book isn't a book: *Agile in a Flash* is a unique deck of index cards that fit neatly in your pocket. You can tape them to the wall. Spread them out on your project table. Get stains on them over lunch. These cards are meant to be used, not just read.

Jeff Langr and Tim Ottinger
(110 pages) ISBN: 9781934356715. $15
http://pragprog.com/titles/olag

Here are three simple truths about software development:

1. You can't gather all the requirements up front. 2. The requirements you do gather will change. 3. There is always more to do than time and money will allow.

Those are the facts of life. But you can deal with those facts (and more) by becoming a fierce software-delivery professional, capable of dispatching the most dire of software projects and the toughest delivery schedules with ease and grace.

Jonathan Rasmusson
(280 pages) ISBN: 9781934356586. $34.95
http://pragprog.com/titles/jtrap

The Pragmatic Bookshelf

The Pragmatic Bookshelf features books written by developers for developers. The titles continue the well-known Pragmatic Programmer style and continue to garner awards and rave reviews. As development gets more and more difficult, the Pragmatic Programmers will be there with more titles and products to help you stay on top of your game.

Visit Us Online

This Book's Home Page
http://pragprog.com/titles/sidruby
Source code from this book, errata, and other resources. Come give us feedback, too!

Register for Updates
http://pragprog.com/updates
Be notified when updates and new books become available.

Join the Community
http://pragprog.com/community
Read our weblogs, join our online discussions, participate in our mailing list, interact with our wiki, and benefit from the experience of other Pragmatic Programmers.

New and Noteworthy
http://pragprog.com/news
Check out the latest pragmatic developments, new titles and other offerings.

Save on the eBook

Save on the eBook versions of this title. Owning the paper version of this book entitles you to purchase the electronic versions at a terrific discount.

PDFs are great for carrying around on your laptop—they are hyperlinked, have color, and are fully searchable. Most titles are also available for the iPhone and iPod touch, Amazon Kindle, and other popular e-book readers.

Buy now at *http://pragprog.com/coupon*

Contact Us

Online Orders:	*http://pragprog.com/catalog*
Customer Service:	*support@pragprog.com*
International Rights:	*translations@pragprog.com*
Academic Use:	*academic@pragprog.com*
Write for Us:	*http://pragprog.com/write-for-us*
Or Call:	+1 800-699-7764